AF505431

# LITERARY CONJUGATIONS

Edited by Richard T. Gray

This series investigates literary artifacts in their cultural and historical
environments. Through comparative investigations and case studies
across a wide array of national literatures, it highlights the interdisciplinary character of literary studies and explores how literary
production extends into, influences, and refracts multiple domains
of intellectual and cultural life.

*W. G. Sebald: A Critical Companion* edited by J. J. Long
and Anne Whitehead

*Speaking Havoc: Social Suffering and South Asian Narratives*
by Ramu Nagappan

*The Linguistics of Lying and Other Essays* by Harald Weinrich,
translated and introduced by Jane K. Brown and Marshall Brown

*Missing the Breast: Gender, Fantasy, and the Body in the German Enlightenment*
by Simon Richter

*The Work of Print: Authorship and the English Text Trades, 1660–1760*
by Lisa Maruca

# THE WORK OF PRINT

*Authorship and the English Text Trades, 1660–1760*

## LISA MARUCA

A ROBERT B. HEILMAN BOOK

UNIVERSITY OF WASHINGTON PRESS

*Seattle and London*

© 2007 by the University of Washington Press
Printed in United States of America
Designed by Ann Kumasaka
12 11 10 09 08 07    5 4 3 2 1



University of Washington Press
PO Box 50096, Seattle, WA 98145
www.washington.edu/uwpress

Library of Congress Cataloging-in-Publication Data
Maruca, Lisa.
The work of print : authorship and the
English text trades, 1660–1760 / Lisa Maruca.
p.   cm. — (Literary conjugations)
"A Robert B. Heilman Book."
Includes bibliographical references and index.
ISBN-13: 978-0-295-98744-6 (hardback : alk. paper)
ISBN-10: 0-295-98744-8 (hardback : alk. paper)
ISBN-13: 978-0-295-98757-6 (pbk. : alk. paper)
ISBN-10: 0-295-98757-X (pbk. : alk. paper)
1. Book industries and trade—England—History—17th century.   2. Book
industries and trade—England—History—18th century.   3. Authorship—
History—17th century.   4. Authorship—History—18th century.   5. Authors and
publishers—England—History—17th century.   6. Authors and publishers—
England—History—18th century.   I. Title.
Z325.M382   2007
381'.45002094309033—dc22        2007016295

The paper used in this publication is acid-free and 90 percent recycled from
at least 50 percent post-consumer waste. It meets the minimum requirements
of American National Standard for Information Sciences—Permanence of Paper
for Printed Library Materials, ANSI Z39.48–1984.

# CONTENTS

# *Acknowledgments*

This book, like all books, is the work of many hands. From its conception, through writing, revising, and finally to production, it has benefited from a collective knowledge much vaster and insights sharper than my own. Through this process, ideas have been shared, mistakes have been corrected, limitations shored up, and prose sharpened. (Needless to say, the project's enduring errors and inadequacies remain my own.) My many collaborators must be acknowledged for their role in bringing the ideas here to print.

To Martha Woodmansee, longtime mentor, teacher, friend, and role model, I owe the largest debt. Her creative classrooms, close reading, careful criticism, and even casual conversations have shaped this project through all its stages. Indeed, her anonymous authorship (in the largest sense of the word) lies behind many a scholar's name. Peter Jaszi is another whose influence is pervasive here; his gentle wisdom and dedicated activism serve as both guide and goad.

Financial and intellectual support was provided at an early stage of this work in the form of an Andrew W. Mellon Dissertation Fellowship. I thank the Mellon Foundation for allowing me to share work and receive advice from the seminar participants. Fellow Case Western Reserve University students Ann Marie Hebert and Sarah Turner must also be acknowledged for reading drafts, strategizing about writing, and providing the balm of friendship for many years.

Jeffrey Masten read a version of chapter 2 at a preliminary stage, saving me from early excesses. A version of that chapter appeared as "Bodies of Type: The Work of Textual Production in English Printers' Manuals" in *Eighteenth-Century Studies* 36, no. 3 (2003): 321–43. I must also thank the anonymous readers and editorial board there whose commentary shaped that piece. Part of chapter 4 appeared as "Political Propriety and Feminine Property: Women in the Eighteenth-Century Text

Trades," *Studies in the Literary Imagination* 34 (2001): 79–99, in a special issue edited by John Dussinger.

A sabbatical leave granted by Wayne State University allowed me to complete work on chapter 3. The faculty in the Department of Interdisciplinary Studies there must be noted for their unflagging interest and encouragement throughout the process of revising this work. Demonstrating the true meaning of collegiality, they continue to serve as exemplars of teacher-scholars and educational activists. Stuart Henry, Roslyn Abt Schindler, and Julie Thompson Klein especially must be recognized for their generous provision of canny advice, as well as concrete logistical and editorial assistance. In this department I have been granted the intellectual space necessary to do true interdisciplinary work.

Series editor Richard Gray also has my appreciation for his enthusiasm and faith that my manuscript could become a book. Both Margaret Ezell and Adrian Johns provided shrewd and careful readings of the entire text, giving generously of their time and vast knowledge. I am grateful to have received their esteemed scholarly support and assistance at such a crucial stage.

Editors rarely receive enough credit. Jacqueline Ettinger, Mary Ribesky, and Jane Lichty have been a pleasure to work with, models of professionalism and always patient with their sometimes wayward author. Their careful questions and painstaking editing have made this a better book.

Finally, I must thank my family. Brenda Maruca instilled in me a passion for books at an early age; Robert Maruca made many sacrifices to provide an education for his children. This book is therefore in no small part a product of their unstinting labor of love. Michael and Shawn Anderson continue to share with me the work of domesticity. Shawn has the unenviable position of son of a writing mother. A burgeoning book lover himself, he freely shares the gift of his fresh perspective. Mike, however, must especially be lauded for years of patience and fidelity, emotional and economic support, throughout the project's duration. It is to him that I dedicate this book.

# THE WORK OF PRINT

I

❦

# INTRODUCTION: PRINTING PRODUCTION VALUES

*The Tears of the Press were but the Livery of its Guilt; nor is the Paper more stained,  than Authors, or Readers.*

—THE TEARS OF THE PRESS, 1681

*We seem to live in an age when retailers of every kind of ware aspire to be the original  manufacturer and particularly in literature.*

—MONTHLY REVIEW, 1766

*We write as cyborgs, inventing the language machines that reinvent us.*

—JEFFREY MASTEN, PETER STALLYBRASS, AND NANCY J. VICKERS, 1997

In 1713 a printer from the outskirts of the British kingdom, one James Watson of Edinburgh, found it necessary to clear the name of what he saw as a debased profession. Using his proximity to the communication technology of his day, he printed, distributed, and sold *The History of the Art of Printing*, his own translation of the anonymous French "The History of the Invention and Progress of the Mysterious Art of Printing, &c." He begins this work with a seemingly innocuous "Publisher's Preface to the Printers in Scotland." Under this misleading neutral, if not almost invisible title, however, is a manifesto that clarifies Watson's intent in reviving this obscure French chronology. Claiming that a spirit of public good underlies "all the Arts and Sciences that are instructive or beneficial to Man," Watson emphasizes that "the Invention, and vast Improvement, of the no less honourable, than useful and admirable Art of PRINTING, ... deserves a very eminent Place."[1] He points to the

"Character of the Men" who were the early printers and "the Marks of Honour paid them" in order to show how "those illustrious Persons were honour'd, and ranked among the best of their fellow Citizens, in those Times" (*History*, 4). No history is written without a specific agenda in the present, and Watson is explicit about his. He wishes to counter a prevailing trend: "Whereas now, we [printers] are scarcely clais'd or esteem'd above the lower Forms of Mechanicks" (*History*, 4).

Watson was not alone in using his resources to promote—and, as we will see, critique—the status of his craft. Instead, his work is representative of a proliferation of text about texts—or, more to the point, print about print—written and produced from within the trade itself. It is also symptomatic of the eighteenth-century discourse of "print anxiety," detailed in the many tracts of the period in which publishing practices are discussed, derided, or decried. My interest, though, is in a specific subset of these texts. In the chapters that follow, I discuss others like Watson: the workers who cast letters, composed pages, and ran the presses; the retailers who sold tracts and books in stalls or shops; and the variety of figures, well known or anonymous, who wrote texts traded in the literary marketplace. Despite their long marginalization within literary history, even—perhaps most surprisingly—within many recent examples of "print culture" studies, many of them were, in fact, remarkably prolific writers. This project explores what I call their "text work." I use this term to encapsulate, without delineating as separate spheres, the labor of their bodies, the concrete product of this work (whether a printed page or the press itself); the texts they wrote; and their representations of all this work—the work as a linguistic construction. This understanding configures writing not as purely the product of a disembodied intellect, but as always concrete and physical, mediated by technology, subject to market forces, and shaped by audience demand. It also posits "print" not just as an output—black marks on white paper—or as merely the physical process of the operation of the press. True, "type," as Harry Carter once famously opined, "is something you can pick up and hold in your hand,"[2] but even those making print (or printing) in this period saw it as more: print is a site in which the book as a tangible, commercial product, subject to the mores of trade and to regulation and control, meets the meaningful text contained within its pages. Thus, I use "text work" to suggest an opposition both to the abstraction and denial of labor usually known as a "literary work" *and* to descriptions of the print trade assumed by historians to provide unmediated access to real-life routines. Such an approach demands that the rhetoric of print be placed alongside the other discursive practices of the period. This allows print workers to emerge as constructing their text work—but always within a broader cultural terrain that, reciprocally, shapes their notions of their labor. By analyzing the representations they circulated, we gain a much broader and more inclusive understanding of material textuality in late seventeenth- and early eighteenth-century London.

## *Material(ized) Print*

N. Katherine Hayles points to the signifying function of books as physical artifacts, a process that operates to make meaning even when (and precisely at the moment that) one is least aware of it. Indeed, she argues that even for "transparent" interfaces, "this very immediacy is in itself an act of meaning-making that positions readers in a specific material relationship with the imaginative world evoked by the text."[3] My interest lies in the ways in which transparency functions to position readers to understand certain elements in a text and ignore others. Literary transparency has been a seductive mechanism, working to render the material nature of print—the business, technologies, and labor of writing—as virtually invisible for well over two hundred years. The study of literature until recently has not been the study of *books*, after all, but the study of *writing*, that is, a special sort of discourse, distinguished as such, and set apart from other forms of discourse by, as Michel Foucault noted, its affiliation with and origins in an author.[4] This looming figure obscures other contributors. Books become merely convenient carrying cases for the author's will and "work"—the abstract literariness—we read. In this regime of reading, the physical medium (page, typography, binding) is screened out through unconscious processes taught to us when we are introduced to the alphabet. Richard Lanham describes the procedure:

> [A]n alphabet that could support a high literate culture had to be simple enough to be learned easily in childhood. Thoroughly internalized at that time, it would become a transparent window into conceptual thought. The shape of the letters, the written

surface, was not to be read aesthetically; that would only inter-
fere with purely literate transparency. "Reading" would not,
except in its learning stages, be a self-conscious, rule-governed,
re-creative act but an intuitive skill, a literate compact exercised
on the way to thought.[5]

While Lanham does point to a time before reading, when individual
letters might be thought of as having a separate, opaque reality, he uni-
versalizes the process through which, one assumes, all members of all
literate cultures forget their childish ways and get down to the task of
really reading—and thinking. I suggest, however, that we interrogate
this transparency, for that which is the most "internalized" or "intuitive"
is that which is also the most ideological. Rather than take the invisibility of print for granted, then, one might usefully examine the text work
of print for alternative configurations.

Before engaging in historical exegesis, however, it may be helpful to
highlight the contingent nature of print's transparency by comparing it
to the development of a more opaque medium; "commonsense" understandings of print-based communication are destabilized when contrasted to alternative technological practices of textual production and
accreditation. The term *production values*, used in the title of this chapter,
usually registers solely within the discourse of film. I intentionally
deploy this term in this alien context, however, to highlight the conflu-
ence of meanings that inform my work and which I elaborate on
throughout this study. *Production values* refers, literally, to the physical
quality of a film or television show. Good production values depend on
numerous variables, including set design, sound, lighting, cinematogra-
phy, and editing. The production of these "values" is thus a collaborative
enterprise, contributed to by many workers. The film industry is markedly different from the book industry in that it credits these workers.
While a film may highlight its director or the famous actors it stars, it
never fails to mention, as it closes, those who brought it materially into
existence. The director may be charged with supervising, with bringing
the disparate elements together, but it is dozens if not hundreds of individuals who are charged with providing a production's literal and figura-
tive value. *Value* here suggests many meanings, all of them applicable to
moviemaking: the perceived image, made up, at the most basic level, of

shades of light and dark registering chemically on film; the artistic worth of the film-as-work, sometimes perceived as being an intrinsic quality, but actually judged by specific cultural and critical standards; and the amount of money that the film-as-product returns to the studio or backers who invest in it.

The film world, except for rare cases or occasional lapses into auteurism, is usually quite frank about the multiple levels of production and reception that structure its participation in the market. Talk of grosses and rankings of summer hits are as common in the popular media as gossip about stars. Even foreign films and "independents," which self-consciously situate themselves outside the crass maneuvers of Hollywood, are judged in terms of their relative financial success (or lack thereof) and their relatively low production costs, especially if they win multiple awards. Even the most "artistic" film, the one positioned the farthest outside of the mainstream, calls attention to itself as the work of multiple hands (even if these hands are seen to be organized by an artiste-director) precisely because of its superior production values.

By contrast, the contemporary book world does not display so prominently its multiple levels of production. Even best sellers are perceived to be the work of one superior man or woman, whether that superiority is seen to be based on fine artistic sensibility or the ability to pander successfully to the base desires of the mass market. Little or no attention is ever paid to the many workers who, like film denizens from best boys to gaffers to costume designers, build the print product from the ground up. A few editors and agents might achieve moderate fame within a small literary circle if they prove their worth by discovering and supporting the unknown genius, but editorial assistants, typists, cover designers, printers, publicists, and sales staff provide invisible if nonetheless essential services, shaping both the product itself and the public's perception of it. There are few credits in a book acknowledging their work.[6]

Thus I come to another meaning suggested by the chapter title. *Production values* refers to those values—the social standards or community agreements as to what is worthy of notice and is best to uphold, and likewise what must be repressed in order to maintain those standards—that are promulgated both *through* the act of textual production and *about* textual production. I have suggested that literary studies has supplied us with a specifically ideological view of history, in which works (not books) are produced only by authors. This study strives to disrupt that history and recover from erasure the workers who set type, ran presses, distributed pamphlets, or organized all these activities, as well as the material components they made, sold, or circulated. In doing so, I show how print technology in the hands of its workers, and in the words of its purveyors, manufactured and circulated its own system of production values. Reading has not always been a process of screening out the physicality of the print product and those who manufactured it. The research presented in the following chapters shows that in the late seventeenth and early eighteenth centuries, many of those most closely allied with bookmaking assumed that their work was indeed visible. They represented themselves not merely as helpers or supporters of authors but as creative collaborators in their own right. They believed that the tangible goods they created spoke for them and that readers read in their books the signs of their contributions. I reveal these values in my analyses of their text work.

I therefore depart from Lanham when, constructing a history that starts with the creation of the alphabet and ends with electronic writing, he asserts that, after Gutenberg and the rise of transparent type, "unintermediated thought," an "unselfconscious transparency," became the "stylistic, one might almost say a cultural, ideal for Western civilization."[7] Lanham is making assumptions about early modern printing based on the logic of today's print culture. Print did not become transparent until the real "work" was understood as existing "behind" the letters rather than inhering in them and was deemed to be the true essence of the book. For this to happen, the creator of the written work—rather than the produced book—first had to be constructed as superior to other sorts of print workers. That idea did not occur in tandem with Gutenberg's invention, as Lanham suggests. Instead, this study shows that our "natural" view of transparency emerged only through a process of linguistic negotiation and contestation played out in the English print culture of the late seventeenth and early eighteenth centuries.


## PRINT AS TEXT

The years covered in this study thus coincide with the end of an era in England, an era in which print workers enjoyed predominant responsibility for the production and circulation of texts. These years also cover, not coincidentally, a particularly active period in the formation of the print culture of London, as a brief overview will suggest. The texts I discuss in the following chapters illustrate changes in the rhetoric and representation of print that accompanied the economic and cultural transformation in the print trade as it developed from a government-regulated, yet loosely defined, enterprise, producing a chimera of texts, tracts, and tales, to a staid and efficient market-regulated business, promoting taste and genteel authorship to a large middle-class readership. The second half of the seventeenth century was marked by much turmoil in the print trade, a term I use in this study to encompass the official guild of Stationers as well as those who worked for, with, and sometimes against them, including unofficial printers, lowly street hawkers marketing cheap pamphlets—and writers. These various participants in the production of texts were the objects of much discursive scrutiny in this period. The monarchy and the public alike worried that the press had toppled one government and could do it again. Anxiety about print—who should print, who was responsible for print, what should be printed, what the effects of print were—became a frequent topic in print. As I detail later, the government moved from straightforward suppression (through the Licensing Act of 1662, for example) to a realization that the press could be used to influence political events, without wholeheartedly accepting either extreme.[8]

The first few decades of the eighteenth century, though calm politically, continued to witness great changes in the print trade. By 1700 printing had begun, as Alvin Kernan notes, "to affect the structure of social life at every level." He details the "very ordinariness" of the everyday print products that became common in this period: "theater bills, newspapers and magazines, hand-bills, bill-headings, labels, tickets, . . . [and] marriage certificates."[9] Social and institutional life depended increasingly on print. Such cultural acceptance of print as an unavoidable fact of life meant booming business for those in the trade. Booksellers began to specialize as customers indicated preferences for old or new fiction, trade manuals, or scholarly material. Reading became a national leisure-time activity as well as a necessity for many middle-class professions, and the now highly commercial trade of printing and publishing reorganized and formed new trade practices to meet the diverse needs of its customers. Networks of distribution grew within London and into the provinces, for example, and the conventions of advertising and reviewing books in newspapers were initiated to inform consumers of what was now a plethora of choices.[10]

While the trade was busy producing new print commodities and new ways to promote and distribute them, it was also active discursively (re)producing itself and its work. Increased business brought with it new forms of print anxiety. Wealth was consolidated into the hands of a few, and changes in economic status reconfigured the network of sociocultural positions. Printers, once a dominant force in the trade, were reclassified as lowly "mechanicks," while booksellers used their affiliation with the rising merchant class to boost their cultural capital. I investigate the effects of this rearrangement in later chapters. Here, though, it is important to note that these new socioeconomic affiliations situated the trade within a new discursive network of manners and morals, which brought new understandings of the role of business and its relation to aesthetic concerns—and restructured the value(s) of print.

This period between the Restoration, when the Stationers lost monopolistic control of the print and publishing market, and the mid-eighteenth century, which witnessed the consolidation of large capital-intensive publishing houses, was also a time of fruitful indeterminacy within English print culture. Indeed, many of the literary categories that later emerged as rigid "natural" dichotomies—text versus book, creative thought versus manual labor, intellect versus economics—had not yet developed into commonsense inevitabilities. Certainly, many print workers, from booksellers to compositors, did not always see themselves as confined to one side of the binary. However, such freedom was not without contestation—nor was it usurped in a sudden, dramatic way. Instead, the terms deployed by text work are multivalenced and over-written with meanings from other spheres. Foucault has written that "[a]n event . . . is not a decision, a treaty, a reign or a battle, but the reversal of a relationship of forces, the usurpation of power, the appropriating of a vocabulary turned against those who had once used it."[11] In these terms, the texts emerging from the print trade can be seen themselves as crucial Foucauldian "events" in a cultural shift in the understanding of this sort of labor. They reveal the complex and sometimes contradictory processes through which a group struggles to garner and preserve enough linguistic capital to fund its version of print.[12]

Indeed, the print market itself can also be usefully understood as a Bourdieuian field. This sort of system is "not the product of a coherence-seeking intention . . . but the product and prize of a permanent conflict"; that is, "the generative, unifying principle of this system is the struggle, with all the contradictions it engenders."[13] The idea of the "struggle," however, is usually employed in literary history (even by Pierre Bourdieu himself) as a way of conceptualizing *aesthetic* debates insomuch as it accounts for the strategies writers and those attendant on them use to authorize the artistic product. This is true, for example, of Clifford Siskin's useful study of the generic and professional reclassification of writing in the late eighteenth century. My argument is much in sympathy with his, especially in his articulations of the ways in which, "as with other kinds of work, the act of writing was subject to conflicts over who could and should use the technology, in what ways, and with what consequences."[14] Paradoxically, however, my study is both broader and narrower: instead of the technology of writing, I am more generally interested in the many technologies of bookmaking, of which I consider writing as just one; more specifically, I focus on conflicts over representations of *one* of writing's manifestations, print.

This distinction is important. The texts by the printers and booksellers I examine—many working before the ideological veil of "disinterest" worked to obscure and defame the economic investments of authorship—do not just legitimate the value adhering to the text work of others, but they produce authorizing representations of print workers themselves, along with their technologies, whether "technology" is used broadly in the Foucauldian sense or in its literal, mechanic sense. This adaptation of the "field of cultural production" allows us to investigate the ways in which writing on print reveals a constant and vigorous negotiation of the source and flow of power within the realms of textual production and circulation. As the case studies I discuss will show, while this linguistic conflict sometimes reflected a straightforward rivalry between divergent economic interests, it more importantly represented a nexus of competing ideologies: different ways of imagining the process of textual creation as it evolved from the glimmer of an idea to the solid book in a reader's hands.

## *PRINTING VALUES*

A brief return to Watson's *Art of Printing* will enable us to see some of
the issues that emerge in treating print as "text work." While Watson's
text is of course unique to his specific time and place, the production
values articulated within it usefully set up some common themes. The
first I discuss is the most obvious and yet the easiest to overlook: its
status as a print text on the subject of print. Stating that his purpose is
to inquire into "how we came to lose that Honour and Respect due to
our Profession, (since the present Age is much more learned, and I
believe as just too, and discerning of Merit as their Ancestors)" (*History*,
4), Watson appeals to his audience's sense of the naturalness of historical progress. By placing his current profession in a larger and grander
narrative, Watson is literally writing—in fact, printing—himself and his
text into the history of print. In doing so, he creates what N. Katherine
Hayles calls a "technotext"—one that "interrogates the inscription technology that produces it."[15] He thus participates in what Hayles has elsewhere described as the "informational feedback loop" of "reflexivity."
The works on print that I take up in this study can be seen as part of "a
movement whereby that which has been used to generate a system is
made, through a changed perspective, to become part of the system it
generates."[16] This changed perspective allows us to see processes that
may have been occluded in a more straightforward reading. As Hayles
suggests, "reflexivity has subversive effects because it confuses and
entangles the boundaries we impose upon the world in order to make
sense of that world."[17] Paralleling M. C. Escher's drawing of the hand
drawing a hand that Hayles sees as emblematic, representations *of* print
*in* print *as* print problematize the art and fiction of boundary making
itself, revealing not only their contingency but their instability in a state
of flux, of construction and reconstruction. The machine printing the
machine is not a fixed or stable essence.[18] This is not to impose on writers such as Watson a postmodern metafictional intent, but to see in their
texts a reflexivity engendered by their proximity to the grounds of material textual production.

Recasting boundaries allows us to see the text work of print as porous
and in dynamic interaction with other discourses. This is a matter not of
straightforward influence but, often, of mutual renegotiation of the lin-

guistic terrain. Watson's text itself bears traces of this struggle. He claims a moral authority by insisting he writes for "the common Benefit of these practicing the Art [of printing] in this Part of Britain; without proposing any other Advantage or Gain by it, but the Improvement of the Art. . . . And since we are, I trust, all of us honest Men, and of better spirits than to propose the Earning of our Bread as the chief and only End of our Labour" (*History*, 5). His need to at once invoke and deny the crude reality of "earning our bread" reveals this as a vexed issue. We can see rhetoric such as Watson's as symptomatic of a cultural dissonance between the competing claims of economics and "improvement" within a maturing and consolidating literary market and a struggle to reconceptualize the role of writing, work, machines, and money within the terms of the polite bourgeois public sphere. While his text is thus part of the larger eighteenth-century cultural-aesthetic project, what is notable here is its manifestation in the printing house itself: the source, the literal engine, of the textual forces that created and sustained Enlightenment values.

Although the works I study in the following chapters all originated in London, it is notable that Watson strikes his defensive pose at a distance from the metropolitan center, in Scotland. When, for example, he laments the fact that "our former Authors have been forc'd to . . . go to other Countries to publish their Writings, lest a learn'd Book should be spoil'd by an ignorant or careless Printer," and urges his brethren to "make it our Ambition, as well as our Interest and Honour, to furnish them with Printers that can serve them . . . well" (*History*, 6), he calls on notions of both ethnic and trade loyalties: Scottish writers are not well served by inferior Scottish printers. While the complex issue of Scottish independence and the thorniness of Anglo-Scottish relations in this period lie outside the scope of this brief analysis, Watson's text does serve to highlight (in its simultaneous denial of and subservience to) the dominant discourse of English print superiority that emanated from London. In doing so, it participates in a discourse of nationalism that was written by and on the print trade more broadly. As the references to both "interest" and "honour" make clear, however, national identity is just one of the many *intertwined* cultural ideologies structuring print. Thus when Watson concludes this section with a rallying cry—"Thus, Gentlemen, we shall have this Honour, which is truly more valuable than immense Sums of Money or opulent Estates, that, for the Glory of our Country, we have retrieved the Art of PRINTING, and brought It to as great Perfection as ever It was here in former Times" (*History*, 6)—he is compressing anxieties about aesthetics and technology, commerce and class, nationalism and nostalgia that, as I show, were played out with a variety of purposes and effects, across different texts, times and cultures of print.

Watson's discourse articulates another important boundary as well. His rhetorical folding of himself into the polite category of honorable gentlemen, "us honest men," and his use of the misleadingly universal and transparent "we" foreground the *gendered* nuance of all these concerns: part of his project is constructing the appropriately gendered man and woman of print. This is most apparent in Watson's construction of an explanatory narrative showing how Scottish print has fallen from its former glory. Seeking an appropriate scapegoat, Watson castigates at some length one Mrs. Anderson, a printer's widow and a shrewd and successful businesswoman in her own right, who controlled Bible printing through her late husband's monopoly as King's Printer. His description of her as the moral decay undermining righteous print and disrupting its natural progress blends notions of religious duty with properly gendered behavior in a manner reminiscent of the period's conduct manuals:

> Nothing came from the Royal Press (as Mrs. Anderson vainly term'd it) but the most illegible and uncorrect Bibles and Books that ever were printed in any one Place in the World. She regarded not the Honour of the Nation, and never minded the Duty lay upon her as the Sovreign's Servant: Prentices, instead of the best Workmen, were generally imploy'd in printing the Sacred Word of GOD. And, in fine, nothing was study'd but gaining of Money by printing Bibles at any Rate ... that no Body could want them. (*History*, 13)

His opprobrium works by linking her unnatural neglect of the chief feminine virtues—her failure of duty, neglect of honor, resistance to subordination, and lack of veneration of the sacred—to an excess of reproduction resulting in faulty progeny, the flawed text. Paralleling the morally righteous endings of other eighteenth-century stories of unsanctioned sexuality and reproduction, Watson uses the standard narrative of the fallen woman to chart the predicted results: "[T]hose, who formerly were her Friends . . . began to be asham'd of her Practices and turn'd their Back upon her" (*History*, 13–14).[19] The metaphor of the press as a sexually reproductive machine has many precedents in early modern culture, of course, which work to express and produce congruent changes in gender and sexuality as well as authorship and technology.[20] Watson's invocation at this juncture, however—though certainly calling on that familiar history—is unique to his period in that it encapsulates anxieties about recent changes in the understanding of male and female identities as they were reconstituted through text work, the print market, the sexed body, and gendered language. It is these changes and these sorts of connections that I explore in the chapters that follow, in which I see gender as a social(izing) category, a performative gesture, a marker of the boundaries of acceptable behavior, and a producer of generic textual distinctions. At the same time, I use gender to discuss the real-life effects on the working bodies of women in print.

In constructing this world of gendered print(ers), Watson freely mixes history, current events, biography, personal vitriol, technical know-how, and advertisement—an odd mix to twenty-first-century readers trained in the genre categories founded in Enlightenment precepts. However, Watson's text is representative of others in this study in the way it segues seamlessly from the political to the domestic to the realms of machine, labor, and trade. For Watson, the circulation of a well-regulated and honorable, indeed, properly gendered, text is inseparable from his more material concerns: the importance of paying well "a good Press-Man, who brings Reputation to my Work" (*History*, 21); the superiority of a Dutch-made press, which worked so well for twenty years that "neither Smith nor Joiner [were] call'd for to her" (22); or the use of good, cold lye to "preserve your Letter and other Materials, or to make your Work beautiful, or to have your Servants appear neat and clean" (23). Finally, he ends his diatribe on the problems of Scottish print with a type specimen that shows off the letterforms he has available in his printing house. This explicit form of "product placement" calls attention to the economic transactions in which the text as printed book must by necessity participate, for it serves to advertise Watson's trade in bookmaking and make *The Art of Printing* itself a form of self-promotion, commercially as well as ideologically. It also serves to reembody his history as a *print* narrative, that is, a manifestation of the carved letterform itself. This type of blending of what would later be positioned as incompatible discourses—objective history versus gossip, art versus economics, narrative story versus typeface—is central to my concerns throughout this study. As Paula McDowell has noted, it is when we venture "into the realm of what seems strange *to us*" that we begin to understand "not only our own literary values and agendas, but also . . . those values' original sociocultural functions and consequences."[21] "Strangeness" can be useful, then, as long as we take care not to make it so exotic that we homogenize its Otherness. Watson's "generic confusion" is *not* a glimpse of a monolithic pre- or early Enlightenment mode of thinking, but a register *through and against which* later dominant constructions of knowledge are being produced. My work thus calls for us to uncover that which, because it resists our common perceptions of the writing-work relationship, remains hidden from view.

## *Author-ized Print*

The template that has been applied most often to this relationship is that of proprietary authorship. The idea that an author is an individual proprietor of intrinsically original "intellectual property" that deserves protection by the laws of copyright is a relatively new one, historically. It is also culturally specific. Based in changing views on genius, individualism, property, and literary production and supported by developments in law, trade, and technology, the concept of authorship slowly gained currency throughout the eighteenth century in England. This new way of looking at literary production and property did not "naturally" evolve within literary history, however, but was contingent on the claims of certain privileged groups with definite ideological interests. Only later did authorship become the dominant and seemingly inescapable way of defining textual and other creative output. In my study, I investigate the way in which authorship, because of its eventual dominance—evidenced by its seeming naturalness—erased all evidence of alternative approaches to writing and the production of texts. I show how it develops in and is deployed against the contested terrain of print.

Watson's text, for example, formulates a technology-based author-function at the same time as he dissolves it, epitomizing a contradiction. Through the act of publishing, the material means of which he has at his ready disposal, the printer Watson author-izes himself as one with a legitimate claim to discursive production. This also casts his topic, "the art of printing," as one worthy of dissemination and debate. While printer and writer are perhaps two separate positions Watson can choose to occupy at distinct moments, his self-representation blurs the boundaries: he is a printer/author reflecting on print-art. At the same time, however, at the moment of his most spirited call to action—the earlier quoted passage in which he urges his fellow printers to improve their art—he subordinates his trade by casting it as one in service to Authors. Such a move seems obvious by today's standards, for this is still our most common way of understanding writing technologies and the people who service them: they exist to be written through; their obvious and proper position is that of invisibility; their aims are subordinate to those who do the superior intellectual work of disembodied, nonmechanical *writing*. This conventional notion of the (non)medium of writing, however, is at odds with the print-on-print materialism that Watson's text also enacts, with its emphasis on the press, pressmen, and the letter as specimen. How do we account for this contradiction?

In order to understand the textual production of this period, we must forego the logic of proprietary and original authorship that structures so much work on print. In fact, close analysis of the texts of print workers reveals, as I show in the chapters that follow, that our current regimes of creative work are often anachronistically applied to the socioeconomic relations of the late seventeenth- and early eighteenth-century literary markets. The texts of print workers reveal hierarchies of labors, attitudes about the creative process, and approaches to the commodification of writing that are often strikingly at odds with those written by the emerging professional author and most studied by scholars today. Most importantly, in multiple ways and with divergent interests, these printers, booksellers, publishers, and distributors cast *themselves* in central roles in the production process. Thus my central thesis is that those who worked within the many professions of the print trade (from printers to publishers to writers) understood books and other print products to be the result of a *collaboration* of many hands and the process of textual production to include not only writing but also the work—and workers—of technology. Indeed, I show that a participant in the print culture of the late seventeenth and early eighteenth centuries would have understood practices of writing, technologies of printing, and even the business of planning, marketing, and selling print commodities all as productive and creative aspects of text making. This was the context in which the purveyors of the press depicted writers as equal or inferior to other print workers.[22] My project thus recovers a collective alternative to anachronistic notions of creativity centered in the singular author, the sole creator of original works. It also demystifies a long-accepted trope in literary studies, that of the disinterested genius whose work transcends the base realities of economics.

However, a specter haunts the assertions of print workers: a counter-discourse that cannot help but shape their arguments. Their declarations, I assert, must also be seen as part of a struggle for textual ownership and control that ensued as a new concept, that of the solitary author as proprietor of his intrinsically original intellectual property (protected in new copyright laws), which slowly gained currency in the mid-eighteenth century. In fact, print workers, in positing themselves as significant creative contributors, were engaging in acts of linguistic self-preservation, for central to the notion of author-as-proprietor was the effacement of print workers from the imagined scene of textual creation.[23] Nonetheless, I do not wish to look back with nostalgia on a utopian pre-authorial past. Certainly, the press has been deployed politically in some manner and in someone's favor since its inception. Rather, I wish to chart how representations shifted to favor an individualized notion of disinterested authorial production while muting the importance of technology and the working body in the construction of print.

There is more at stake than giving print workers their moment of glory. This struggle was not an isolated "labor issue," with effects confined merely to title-page practices or the domain of copyright, but was shaped by and had ramifications for larger social discourses. For example, as we saw in James Watson's use of Mrs. Anderson as the fallen woman of print, many of the texts emerging from this realm use images of the sexed body and properly gendered behavior to categorize print products and make normative their particular view of print propriety. My analysis of the print trade's depiction of their work calls attention to the ways in which they asserted their importance through a rhetoric of hierarchical and binary sexuality and gender. This articulation of authority in gendered terms in turn affected the many, often invisible, women who worked in these trades. In fact, these representations, while not excluding women from writing and the print trades, helped to limit the types of writing and work in which they were authorized to participate.

## WORK ON PRINT

This book is by necessity interdisciplinary, encompassing labor and guild history; theories of class and economics; the history of science and of technology; the legal history of textual control and regulation, from licensing to copyright laws; the history of the book, publishing, and bibliography; new media theory; and eighteenth-century understandings of gender and sexuality. In my attempt to weave together these various and sometimes conflicted strands, I have been assisted by the work of numerous scholars representing several larger fields. I have discussed my debts to the theories of Michel Foucault and Pierre Bourdieu in constructing a methodological framework, but specific interpretive strategies, readings, and new histories emerging from early modern and eighteenth-century culture and literary studies have been helpful as well. A detailed analysis of my reliance on and departure from individual applications is best explored in the context of the individual chapters that follow. Nonetheless, an understanding of this project's self-placement within recent scholarship may help clarify my broader aims.

This study is, not surprisingly, indebted to earlier work on the history of print, from Elizabeth Eisenstein's groundbreaking *The Printing Press as an Agent of Change* (1979) to Alvin Kernan's *Samuel Johnson and the Impact of Print* (1987). Eisenstein, following Marshall McLuhan's media theory, first allowed us to see how a relatively simple machine could reshape knowledge itself. Walter Ong's work defining cultures of orality, literacy, and print served to buttress this idea. The idea of "print logic" that emerged privileged abstraction, uniformity, repeatability, visuality, standardization, linearity, and quantification.[24] This logic extended beyond the format of books, Kernan insists, and affected the framework of human thought and society: "Print logic began to shape mental structures, imparting a sense of the world as a set of abstract ideas rather than immediate facts. . . . [A]s print logic changed mental structures, the social world was also changed by the increasing numbers of people whose minds were programmed by print logic. Rationalism, idealistic philosophy, consumerism, capitalism, and nationalism . . . are all . . . inevitable consequences of movable type."[25] A single piece of machinery, the printing press, is thus charged with nothing less than the wholesale makeover of Western culture. Though Eisenstein's work itself is more subtly nuanced, her study does sometimes imply a technological essentialism in which the duties of master printers or authors become merely inevitable effects of an always already installed technology. While I detail the problems with such a construction in chapter 2, I stress here that inevitable and monolithic effects can be avoided by focusing on print as linguistically constructed in the context of a series of arguments, debates, local material practices, and minor rhetorical adjustments.

My work also relies on the archival studies undertaken by those following Eisenstein. Originally marginalized within their disciplines of English or history, or relegated to what was then considered the obscure field of library studies, scholars within the interdisciplinary field of the "history of the book" now have become more prominently institutionalized. With its vigorous investigation of the physical aspects of print production, such as paper- and ink-making, letter founding, composing methods, work organization, distribution, circulation, consumption, and so forth, book history is a field, in short, "that, broadly defined, promise[s] to cover the whole history of the creation, diffusion, and reception of the written word."[26] However, much of this scholarship is still marked by a positivist bias, an empirical agenda, and an investment in narratives of natural progress, whether aesthetic or economic. A benevolent if not liberating literacy is depicted as arising to enable cultural progress, a process by which, James Raven has complained, print culture is viewed as "part nursemaid and part chronicler."[27] These studies are often author-centric, existing, in many cases, solely for the purpose of enabling our appreciation of Shakespeare or other canonical "greats." Larger cultural forces are ignored or taken for granted as a stable background against which business or craftsmanship proceeds independently. Lacking a theory of representation, they ignore the discursive environment in which the trade participated.

More recent projects within eighteenth-century "print culture studies" have avoided technological determinism and teleology by examining individual agency and the social construction of technology. However, much research in this sector of literary studies, despite its more sophisticated theoretical approach, is in fact also still primarily author-centric and focused on a select canon of texts.[28] Thus we have Alexander Pope on Edmund Curll, Laurence Sterne on typography, or Samuel Johnson on professionalization—while the workers who actually made print available are largely ignored. My analysis tries to bridge this gap by reinstalling as an essential component of the literary culture of this period the many and varied voices emerging from the trade itself. In that goal I have been enabled by Adrian Johns's groundbreaking attempt to displace a neutral, objective, and standardized print as the transparent medium through which scientific texts could be safely circulated. In almost overwhelming detail, he shows how what was later considered inherent to print was in fact propagated by those within the trade in an attempt to authorize and legitimate their businesses. By complicating these printing practices, he forces us to reevaluate almost all that we have taken for granted about the texts that emerge from this trade.[29] Nonetheless, as brilliant as he is in unearthing debates within the print world, he rarely places them alongside other cultural texts—so there is no context for understanding the broader *social* work of print outside its own domain. Without a sensitivity to sociolinguistic concerns, we cannot see the polyvocality of print—an aspect I believe is necessary to understand print as text work. My project thus can also be seen in relation to McDowell's call for "a new model for the study of the literary marketplace as a whole," one that "break[s] down disciplinary and conceptual boundaries which separate the study of texts' ideological content and form (literary criticism) from the study of their physical production (publishing history)."[30] Her work specifically calls attention to the role of unruly women printers and radical religious orality in the production of the eighteenth-century bourgeois public sphere. Her study is an exemplar of how to combine literary theory with material sources in an analysis of textual production that questions print culture's hierarchy of margin and center.[31]

Most influential to my work, however, has been the now substantial body of work deconstructing authorship as a timeless and universal category.[32] As groundbreaking as this work was when it emerged more than a decade ago, however, the problem with many of the studies that have followed since is, ironically, the author-centric nature of them: seldom are other ways of imagining textual agency and creativity reconstructed. Authors and booksellers are all too often always already opposing parties; the fact that they once worked in tandem, or that the art-business hierarchy they represent was ever conceptualized differently, is rarely acknowledged. Unfortunately, this has the unintended consequence of casting the proprietary author as the natural and inevitable result of literary market forces—an issue this project hopes to address. I believe that an analysis of the text work of print supplements the scholarly work demystifying the "author function," but with a significant difference: it shifts attention away from authors by examining other important contributors to, and alternative ways of understanding, the making of books. This is an important distinction, for focusing more attention on the "rise of the author" operates (if inadvertently) as a teleology that evacuates other types of print workers from the imagined scene of textual creativity.

Finally, my belief in the importance of studying the material technologies of writing has been influenced by recent studies in information theory and electronic writing. Lanham, for example, describes the surface play computers make possible that disrupts the seeming transparency of type:

> I can enlarge the print if my eyes get tired, reduce it to check format and page layout, flow it around illustrations if I want. I can redesign the very shapes of the letters, zoom in on them until their transparency becomes an abstract pattern of separate pixels. I can alter the alphabetic/graphic ratio of conventional literacy in dozens of ways. . . .
>
> The textual surface is now a malleable and self-conscious one. . . . The textual surface has become permanently bi-stable. We are always looking first AT it and then THROUGH it.[33]

Although this sort of manipulation is now almost as natural as staid print, Lanham explains how it has nonetheless "turned a lot of commercial practices and relationships upside down along with our traditional notions of literary and cultural decorum."[34] What this new technology enables, in short, is a "turning upside down" of what Lanham in the previous passage termed Gutenberg's "transparency" of print. For the historian of print, however, such rhetoric encourages new investigations into the supposedly stable, solid realm of early modern typography. For master printers, who ordered type to be cast according to certain specifications and monitored compositors' use of different fonts in the creation of the print page, was type ever transparent? Despite the incorrect assumption of many electronic media critics that the destabilization of text is a recent phenomenon, studies such as theirs do call our attention to the surface features of older texts in useful ways. I discuss some of the meanings of different type styles in chapter 2, for example, and parts of my fourth chapter would be difficult if not impossible to convey if not for my word processor's ability to mimic seventeenth-century typography. Thus new technology provides both an example and a tool with which to explore the old.

Similarly, work on postmodern information systems more broadly understood has also been helpful in allowing me to revisit older communications media. Donna Haraway's attention to "women in the integrated circuit" in her famous "Manifesto for Cyborgs" broke new ground in theorizing the body-technology-gender nexus; her essay serves as a model for ways to think outside the Enlightenment dualism of man versus machine. Shoshana Zuboff's prescient analysis of workers' relationships to computerized information in factories and offices in *In the Age of the Smart Machine: The Future of Work and Power* (1988), especially her treatment of the importance of embodied as opposed to "scientific" forms of knowledge, allows me to better theorize printers' bodies in relation to their work and their machines.[35] Similarly, it is N. Katherine Hayles's immersion in cybernetics, postmodern fiction, and electronic literature that leads to her call for a "media-specific analysis" as central to literary studies, insisting that "without it we have little hope in forging a robust and nuanced account of how literature is changing under the impact of information technologies."[36] Hayles's work itself, though, centers on contemporary art-texts that foreground their own physicality, and she does not suggest that these works are part of a tradition of technotexts. In order to fully comprehend the way new media are reshaping old genres, assumptions, and practices, however, we must first understand the materiality of the past, in all its rich and varied manifestations. We must not deny its unique complexity by projecting our own anachronistic reading practices onto its forms. We need to rethink materiality and make it central again—by tracing the history of its disappearance.

In the following chapters, I look at a wide range of textual sites from which the production values of the print trade emerge: printers' manuals, booksellers' correspondence and autobiographies, pro-censorship tracts, and court documents from seditious libel trials and pleas from prison, in addition to works of fiction, such as Samuel Richardson's *Pamela*, and the voices of canonical authors who have grumbled about the sloppy work of printers or the exorbitant demands of booksellers. The chapters present individual case studies, each focusing on one of the variety of professions within the British print trade. I thus show that the renegotiation of the concepts of print worker—from a key contributor to the making of books to an invisible body to be written through—is not an isolated phenomenon but takes place in a number of diverse sources and reveals its effects in a variety of discrete practices. I call attention to texts and practices rarely closely examined, arguing that without understanding the role of print workers as textual agents, we cannot properly assess the workings of the eighteenth-century literary market. In uncovering these various cultural "moments," however, I am not interested in weaving a seamless narrative of influence and institutionalization of ideas, or in "proving" empirically that each individual I discuss fully grasped the implications and ramifications of these ideas on the broader culture. Similarly, I do not wish to imply that the voicing of opinions, or the textual traces of such opinions, is tantamount to their belonging to an accredited and coherent class of ideas—or even that stakeholders within a linguistic site of struggle understood themselves as such. Because I believe that discursive shifts are subtle, complex, and even contradictory, I strive to examine the *multiple* ways in which similar representations get played out across a wide spectrum of individualized interests and investments in the literary marketplace. By examining the local discourses invoked in constructing both dominant and counter discourses, I therefore disrupt the notion of an inevitable "logic" that runs through many studies of authorship and print culture.

Chapter 2, the first of the four case studies, shows that even the most basic, material unit of the trade—the print letter itself—cannot be viewed as a stable or fixed essence. Here I examine the shifting, ideologically situated and contested representations of print texts and technologies in two representative printers' manuals: Joseph Moxon's 1683–84 *Mechanick Exercises on the Whole Art of Printing* and John Smith's 1755 *The Printer's Grammar*.[37] Written more than seventy years apart, these manuals project vast differences in what constitutes the creative act of bookmaking. I also discuss the ways in which each manual reflects changing discourses of sexuality and gender support in its construction of an orderly print. To Moxon, who called his manual a "piece of typographie," books are equal parts sweat, labor, and letters. Workers' bodies are part of the construction process; indeed, they cannot be separated from the machinery they operate. His manual celebrates the heterosexual working bodies of print, the laborers whose physical production of print is as important as the text supplied by writers. In Smith's manual, however, the bodies of labor disappear into an authoritative masculine font. His naturalized gendering of a (now) invisible print privileges only the Author, who controls the text and whose disembodied intellect transcends the physical book.

Chapter 3 moves from those who worked to make print to those who sold it—and, just as often, originated ideas for products that they funded, supervised, and distributed. Booksellers—their trade's appellation itself giving short shrift to their long line of duties—have long been controversial characters. I show, however, that the various insults hurled at "Grub Street" are, in fact, indications of its status as a zone of representational conflict. In contrast to many literary histories that ignore the work of booksellers—or at best bracket them to the realm of the amusing anecdote—I analyze the discourse of the immoral bookseller as part of a larger early eighteenth-century manifestation of "print anxiety," a cultural debate about the nature of print texts and the ways in which they should be produced, controlled, and profited from. I examine traces of this contestation in the language of booksellers, focusing on three central and representative figures, Francis Kirkman, John Dunton, and Robert Dodsley, whose writing together spans the period I cover and reveals changes in the trade's understanding of the role of the proper proprietor of print. The ideology of the bookseller as revealed in the texts of Kirkman and Dunton is one in which booksellers themselves are the creative protagonists of a commercial print. However, as Dodsley's self-construction as "the Muse's Midwife" makes apparent, the rise of the author, and the discursive removal of published writing from the realm of physical labor and material economics, led to a midcentury rhetoric that cast booksellers as secondary to the intellectual requirements of a transcendent, authored text.

Chapter 4 also takes up an alternative to proprietary authorship by examining the discourse of the regulated text circulated by those in the socioeconomic margins of the trade. This chapter focuses on those whom we might better understand in our own parlance as distributors or small retailers, termed in their own time *trade publishers*, who ran small shops and worked closely with both *mercury women*, who could have small pamphlet shops or market stalls, and *hawkers*, who cried their wares on the streets. Indeed, the author as an accountable agent, I assert, emerged in England only as an entity intrinsically connected to a variety of legally responsible agents within the trade. This chapter takes up the rhetoric of licensing, sedition, and libel, illustrating the ways in which, rather than being purely repressive, these laws were crucial in the production of certain forms of Enlightenment discourse. Thus even literature outside the usual purview of censorship, such as the ostensibly "apolitical" genre of the novel, felt the ripple effects of textual regulation. To illustrate my point, I describe in detail the resistance strategies utilized by mercury women, pamphlet distributors charged with handling political tracts and frequently shouldering the responsibility of their writing and printing. On the front lines of dangerous textuality, the mercuries deployed the rising rhetoric of middle-class femininity later taken up as a defining feature of the properly feminized eighteenth-century novel. I conclude that the regulations governing the print trade produced a form of morally authoritative discourse best represented by the woman author: the trade's positioning of women as the agents responsible for the regulated circulation of virtuous texts allowed women writers to flourish at midcentury, just as women print workers disappeared.

I explore the links between authorship and gender in more depth in chapter 5. This chapter, the final case study, completes my description of the shift from the cultural privileging of the print worker to that of the author by focusing on one individual, Samuel Richardson, who, at the same time and in often contradictory ways, encapsulated both roles. I examine some of the ways in which his work as a printer fundamentally shaped his understanding of, indeed his construction of, his status as a writer and how his ideological concerns as a novelist writing for and about women affected his views on the appropriate circulation of the material print product. I argue that to Richardson, creator of the popular and beloved heroines in distress, Pamela and Clarissa, and the feminized hero, Sir Charles Grandison, intellectual property was always already *gendered* property, linked intimately to the rules of sexual propriety and proper feminine behavior. Through a detailed analysis of a series of public and private discursive events—letter writing, advertising, and, eventually, the writing of the continuation of *Pamela*—which took place shortly after the publication of Richardson's first novel in the fall of 1740, I show how, by midcentury, the obfuscating discourse of patriarchal authorship had trumped the more explicitly mercenary concerns of trade. Thus, I argue, intellectual property in the feminine form of the novel cannot be understood without recourse to eighteenth-century ideologies of gender.

In the end, print workers' discursive acts of self-preservation failed—the proprietary author won the battle for control. As we can see in literary studies' adoption of the discourse of "the-man-and-his-work," the dominant view of textual creation became reified and naturalized as the only possible understanding of it. The fact that alternatives ever even existed was forgotten. They were rendered invisible by the strength of the discourse that succeeded it. Thus what I am undertaking here is an almost archeological recovery, reconstructing from shards of misunderstood texts an ideology once commonplace. To do otherwise, to ignore the text work of print, is to ignore the rich material history that lies at the boundary of "text" and "book"; to view this process of production only through the eyes and ideologies of authors is to accept as "truth" a singular perspective. By recovering the texts of these print worker-writers, and by examining their shifting understanding of their domain and the representations they deployed, I hope to expand our notion of what constituted legitimate print, authorship, and creative work in this period of transition.

# 2

# *Printers' Manuals and the Bodies of Type*

*Book, is either numerous sheets of white paper that have been stitched together in such a way that they can be filled with writing; or, a highly useful and convenient instrument constructed of printed sheets variously bound in cardboard, paper, vellum, leather, etc. for presenting the truth to another in such a way that it can be conveniently read and recognized. Many people work on this ware before it is complete and becomes an actual book in this sense. The scholar and the writer, the papermaker, the type founder, the typesetter and the printer, the proofreader, the publisher, the book binder, sometimes even the gilder and the brassworker, etc. Thus many mouths are fed by this branch of manufacture.*

—*ALLGEMEINES OECONOMISCHES LEXICON*, 1753

*[T]here has always appeared to me, something monstrous in the existing relation between Author & Bookseller or Publisher, as regards remuneration . . . — a positive reversing of the natural order of things, as we find it obtains in all matters else—a subservience (pro tanto) of the spiritual to the material.*

—WILLIAM WORDSWORTH, MANUSCRIPT FRAGMENT, 1838

On the first page of *Mechanick Exercises on the Whole Art of Printing* (1683–84), Joseph Moxon dedicates what he calls his "Piece of Typographie" to the several partners who ran the Press at the University of Oxford. Of course, Moxon's text is a piece *on* typography in that typography is one of the many topics he covers in his expansive treatise. But his volume is also, inevitably, a literal piece *of* typography, as are all printed books. While Moxon, who was a part-time printer, typefounder, and writer, in addition to his regular work as a hydrographer and mathematical instrument maker, had personal and financial reasons to point to the material nature of his text, it is also evident throughout his text that he regarded the mechanical aspects of bookmaking as just as important as, if not superior to, the intellectual.[1] In the past twenty-five years or so, scholarship in the "history of the book" has *re*discovered the significance of these physical aspects of texts such as paper- and ink-making, letter founding, composing methods, work organization, distribution, circulation, and so forth. John Feather, in an essay defining this field of inquiry, tells us what Moxon might have: "[O]ur understanding of a text is ultimately influenced by the physical form of its presentation."[2]

In this chapter, however, I would like to press Moxon's implications a bit further. *Mechanick Exercises* makes it clear that the text is not only *influenced* by its physical form, but *is* that physical form. I say this wary of the essentialist view of technology such a statement can engender. For example, technological determinism is implied in much of Elizabeth Eisenstein's otherwise groundbreaking *The Printing Press as an Agent of Change,* in which she outlines the "communications revolutions" wrought by Gutenberg's invention. True, her work remains a fundamental and comprehensive overview of the social changes that derived from the new medium of print, but the work's very title explicitly credits the *technology itself* with subsequent cultural transformation. She does seem to address this as a potential problem when she writes in her preface that she "would have liked to underline the human element in my title by taking the early printer as my 'agent of change,'" conceding that "certain master printers" are the "unsung heroes" and the "true protagonists of this book." Nonetheless, she goes on to insist that "impersonal processes involving transmission and communications must be given due attention," and in the text that follows, the work of master printers and others in the print trade becomes merely an effect of an always already installed technology.[3]

Michael Warner points to the pitfalls inherent in relying on this "Whig-McLuhanite model of print history," claiming that most historians of the book "at some level . . . suppose printing to be a nonsymbolic form of material reality. Printing, in this view, is naturally distinct both from rhetoric, . . . and from forms of subjectivity. . . . It is mere technology, a medium itself unmediated."[4] This technology is seen as an implacable force, whether for good or evil. Once set in motion, its inexorable drive—the very motor, perhaps, of human progress—cannot be resisted. It remains to historians only to chart the detritus (be it composed of constitutions, novels, bills of sale, or ideologies of individualism) it leaves in its wake. It is clear that from within such a narrative, "politics and human agency disappear. . . , whether the agency be individual or collective, and culture receives an impact generated outside itself."[5] This understanding of print has let us easily give the printing press credit or blame for such vast and complex cultural conditions as literacy, democracy, and capitalism; for reading and writing regimes such as authorship and intellectual property; and even for more local institutional practices like literary hermeneutics and scholarly editing.[6] This attitude lingers into analyses of our own late- or post-print era as well: theories of hypertext and electronic writing often assume that regimes that rose directly and inevitably as a result of print are toppling as the essentialized technology of the computer becomes dominant.[7] Those less enthusiastic about this latest "revolution" ironically rely on a similar understanding of the human-machine equation. For example, Neil Postman, a critic of recent innovations in communication tools, claims that "once a technology is admitted, it plays out its own hand; it does what it is designed to do. Our task is to understand what that design is."[8] This common understanding of the "invisible hand" of the machine is, in fact, an effect and not a cause of attitudes such as Postman's. One of the goals of this chapter is to locate the cultural shift that brought us ideas like this.

Such determinism can be counteracted, I believe, by examining more closely the multiple possible and actual uses of a machine in the hands of variously ideologically situated owners and workers—indeed, by looking back at the human element to which Eisenstein herself alludes. This is not to take these up as essentialized bodies (or homogenized classes of bodies) as opposed to machines, but to examine them as agents of print, if they are also at the same time subjects of print. Therefore, when examining the physical form of print, I do not oppose it to or divorce it from the metaphysical text but assert that this supposedly solid essence is in fact always ultimately textual.[9] Such an analysis does not suppose that machines or media inevitably contain certain powers or must shape the culture according to an intrinsic plan. However, it does acknowledge the especially slippery nature of print as a self-advertising discourse, invisibly mediating itself through itself. To disrupt its tautology and to reenvision it as the graphic, visible tool that it is, we must turn to the rhetoric of print, to print as a human-linguistic construct. In this chapter, then, I take up some early examples of books about books.

A useful place to examine the representations of print technology is in printers' manuals, the self-reflective texts by printers about printing. These books about books attempt to describe, analyze, standardize, and regulate their craft and trade. Much attention has been paid to the role print played in spreading technical knowledge but little to those texts that turned, in an almost Borgesian self-reflexivity, onto themselves, describing the process of their own construction. Manuals describing the trade of printing were uniquely situated within a dynamic of information circulation, illustrating, as they did, the very mechanisms of the dissemination of technical knowledge. By revealing the literal nuts and bolts of print, these manuals made opaque what might otherwise have been a transparent medium, making the medium—long before McLuhan—the message. From these manuals, then, we can begin to glean the local and historical meanings of print and see it not as a fixed essence but as an active and ever-changing ideological tool.

I am using Joseph Moxon's 1683–84 *Mechanick Exercises* and John Smith's 1755 *The Printer's Grammar* as representative examples of these printers manuals. Certainly they were considered such throughout the eighteenth century: Moxon's text, "the first comprehensive [printers'] manual in any language," stood as the primary source of information on printing for the first half of the century, and Smith's was the most widely copied for the next hundred years.[10] These two texts are also representative in that they each appeared after periods of dramatic upheaval within the trade. Moxon's text came after a period of great flux within the printing businesses spurred by the political upheavals of Restoration England and the debates over the relative freedom of the press. Smith's text, too, responds to a half century of legal and economic changes that solidified the market for print products. I argue that both printers' manuals not only reflect these changes in their trade but react to them in ways that produce specific ideological regimes. Operating as prescriptive as well as descriptive projects, the manuals strive to regulate the trade after periods of unruly growth.

As part of my examination of these ideologies of print, this chapter attempts to recover the print workers' role as it was once understood by contemporaries in the print trades and perhaps even by readers and writers. In Moxon's manual, I argue, the body of print emerges as a working body, a laborer whose physical construction of print is every bit as, if not more, important than the writer who supplies text. Indeed, the print worker is understood as a *collaborator* in the construction of the meaning of the print text. By the time Smith wrote his manual, however, the working body had dissolved into the subject writing, the transcendent Author, whose disembodied intellect is privileged over the physical book. Typography was thus conceived of as a transparent manifestation of the Author's will. One of my goals, then, is to chart the history of the erasure of the printer from the scene of textual creation, to reclaim a discourse lost in the naturalization of print.

Printing, however, is but one human activity among many, and it must be viewed in its larger cultural context. In both Smith's and Moxon's manuals, the representation of orderly print (held up as an exemplar against unauthorized forms and potential typographical chaos), and the proper role of printer and writer within that order, is buttressed by other technologies of management: in both texts, as I show, the arguments for typographical regulation rely on discourses of sexuality and gender. These writers, however, writing in historical situations seventy years apart and promoting their own particular agendas, each construct a different interpretation of what it means to be a man (and by inference a woman) in and of print. The changing notions of authorship and print work in this period both reflect and reproduce changing notions of sexed bodies and gendered behavior. *Mechanick Exercises* and *The Printer's Grammar*, then, usefully frame an important transitional period in the history of publishing, a period that reconstructed the meaning of that "piece of typography" we call "book."

## "THE LANGUAGE OF ARTIZANS": PRINTING MANUALS FOR THE "MECHANICK ARTS"

A brief history of manuals such as these may be useful for understanding their strategic location within changing notions of intellectual work and the economies that support it. While Moxon's and Smith's texts were, as I have indicated, prototypes within the print trade, they would have seemed familiar to an audience acquainted with the larger "how-to" genre of manuals. Printers' manuals were part of the early modern European "proliferation of books on the business arts," that is, the larger and longer historical trend in publishing descriptions and categorizations of the trades in general.[11] In England specifically, the publication of the first printers' manual can be seen in the context of two more specific related trends: the relative loss of guild power and the popularization of science. Manuals such as Moxon's may have contributed to the former: Eisenstein relates that individual trades were not always pleased to have their secrets revealed, and writers of these manuals risked the wrath of their colleagues who preferred to mete out such knowledge only to those who followed the traditional paths of apprenticeship.[12] The London-based guilds were further threatened by political movements against monopolies that accompanied the slow but steady growth of industry outside city walls and in the provinces. At the same time, the development of an increasingly retail-based economy required tradesmen to start their businesses with more capital, which limited the number of those who, as masters of their trade, could set up their own shops. The necessity of taking advantage of economies of scale led to the creation of proto-factories requiring specialization and a division of labor that did not always overlay well onto existing guild structures. Thus while livery companies still existed throughout the eighteenth century, these changes disrupted the once clear path from apprentice to journeyman to master, and guild power was radically diminished.[13]

In the case of the print trades, these factors were exacerbated by the loosening of restrictions on printing throughout the last thirty years or so of the seventeenth century.[14] In the early seventeenth century, the Stationers' Company had been able, with the cooperation of the Crown, to control not only who printed but what was deemed printable, that is, what was not considered blasphemous or seditious. The political upheaval of the 1640s and 1650s, however, was accompanied by, indeed, arguably constituted by, an outpouring of unauthorized printed texts. When Charles II was restored to the throne in 1660, the Stationers' Company looked to the government to help it reestablish the authority it had lost during the civil war and prevent the many unofficial printers who had flourished during those years from continuing to take business away from company members. The nervous Crown, which had learned all too well the potential power of the press, was happy to oblige—but the company was not completely pleased with the results. The Licensing Act of 1662 reinstated most of the company's prerogatives except one important one: although printers, in order to publish legally, had to be one of the Stationers, the Stationers would no longer be trusted to enforce their own pre-publication censoring. Instead, a licenser was appointed who reported directly to the secretary of state. The first licenser, the notorious Roger L'Estrange, was much despised by the Stationers, but even he could not keep the press under control in times of political duress, as the Exclusion Crisis of 1679–81 revealed. The Crown gave up its most stringent efforts to censor, though, as it realized the press was better channeled than suppressed: by 1695, the government had polarized into two parties, Whig and Tory, both of which relied on printed material to garner support and besmirch the opposition. Thus when the Licensing Act was up for renewal, it was rejected by Parliament. The Stationers' Company from this point would seek other means, both legal and discursive, to control its trade, but despite its efforts, it had ceased, like many other guilds, to be a dominant force in an increasingly entrepreneurial and commercial trade.[15] Unofficial printing outside the guild continued to flourish.

Joseph Moxon was one such entrepreneur, the prototypical printer of this new era. He was not one of the twenty authorized printers in London.[16] As a freeman of the city (a member of the Weavers' Company), Moxon may have been protected by a 1614 legal decision that allowed any freeman to practice any trade. His position as official hydrographer to the king may also have allowed him printing privileges.[17] In any case, outside the still closed ranks of the Stationers' Company, he could freely give away "secrets."[18] It is not necessary to believe he wrote deliberately in defiance of the company, however; after all, his work on printing was part of a larger set of *Mechanick Exercises, or The Doctrine of Handy-Works*, the first volume of which described the work of smiths, joiners, carpenters, and turners. His goals were perhaps more narrowly financial: by publishing these volumes he declared himself an expert on the "mechanick arts" and so advertised himself as not only a knowledgeable printer but also a reliable hydrographer and maker of maps, globes, and mathematical instruments.[19] More broadly, though, these texts announced that he was part of what Eisenstein has termed the "new scientific ethos" that linked trade and technology.[20]

It was perhaps his interest in this linkage that gained Moxon a membership in the nascent Royal Society, which proposed as one of its first projects a collectively written catalog and history of the trades.[21] Even before the founding of the Royal Society, Samuel Hartlib, Robert Boyle, and William Petty had discussed the creation of a *"gymnasium mechanium* or a college of tradesmen . . . for the advancement of all mechanical arts and manufactures."* Petty stressed that in such a school "the history of arts or manufactures might first be undertaken . . . , wherein should be described the whole process of manual operations and applications . . . with the necessary instruments and machines, whereby every piece of work is elaborated, and made to be what it is."[22] While never completed, this project was a predecessor to the Royal Society's plan in 1667 to publish a *"Catalogue* of all *Trades, Works*, and Manufactures," also largely illusory.[23] When Petty envisions the audience for the history of trade he is proposing, he refers to customers, scholars, divines, students, and mathematicians, among others, but he does not mention those who might actually work in the trade.[24] Certainly, tradesmen were not asked to author such texts. The implicit purpose of Petty's—and later, the society's— plan was to disseminate the technology behind the trades so that superior minds might, upon studying this technology, improve it, leading to more efficient—and thus more profitable—systems of manufacture.

Understanding Moxon's affiliation with this Royal Society project thus sheds new light on his manuals on "handy-works" and printing. It contradicts the view, long implied by bibliographic scholars, that printers' manuals were written for printers, a view that has justified treating Moxon's manual and those of his followers as transparent windows onto the world of professional printing.[25] Instead, Moxon's participation in the Royal Society suggests that his was not a manual for printers but one specifically for outsiders. Despite the Stationers' Company's loss of power, most printers still learned their trade through apprenticeship and would have no need for such a book.[26] Moxon's own views on who his audience should be are indicated in the preface to the first volume, *Mechanick Exercises, or The Doctrine of Handy-Works*:

> I See no more Reason, why the Sordidness of some Workmen, should be the cause of contempt upon *Manual Operations*, than that the excellent Invention of a *Mill* should be dispis'd, because

> a blind Horse draws in it. And tho' the *Mechanicks* be, by some, accounted Ignoble and Scandalous? yet it is very well known, that many Gentlemen in this Nation, of good Rank and high Quality, are conversant in *Handy-Works*.... How pleasant and healthey this their Divertion is, their Minds and Bodies find; and how Harmless and Honest all sober men may judge?[27]

While this does not tell us who *did* read Moxon, it does show how he positions his book: it is meant for those readers who might need convincing to look past the "sordidness of some workers" (and not blink at his blunt comparison of them to a blind horse) and with the leisure to read for "divertion" rather than necessity. Indeed, such recreational pursuits in the upper class were publicly sanctioned: according to David McKitterick, London printer George Palmer did teach the young Duke of Cumberland, son of George II, how to print in 1731, prompting the *Craftsman* to remark that aristocratic printing was "a much more polite, as well as more instructive Amusement for Themselves and their Heirs, than the modern fashionable Diversions of Billiard-Tables and Fox-Hunting."[28]

Elsewhere, though, it is clear that while such work might have been used for the setting up of entertaining hobbies or merely to satisfy intellectual curiosity, a more serious goal was also attached to the larger Royal Society project of which Moxon's manuals were a part. This agenda is made manifest when Moxon explicitly contrasts the worker with the scholar in the same preface: "The Lord Bacon, in his Natural History, reckons that Philosophy would be improv'd by having the secrets of all Trades lye open; ... that *the Trades themselves might, by a Philosopher, be improv'd*."[29] This mirrors earlier writing: John Evelyn, writing in 1662, even asks workers to participate in this project, assuming condescendingly that it is in their own best interest:

> I could wish, with all my heart, that more of our workmen would ... impart to us what they know of their several trades and manufactures.... For what could so much conduce to their profit and emolument? When their several mysteries being subjected to the most accurate inspection and examen of the more polite and enquiring spirits, they should return to their Authors again so greatly refin'd and improved, and when (through this

means also) Philosophy her self might hope to attain so considerable progress towards her ultimate perfection.[30]

Thus we see that the Royal Society's celebrated call (in Thomas Sprat's *History of the Royal Society*) for the use of "the Language of Artizans, Countrymen, and Merchants," then, was not so much a recognition of the expertise of these groups as a concern that, without help from the higher classes, trade would founder.[31] Here, philosophy's opposition to manufactures, a form of mind-body dualism, marks a class difference, a privileging of brainpower over brawn.[32] Such distinctions grew in part from a perception of economic threat from below. Philip Ayres, for example, admonishes gentlemen to manage their estates more wisely "to prevent this growing mischief that the wealth of the Nation be not transferred from the Ancient Nobility and Gentry in England, to the Commonality, and to the Mechanicks and Mean Spirited Men (who have acquired a great dexterity in getting and gathering together Riches)."[33] They also worked to abet the British colonial project, as Moxon's preface to the first volume of the *Handy-Works* implies: "Nor would I have you understand, that when I name the Mechanicks, I mean the rough and Barbarous sort of working which is used by the Natives of America and some other such places." He claims that this work is inferior since it does not utilize the "good and ready Rules of Art" and that "what they do, is done by Tedious Working, and he that has the best Eye at Guessing."[34]

That Moxon's manuals were written or used to promulgate a social hierarchy is perhaps not surprising. What is notable, however, is the means by which this was happening. It is easy to overlook the fact that Moxon and his Royal Society friends are promoting the use of a hitherto underutilized medium. They are advocating, in short, that the mysteries of manufacture be "returned to their Authors" through the *printed* words of an author. Books were meant to improve an apprenticeship system that construed learning as inseparable from physical labor. While guilds had carried on for hundreds of years, using oral transmission to pass on trade secrets to apprentices and journeymen, the transformation of these somatic ways of knowing into print information made guild techniques the business (in both senses) of the literate and educated classes, allowing them to buttress their power—and personal finances—

by increasing their knowledge of once mysterious techniques.[35] This alteration in the *technologies* of learning, from orality and other embodied forms to print and pages, is significant enough that Moxon is compelled to comment on it in the preface of his first volume:

> I thought to have given these Exercises, the Title of The Doctrine of Handy-Crafts, but when I better considered the true meaning of the Word Handy-Crafts, I found the Doctrine would not bear it; because Handy-Craft signifies Cunning, or Sleight, or Craft of the Hand, which cannot be taught by Words, but is only gain'd by Practice and Exercise; therefore I shall not undertake, that with the bare reading of these Exercises, any shall be able to perform these Handy-Works; but I may safely tell you, that these are the Rules that every one that will endeavor to perform them must follow; and that by true observing them, he may, according to his stock of Ingenuity and Diligence, sooner or later inure his hand to the Cunning or Craft of working like a Handy-Craft, and consequently be able to perform them in time.[36]

As we see, this conversion is not necessarily a smooth one. Moxon is usually a writer of direct prose, so his convoluted syntax here is evidence of his struggle to fulfill the demands of competing ideologies: the hand versus the eye, practice versus reading, embodied muscle memory versus print information. He comes to an uneasy compromise, for while he cannot guarantee that reading alone will teach these crafts, as a producer of books he cannot concede either to the domain of pure "handy-craft," in which the body learns only through "practice and exercise." He does make print primary, refusing to use "handy-craft" in his title, but has to admit the body is necessary. Here he differs from his Royal Society companions who emphasized philosophy alone. He sees the intellect and the body working together, a belief that becomes more obvious in the main text of his printers' manual. Despite this caveat—an important one, as I detail—Moxon is, at least momentarily, strategically placing his text within the ideological camp of this relatively new technology, with its associated social affiliations.[37] The silent book has replaced the physical intricacies of the guild training system: anyone who can read becomes a virtual apprentice.[38]

Understanding the audience for these printer's manuals helps us understand the ideology they promulgated: they are not so much about the literal printing process as about the idea of print. They argue for what print should be and could do, not necessarily what, in a factual, objective sense, it was. By placing these manuals in the social context of the intellectual production of knowledge, I am not conceding to the Royal Society's dictate of where such information belongs but acknowledging these texts as producers of very specific views about the uses of print, the meaning of print, and the role of print in social transformation. In short, I see Moxon's work, and printer's manuals in general, as a statement of the values of print culture itself.

## THE BODY OF KNOWLEDGE: JOSEPH MOXON'S SEXUALIZED TRADE

If, in his preface, Moxon marks the worker as "sordid" and sleights as "handy-crafts," while at the same time contradictorily insisting on the importance of the body and its labor, his volume on printing is much less ambiguous. His preface had to sell his multivolume work, and he may have wanted to attract an audience like his friends in the Royal Society and other men of "good Rank and high Quality" by "classing" his text in opposition to workers. Moxon, however, was also a worker himself, or at least worked closely supervising them in the printing of books and the constructing of mathematical tools. His multiple roles placed him on the boundary between the laboring and the thinking classes, and his preface reflects this uneasy ideological positioning. Despite his use of the Royal Society's rhetoric, however, his volume on printing suggests that the true force behind the popularization of science and the promulgation of technological expertise is not "philosophers" but working men and their tools, men carving letters, boiling pulp, building presses, laying out pages. In short, it indicates that knowledge was disseminated only through sweat and labor and letter—three terms that, I show, cannot be separated. While the Royal Society worked to place technical information into the hands of an educated elite who sought to control the trade-knowledge nexus, Moxon, perhaps inadvertently, demystifies this realm by showing it to be intrinsically grounded in the physical: knowledge is ink on paper and, as such, belongs to the artisans and laborers who constructed it.

In the printing terminology of the period, a "body of type" meant a complete run of letters of all one font and size, such as French Canon, Greatprimer, Pica, and so forth. Dismembered body parts of a more familiar sort, however, litter Moxon's text: heads, cheeks, faces, mouths, tongues, feet, and toes, among others. These are, of course, not literal human remains but the terms given to various mechanical parts and tools related to the work of printing; nonetheless, their overwhelming presence seems more than an accident of etymology. The ghostly bodies formed by these parts evidently have a sex and, indeed, are made to have sex, for, Moxon tells us in a passage on the casting of letters for type, "[t]he *Female Block* is such another *Block* as the *Male Block*, only, instead of a *Tongue* running through the length of it a *Groove* is made to receive the *Tongue* of the *Male-Block*" (*ME*, 181). While the male-female terminology used to describe insertable objects, such as water pipes, lingers even today, the *Oxford English Dictionary* traces one of its earliest usages to Moxon. His prosaic manner in deploying such terms, however, suggests that this description was not uncommon, at least within the trade. Such usage may originate in the views on sexuality that dominated England prior to the late eighteenth century (and were indeed commonplace in Europe for thousands of years), views that held that women's sexual organs were the same as men's, only inside out. Men and women, like the male and female blocks, were essentially biologically the same, with penis and testicles revealing themselves as vagina and ovaries in half the population. Thomas Laqueur suggests that men and women construed in these theories were understood not as radically dimorphic but as part of a biological continuum.[39] In Moxon, these relatively undifferentiated bodies do the cultural work of print: their mechanistic heterosexual coupling is an essential part of the creation of words. In this passage on the work of the letter caster, for example, he describes this process in intense, almost lascivious detail:

> When his *Stick* of *Letters* is thus transfer'd to the *Male-Block*, He claps the middle of the *Male-Block* into his left-Hand, tilting the *Feet* of the *Letter* a little upwards, that the *Face* may rest upon the *Tongue*, and then takes about the middle of the *Female-Block* in his right-Hand, and lays it so upon the *Male-*

> *Block*, that the *Tongue* of the *Male-Block* may fall into the *Tongue* of the *Female-Block*. . . . So that when the *Knot* of the *Male-Block* is lightly drawn towards the *Knot* of the *Female-Block*, or the *Knot* of the *Female-Block* lightly thrust toward the *Knot* of the *Male-Block*, both *Knots* shall squeeze the *Letter* close between them. (*ME*, 186–87)

So, apparently, from the sex of machinery, a unit of language is born.

Another body also intrudes in the love scene above, however: the "he" whose left and right hands are moving things along. In Moxon, human bodies intrude into the scene of printmaking as much as mechanical ones. These bodies are mostly, as in the passage above, working bodies, for in Moxon labor is never abstract or disembodied; the printed product does not appear magically out of machinery. Moxon's working bodies— almost without exception male bodies—are resolutely physical: they sweat, smell (both actively and passively), eat, drink, grow weary, punish and are punished, and even, in one alarming passage, "Piss Blood, and shortly after dye" (*ME*, 324). Some even marry and have children, and while their couplings are not literally depicted, they underlie Moxon's construction of the printing process: mechanical reproduction cannot exist without its earthy counterpart. Despite the material and sensual nature of these bodies, however, they are not independent of the trade and cannot be separated from the printing process. The possibility of workers' marrying, for example, is listed in a section describing customs of the "Chappel," or printing house. It is not that workers' bodies belong to the chapel; rather, they together make up the larger laboring body that *is* the chapel. Early in his treatise, Moxon explains briefly the way this entity works: "[T]he Master Printer is the Soul of *Printing*; and all the Work-men [are] members of the Body governed by that Soul subservient to him" (*ME*, 12).[40]

Because the workers' bodies are in fact merely parts of this larger body, they cannot be separated from the other body parts occupying the printing house, the mechanical ones. It is the intermingling of the human and mechanical that forms the body of type, as seen in this passage on letter casting I excerpt below. First, though, it useful to remember that Moxon, who had served as a letter cutter and typefounder himself, was intimately familiar with this process. He knew how divorced it was from the flat, linear, abstract product of the printed page. For even though the making of letters might involve the use of written or print models, letter cutting, the method of creating the steel punches that in turn formed the matrices (the "negative space" that held the metal for the final type), was, as Warren Chappel points out, a "sculptural process . . . carried forward by direct and plastic means." Chappel further explains that "even in the use of engraving tools, type-cutting calls for handling that is much more related to scraping and paring than delineating."[41] Similarly, typefounding was also a process that required—to make a point that is obvious but bears repeating—quick and precise *movement*. Here, for example, Moxon describes the typecaster fitting together the two sides of a mold around the matrix and pouring in the molten metal that will rapidly become hard type:

> Now he comes to *Casting*. Wherefore placing the under-half of the *Mold* in his left hand, . . . he clutches the ends of its *Wood* between the lower part of the *Ball* of his Thumb and his three hind-Fingers. Then he lays the upper half of the *Mold* upon the under half, so as the *Male-Gages* may fall into the *Female-Gages*, and at the same time the *Foot* of the *Matrice* place it self upon the *Stool*. And clasping his left-hand Thumb strong over the upper half of the *Mold*, he nimbly catches hold of the *Bow* or *Spring* with his right-hand Fingers at the top of it, and his Thumb under it, and places the point of it against the middle of the *Notch* in the backside of the *Matrice*, pressing it as well forwards towards the *Mold*, as downwards by the *Shoulder* of the *Notch* close upon the *Stool*, while at the same time with his hinder-Fingers as aforesaid, he draws the under-half of the *Mold* towards the *Ball* of his Thumb, and thrusts by the *Ball* of his Thumb the upper part towards his Fingers. . . .
>
> Then [he] takes up the *Ladle* full of *Mettal*, and having his *Mold* as aforesaid in his left hand, he a little twists the left-side of his *Body* from the *Furnance*, and brings the *Geat* of his *Ladle* (full of *Mettal*) to the *Mouth* of the *Mold*, and twists the upper part of his right-hand towards him to turn the *Mettal* into it, while . . . he Jilts the *Mold* in his left hand forwards to receive the *Mettal* with a strong *Shake* . . . into the *Bodies* of the *Mold*. (*ME*, 169)

For the most part, Moxon's italicization of printing terminology in this passage and throughout his text clarifies for the reader whether body parts belong to sentient beings or inanimate objects—the "*Shoulder*" of the notch versus the "Fingers" of the caster, for example. However, a few typographical slippages reveal that this dichotomy may not be completely stable. Throughout, the "Ball" of the caster's thumb is italicized, as if this too were a piece of machinery, located precisely at the place where the two domains, human and machine, most often intersect. Later, the caster's entire body becomes italicized and therefore, in typographic terms at least, a unit of print technology, congruent to the body of the mold, or even the body of type being made. We might relate this to Moxon's own experience: he knew firsthand the complex interplay among human intellectual intention, the physical embodiment of that intention, and the tools designed to achieve that intention. How much more nebulous might these boundaries become when re-presented in the process of writing, then printing, this description? Though patterns of italicization, spelling, punctuation, and such are today usually called "accidentals," this does not mean that, in the period before widespread standardization, they were used carelessly. We may read "accidentals" as makers of meaning, whether purposefully or unconsciously employed.[42] Thus, it appears possible that Moxon (or perhaps his "collaborator," the real-life compositor setting type for this book) could momentarily forget the difference between the body of type and the human body.[43]

Even the construction of the sentences in this passage reflects this confusion. Although through most of this description the caster instigates the work through his body's actions—he clutches, lays, clasps, presses, and so on—as he brings the male and female gages together, the "*Foot* of the *Matrice* place[s] it self upon the *Stool*," acting, so it seems, independently, hopping up on this piece of human furniture with its nimble human appendage. This blurring of the line between object and body suggests that Moxon's workers are ultimately cyborgs, a "hybrid of machine and organism."[44] It does not mean, however, that they have been reduced to mere cogs in a lifeless engine of print. The "mechanical exercises" that make up the "whole art of printing" are always human exercises as well. It is the *coupling* of man and machine that produces the body of type, as is apparent in the many illustrations Moxon includes in his manual (see figs. 1 and 2). The printed page, then, always bears traces of both bodies' labor. Despite Moxon's prefatory comments on the "sordidness" and "ignoble" nature of mechanic toil, then, his book is not a product alienated from the sweat of the worker but one in which the hand of labor is always apparent.[45]

Fig. 1: *Making letters: through the coupling of man and tool, a unit of type is born. (Joseph Moxon,* Mechanick Exercises on the Whole Art of Printing, *1683–84, ed. Herbert Davis and Harry Carter, Dover Publications, 1958. Private collection.)*

Fig. 2: *Pressing books: Moxon's depiction of the printing process conjoins material products with human labor. (Joseph Moxon,* Mechanick Exercises on the Whole Art of Printing, *1683–84, ed. Herbert Davis and Harry Carter, Dover Publications, 1958. Private collection.)*

## A Disembodied Product: Smith's Transparent Authorship

While Moxon's own text may have undermined his intentions to replace bodily knowledge with a regime of reading, the discourses supporting those intentions did eventually become dominant. Almost seventy years later, in John Smith's *The Printer's Grammar*, the human bodies have disappeared from the scene of printing. No major changes in the printing process itself can account for their elision: workers proceeded for the most part, just as they had in Moxon's time, still sweating in workshops with the same tools and machines. Printing, however, had become a large, vital, even indispensable, business, and knowledge became an essential commodity. As literacy spread, and became an important vehicle for both entertainment and information, the demand for printed material increased. Booksellers became the privileged members of the trade, often managing all aspects of the bookmaking process from hiring writers, to contracting printers, to supervising networks of distributors. As those at the top of this capital-intensive trade became wealthier, they often adopted the bourgeois value system of their readers, looking down on the physical labors of "rude mechanicals." In this thriving market, the question of who owned what words became a crucial issue, and debates arose over the implications of terms such as *authorship* and *piracy* and over the ramifications of the 1710 Act of Anne.[46] While little is known about Smith's own life and social positioning, his text must be understood in this context: print was now the institutionalized means of communication for a reading market.

The effects of this market-driven understanding of print can be seen in both the content and style of Smith's manual. His text does not describe the sweaty, human scene of printmaking, but prescribes a system of typographical classification and workplace regulation that will result in a proper, that is, uniform and standardized, page. Indeed, he rarely discusses workers themselves, only opaque objects and timeless methods. His opening sentence sets the tone:

> Conformable to the General method which is observed in Grammars, we begin *this* also with the Principles therof, viz. LETTERS; with this difference, that instead of applying their signification, as in others, to the art of speaking and writing some particular language, we shall consider them as the chief Printing-Materials; and in the course of this Chapter treat of their Contexture, Superficial shape, and such Properties as come under the cognizance of Printers, Booksellers, and others who have a judgement of Printing.[47]

Here he makes it clear that letters—by themselves, without even the supporting context of language to help them make sense—are to be the subject and object of his text, while those who create, place, and distribute those letters are relegated to a relatively distant position. Unlike Moxon, who often uses the name of the type of workman (caster, dresser, compositor, pressman, etc.) as the subject of the sentence, pairing it with an active verb, Smith's sentences are frequently, fittingly impersonal: "That Italic letter was not designed to distinguish proper names in, nor for several other uses which it now serves, might be readily proved" (*PG*, 13). As in this example, the verbs throughout the manual are often passive or state of being, and the subjects of sentences often abstractions, or at best generic "we" constructions that evacuate specific human agency from the scene of print. This abstract and ungrounded nature of his view of the printed text is highlighted in the several charts and tables that are interspersed in his treatise, privileging formula over actual procedure and numeric symbol over the work of hands (see figs. 3 and 4). The difference in the underlying ideology here is especially striking when we compare the tables to Moxon's many illustrations of the interaction between people and mechanical tools.

The only bodies that seem to count for Smith, then, are the bodies of type—but these bodies trouble him. His chief complaint, reiterated frequently, is that the bodies of type in England are not standardized, that is, that the font of one body, Greatprimer or Pica, for example, often varied in height, width, and depth from founder to founder or house to house. In Smith's view, this not only wastes money but can wreck havoc in the orderly workplace. He also worries incessantly about the variations in usage of italics, capitals, spelling, and punctuation. His text is thus full of prohibitions and regulations, "should not" and "ought to," in addition to his instructions, tables, charts, and mathematical calculations. Clearly, his ultimate goal is the regulation of these unruly bodies of type.

In the process of ordering typography, however, he endows it with the human characteristics otherwise missing from his agent-less text. Although I have shown how the print worker is replaced in this manual by the printed letter itself, in a striking "return of the repressed," the body reemerges to provide order to potential chaos: typography is understood here through mid-eighteenth-century notions of the sexed and sexual body. Just as the structure of detached Enlightenment objectivity supports Smith's distanced and impersonal prose, Enlightenment sciences of the body inform his understanding of the proper use of let-

*A TABLE of the present Sizes of Letter.*

| | Contains m', in a Foot, | |
|---|---|---|
| French Canon | — | 18 and a Gr. Pr. |
| Two-lines Double Pica | — | 20 and ¾. |
| Two-lines Greatprimer | — | 25 and an n. |
| Two-lines English | — | 32 |
| Two-lines Pica | — | 35 ¾ |
| Double Pica | — | 41 and an n. |
| Paragon | — | 44 and an n. |
| Greatprimer | — | 51 and an r, flat. |
| English | — | 64 |
| Pica | — | 71 and an n. |
| Small-pica | — | 83 |
| Longprimer | — | 89 |
| Burjois | — | 102 and a space. |
| Brevier | — | 112 and an n. |
| Minion | — | 128 |
| Nonpareil | — | 143 |
| Pearl | — | 178 |

*A BILL of Pica Roman, and Half a Bill of Italic, weigh 800 lb.*

LOWER-CASE

| | | To be cast | | |
|---|---|---|---|---|
| | | More. | Lefs. | In all. |
| a | 7000 | 500 | | 7500 |
| b | 1600 | | 400 | 1200 |
| c | 2400 | | 900 | 1500 |
| d | 4000 | 800 | | 4800 |
| e | 12000 | 1000 | | 13000 |
| f | 2000 | 500 | | 2500 |
| g | 1600 | | 300 | 1300 |
| h | 6000 | 500 | | 6500 |
| i | 6000 | | 2000 | 4000 |
| j | 600 | | 300 | 300 |
| k | 1000 | | 100 | 900 |
| l | 3000 | | | 3000 |
| m | 3000 | | 1000 | 2000 |
| n | 6000 | 500 | | 6500 |
| o | 6000 | 1000 | | 7000 |
| p | 1600 | | 600 | 1000 |
| q | 600 | | 300 | 300 |
| r | 5000 | 1000 | | 6000 |
| s | 3000 | | 500 | 2500 |
| ſ | 2400 | | | 2400 |
| t | 7000 | 500 | | 7500 |
| u | 3000 | | 1000 | 2000 |
| v | 1000 | | | 1000 |
| w | 1600 | 400 | | 2000 |
| x | 400 | | | 400 |
| y | 1600 | 400 | | 2000 |
| z | 400 | | 200 | 200 |
| & | 400 | | 200 | 200 |
| | 90200 | | | 89500 |

CAPI-

FIG. 3. *"This table is drawn up to shew the Size which each Body of Letter, here specified, now has"* (Smith, 26). *He goes on to complain of the irregularity of the casting process which results in letters of the same Body being different sizes. (John Smith,* The Printer's Grammar, *1755, ed. D. F. Foxon, Gregg Press, 1965. Wayne State University.)*

FIG. 4. *A table showing the contents of a "bill," or 500 pounds, of Pica Roman (Smith, 42). He hopes to modify the Bill "so as to make a Fount of Letter turn out more perfect" (46). (John Smith,* The Printer's Grammar, *1755, ed. D. F. Foxon, Gregg Press, 1965. Wayne State University.)*

ters. Unlike Moxon's copulating machinery, however, Smith's type does not directly reveal its physicality but signifies a binary gender—a subtle yet important difference that reproduces a view of sex and gender new to this period. Male and female bodies, instead of being perceived as points on a hierarchical but unitary continuum, were now seen as rigidly distinctive.[48] Gendered behavior was thought to be rooted in these differences, rather than arising from merely a correct adherence to cultural precepts. This "empowerment of the natural," as Michael McKeon has termed it, lent authority to sociocultural norms, which became the locus of attention in eighteenth-century discourse.[49] Gender difference was treated "as a strictly dyadic, experientially articulated and socially mediated expression of sexual difference rather than as ontologically distinct from it."[50] In other words, the biological basis of gender, considered a "given," simultaneously lent credence and allowed attention to be diverted to descriptions/prescriptions of behaviors in the separate spheres of male and female activities.[51] The connection between body and behavior was so obvious it could be ignored.

Smith's text relies on this kind of naturalization. Producing a predictably structured hierarchy of binary gender roles, he personifies type into implicitly masculine and feminine forms, whose outward behavior and appearance reveal the inner virtues appropriate to their roles. For example, Smith lobbies for the increased use of his favorite letterform, the "*good* Roman" (*PG*, 4). This letter, when made well, "is generally cast of good metal, and to stand true, and exact in line, besides well dressed; no wonder that it has recommended itself into the most considerable Printing-houses in this city" (*PG*, 7). In other words, this venerable Latin patriarch (the roman's ancient connections are always stressed) has been transformed into the modern, upright bourgeois citizen of England—by connotation male—whose contained, dignified demeanor makes him welcome in the best houses and marks him as worthy of widely disseminating information in a standard, measured, and rational manner. Print has been transformed from the unruly partner in sedition so reviled in post-Restoration diatribes into something suitable for reasoned discourse in the public sphere. Of course, Smith cautions, he does not "pronounce all Letter good which is new; but only such as has the necessary accomplishments as well in its appearance, as substance" (*PG*, 4), but outside appearance is often connected to the solid weight and heft of a virtuous soul. The link to the economic values of the rising middle class—who of course represented the largest body of readers—is also clear: the roman's virtue is also his profit, Smith explains, for a letter that is cast of good metal will last "so long as till it has paid for itself, besides good interest for its long credit; thereby to ease the charges of such sorts of Letter as never make a return neither of the principal nor interest" (*PG*, 9). The accomplished and profitable roman, then, keeps the printing house solvent, just as middle-class behavioral norms were believed to stave off simultaneously financial hardship and the moral decay of poverty. Indeed, Smith's description of this letterform might have come from an eighteenth-century conduct manual, such as *The Art of Governing a Wife, with Rules for Batchelors* (1747), which dictated that a good husband "be sober in speaking, easy in discourse, faithful where he is entrusted, discreet in giving counsel, careful of providing his house, diligent in looking after his estate, . . . vigilant in what relates to his honour, and very stayed in all his behavior."[52] Similarly, Lord Chesterfield proposes that his son follow the internalized dictates of the eighteenth-century economic man even when it comes to intellectual activity, explaining "the right use of your time . . . is laying it out to immense interest; which, in a very few years will amount to prodigious capital."[53]

Smith contrasts the characteristics of masculine fonts with those he seems to consider feminine. The italic, he argues, if used properly and within specified confinements, can serve as a useful and decorative feminine companion to the roman. It is specifically an object of display whose feminine graces are a point of national esteem: it has a "soft and tender face," Smith proudly states, which "is now in England of such a beautiful cut and shape as it never was before" (*PG*, 13). In order to present this type to its best advantage, the letter cutter, much like a good dressmaker, need take care "to keep the slopings of that tender-faced Letter within such degrees as required for each Body" (*PG*, 16): just as proper attire both molds the woman's shape to a required feminine aesthetic and marks her social position, the letter dresser regulates the form of the individual letter to suit its textual classification.[54] Smith is interested as well in keeping the italic within proper cultural boundaries, deploying it only in the places where it can do its rigidly defined "women's work." It should never be used for the main part of the text, he asserts, only "for varying the different Parts and Fragments" (*PG*, 14), like prefaces and dedications. Though these items are, of course, extraneous to the main (masculine) text, they do still serve an important function. Introductory writing moves the reader from the public realm of buying a book to the private realm of the writer's innermost thoughts and feelings. According to conduct literature of the time, women were especially suited for this sort of sociability: as John Gregory puts it, "[T]he temper and dispositions of the heart in [women] make [them] enter more readily and warmly into friendships than men."[55] Thus a feminine font prepares the reader for the intimacies of the reading experience, culturally coded as private.[56]

This ideology has a material history as well. As the form of English typography most closely linked to handwriting, existing on the border between pen and print, italic facilitated the transition from personal manuscript to market commodity. The italic hand was traditionally (from the Renaissance) a woman's hand, though it became in the seventeenth century the hand of the signature, the mark guaranteeing authenticity.[57] Italic prefatory material, though printed, can thus be seen as working to authenticate the mass-produced, impersonal contents inside the book by erasing the print shop as mediator between author and reader. (The ramifications of this erasure are discussed below.) Structurally, then, the italic is the feminine object of exchange between the implicitly masculinized reader and writer. As such, it is analogous to the eighteenth-century woman on the marriage market, set up as an aesthetically and sexually desirable lure, bounded by taste and propriety, in order to trade intimacy for her father's or husband's social position and mobility. Just as the "authentic" feelings stirred by the romance plot and contained within the companionate marriage masked women's position as a marketable commodity, the italic softened and made personal a cold market exchange: money for print text.[58]

Smith does make clear that the italic is a fragile vessel of feeling: like the midcentury women of sensibility, it possesses "a particular delicacy" (*PG*, 16). The virtue of the italic's sensibility, however, is also the quality that can lead to its downfall, for it lacks the rationality necessary for true self-control.[59] In his diatribe against the overuse of the italic, then, Smith echoes the texts used in the prostitution reform movement, texts that told the story of women led by passion to the nadir of feminine humiliation. Smith, like reformers in other spheres, longs for the days of the italic's "former purity" but consoles himself that "yet may it be hoped that their parading so *very* promiscuously may be prevented" (*PG*, 14). His sentence construction here too is telling: he does not complain about printers misusing the italic; instead, the out-of-control italic parades itself around, like brazen hussies on display in Covent Gardens. The view of the italic as promiscuous may also be linked to its etymological origins as the Italian hand, for Italians, especially Italian women, were thought to be amorous and intemperate.[60] It seems that only an accident of geography links the fallen "Italian" to the noble "Roman," who signifies the stability of Augustan classicism; the Englishman is the true descendent of the Roman citizen, and the roman font his appropriate medium.[61] Thus the italic is the dark other of the roman, the projection of its excess, in terms that rely on discourses of gender and nationalism.

These visions of the italic running amok trouble Smith because they upset the natural order and balance of his typographical universe. An indiscriminate mixing of the fonts leads to an unclear hierarchy and a devaluation of both types: "What a pity," Smith laments, "that two such significant Bodies as Roman and Italic . . . should sometimes be maimed in such a matter as not to be known which of the two has the advantage of the other. It is therefore to be wished, that the intermixing Roman and Italic may be brought to straighter limits, and the latter be used for such purposes as it was design'd for" (*PG*, 13–14). Indeed, the roman letter "suffers by being interlarded with Italic" (*PG*, 13) in that its usual bold appearance is diminished. Feminine type outside its sphere is a castration threat even to that most phallic of letters, the capital. "Large capitals," Smith asserts, "make a fine appearance in Inscriptions, Titles, or other matter, where their beauty is not invaded by Italic, but where they present themselves in their erect position, by themselves. But their bold and distinguishing aspect is greatly obstructed by . . . Italic" (*PG*, 50). Erect and by itself, free of the polluting italic, Smith's ideal roman letter represents a solitary, self-contained masculinity.

Smith's gendered bodies of type have important ramifications for the understanding of the role of print technology and print workers in the mid-eighteenth century. Despite—or perhaps because of—his almost obsessive attention to the proper appearance and spheres of type, and his discussion of letters as the sexed subjects of typography, Smith's regulatory discourse serves, paradoxically, to make print *invisible*. Black letters on white pages, used rationally and without excess, no longer needed to be thought of as material products constructed through the labor of man and machine according to arbitrary or contingent conventions: embodying gender itself, they were as natural. Thus, the ideal print product is to Smith an inhuman yet decidedly masculine consciousness, not reliant on the labor of workers. Indeed, acknowledgment of the work of print—much like any suggestion of the artificial construction of gender—would threaten the stability of its normative categorization. That this is a markedly different view from that expressed in an earlier period is best emphasized by comparing the conclusions of the two manuals. *The Mechanick Exercises* ends with an image of human celebration as Moxon describes the trade's May Day feast: "This Ceremony being over, such as will go their ways; but others that stay, are Diverted with Musick, Songs, Dancing, Farcing, etc. till at last they all find it time to depart" (*ME*, 331). Such warm festivity is nowhere to be found in *The Printer's Grammar*, which concludes with a list "Of Physical Signs and Abbreviations," emphasizing the rupture between language and the physical world, in which signs refer only to other signs in an endless deferral (see fig. 5).

The headpiece for the first chapter of Smith's text is the most telling, however (fig. 6). The book—or, rather, The Book—is held aloft by angels, trumpeting as if proclaiming the word of God. This is an important modification on the Stationers' Company's crest (reproduced in fig. 7 and still used today on the Stationers' Company's Web site and fliers) and would have been recognized as such.[62] Here, the final product of absent work supersedes—is literally held above—the medieval symbolism that represented tradesmen situated in the political and economic environment of the London guilds. Instead, the book claims divine authority, a supreme logocentrism. No humans, much less sweaty laborers, were necessary in its creation; it results from the proper and complementary organization of interiorized gendered behavior, not from messy sexual machines.[63] Its conception is truly immaculate.

## Conclusion: Rising Authors, Receding Print

Historically, Smith's view of the book became dominant, while Moxon's was "disappeared." Even as Smith wrote, courtroom battles and aesthetic proclamations were consolidating a view of authorship that was commonsense by the end of the century.[64] The godlike source of Smith's text morphed into a secular, interiorized version: it became the solitary, original, and implicitly male genius, who creates because he is born to it and is compelled by an almost spiritual calling—not because he is one among a number of workers in the print trades. The finished work of genius is pure transcendent mind, unsullied by bodily concerns or effects. More than a decade of critical work in the field of authorship studies has done much to demystify such claims, of course, yet there is still a sense in much writing that the emergence of the author was inevitable, given the discourse of possessive individualism and the rise of the capitalist market economy. In fact, print itself is seen to have caused proprietary authorship, constructing a stable, marketable persona, the Author, in contrast to the more fluid identities allowed in networks of manuscript

℞ Stands for *Recipe*

℔ for a Pound

℥ for an Ounce

ʒ for a Drachma

 Э for a Scruple

j ſtands for 1 ; ij for 2 ; and ſo on.

ſſ ſignifies *ſemi*, or half

gr. denotes a Grain

One Pound makes 12 Ounces

One Ounce contains 8 Drachma's

One Drachma is equal to 3 Scruples

One Scruple conſiſts of 20 Grains

One Grain has the weight of a Barley-corn

M. ſignifies a Handful

P. means ſo much as can be taken betwixt the ends of two fingers

P. æq. ſtands for Equal parts

ana. ſignifies, So much of one as of the other

q. s. As much as is ſufficient

q. p. As much as you pleaſe

ſ. a. According to art.

## F I N I S.

*F*IG. *5: The last page of* The Printer's Grammar: *No messy human bodies disrupt Smith's neat system of signs and measures. (John Smith,* The Printer's Grammar, *1755, ed. D. F. Foxon, Gregg Press, 1965. Wayne State University.)*

FIG. 6: *The headpiece for the first chapter of* The Printer's Grammar: *the book as divine production. (John Smith,* The Printer's Grammar, *1755, ed. D. F. Foxon, Gregg Press, 1965. Wayne State University.)*

exchange. As Margaret Ezell notes, "[P]rint publication takes on the role of the revolutionary force, usually represented by male writers eager to seize new opportunities."[65]

The printers' manuals under study here, however, help us understand that this heroic author is an ideological rather than a technological outcome. Eisenstein comments that "in the seventeenth century, many scholars and intellectuals were on much closer terms with print shops and typographers than they had been since the industrialization of print led to new divisions of labor. . . . How this growing distance from printing plants has affected the attitudes of men of knowledge remains to be assessed."[66] Comparing the representation of work practices in Moxon and Smith allows us to measure this "distance." In its recognition of the collaborative nature of creative and intellectual work, this statement encourages us to view the early print era as fundamentally different from later regimes of authorship. Eisenstein's own work, however, does not bear this out. Instead, she still privileges the writing part of the equation,

FIG. 7: *The Crest of the Worshipful Company of Stationers and Newspaper Makers, still used by this organization, which is a Livery Company of the City of London as well as a modern-day professional association. Reprinted with permission of the Stationers' Company.*

seeing the printer as an important but nonetheless secondary vehicle for the Renaissance humanist: publishers "served men of letters not only by providing traditional forms of patronage but also by acting as press agents and as cultural impresarios of a new kind."[67] The printers in Moxon's manual, however, are much more than mere instruments of a higher power, allowing us to see that the "closer terms" of writer and printer were indeed a model of fruitful and productive synergy. We have seen how Moxon casts workers (with tools and machines) as crucial to the art of bookmaking. That they are much more than mere instruments of a higher power is also apparent the few times he does address the role of writers. To Moxon, as well as many others in his period, a text producer was only one contributor to the making of meaning. Indeed, he describes the job of the compositor as not only aiding the author in articulating his points but sometimes even supplanting him: "[I]t is Necessary," Moxon tells us, that "the *Compositers* Judgement should know where the Author has been deficient, that so his care may not suffer such Work to go out of his Hands as may bring Scandal upon himself, and Scandal and prejudice upon the *Master Printer*" (*ME*, 219). In the hierarchy of Moxon's printing house, then, the compositor's first duty is to his Master, not the writer, who cannot always be trusted to provide a coherent text. It is only by working together with a fruitful and productive synergy that a worthy text is completed.

This dynamic is not unique to Moxon. Adrian Johns calls our attention to the important and creative role played by those who made books in this period: "[W]hen written materials were reproduced in print the process was by no means one of slavish reproduction. . . . The written sheets represented a fallible, and perhaps incomplete, record," and alterations were easily made "because they held in their hands no sacrosanct text at risk of desecration."[68] A contemporary of Moxon, Andrew Marvell, also comments, though satirically, on the ways in which typography helps readers in the case of authorial incompetence. Describing a writer's use of ambiguous flower conceits, he exclaims, "And to this succeeds another Flower, I am sure, though I can scarce smell out the sence of it. But it is printed in a distinct Character, & that is always a certain sign of a flower. For our Booksellers have many Arts to make us yield to their importunity: and among the rest, they promise us . . . that wheresoever there is a pretty Conceit, it shall be marked out in another Character."[69] Marvell's judgments of such writing aside, it is clear that it is the bookseller's recourse to his "arts"—in this case the use of a different typeface or letterform—that provides the text with its legibility; he hints (if scornfully) at the powers to which readers must "yield." More serious accounts, written from within the trade, of the involvement of print workers in "creative" or intellectual aspects of text making, such as writing, translating, and conceptualizing and managing print projects, can also be seen in the autobiographies of the booksellers Francis Kirkman and John Dunton, as I show in the next chapter.

In Smith's manual, on the other hand, we see a gap between printer and writer, and a concomitant change in knowledge production. Smith—writing at least fifty years before true industrialization, when Eisenstein dates this important change in labor practices, yet representative of the ethos of the second half of the century—insists that writers actively participate in the composing process, even in the selection of accidentals, in order to make their minds more transparently evident in the text: choosing a mode of emphasis, he insists, helps to "inform the Compositor of an Author's intention" (*PG*, 51). The former's duty is obviously to encapsulate the latter. Unlike Moxon, Smith does not trust his compositors even with the task of punctuating properly, for to him the smallest mark on a page is fraught with authorial importance and part of the Author's near theological immanence. The compositor is merely an amanuensis; he should leave no mark of his own personality, no unique quirks in spelling or punctuation. Thus he stresses that "it is impossible for a Compositor to guess at an Author's manner of expressing himself . . . and if [the Author] would have the Reader imitate him in his emphatical delivery, how can a writer intimate it better than by Pointing his Copy himself?" (*PG*, 86). In this model of the delegation of production duties, print workers acquiesce to the Author's will, anticipating the reader's later subordination. The resulting division of labor places genuinely creative work in the Author's garret and constructs the print shop as merely a factory in which lifeless pieces, meaningless in and of themselves, are assembled to hold the Author's mind. Typography only exists to be written and read *through*, to invisibly convey the soul of writing. (The effects of such a viewpoint on the lives of booksellers I explore in the next chapter.)

As the century waned, such attitudes persisted, bolstered perhaps by the growing popularity of ideas promoting natural genius, authorial originality, and "authors' rights." Even into the nineteenth century, printers' manuals were not only acknowledging but virtually copying Smith's text. Caleb Stower, who calls Smith's *Grammar* the "groundwork" of his own 1808 *Printer's Grammar*, and who appropriates much of Smith wholesale into his own text, is even more explicit in advising authors to mark texts as carefully and precisely as possible.[70] His chief advice to compositors is to adopt a "system" that allows for expediency, accuracy, and uniformity. He does address the bodies of workers in chapter 13, but they are relegated to mechanical processes, seemingly isolated from text making, and semantically removed from words on pages—except when their sloppiness causes smudges to the proofs. In fact, it is clear that the workplace itself is now subject to textualized rationalism: Stower strongly suggests posting in the office detailed "rules and regulations" so as to "preserve order and regularity."[71]

The movement from Moxon's embodied print to Smith's metaphysical text thus allows us to glimpse some of the ways in which the ideology of authorship began to reconstruct the printing house and reconstitute the ways in which print work was understood. Moxon describes a time when the physical labor of print workers was still valued, and the final book was thought to bear traces of their presence. Thus Moxon's text represents what Francis Barker has described as "a discursive situation before production has quite 'disappeared' into . . . the closed factory, or at the level of representation, into the conventions of the bourgeois naturalism which has nothing to do with nature, and everything to do with naturalizing the suppression of the signs of the artefact's production."[72] Smith's idealized text, however, erases work by positing a natural, scientifically categorized body of type. The print product becomes a dimorphically gendered entity: standardized, consistent, and therefore transparent. Smith's typography, then, bypasses the workers who cast, dress, set, and press the type and instead signifies directly to the disembodied mind of the writer.

One must be wary, however, of idealizing Moxon's print shop. I have purposely used Donna Haraway's term "cyborg" to describe his mechanistic coupling of man and machine, for her term, while celebrating the "pleasure in the confusion of boundaries," sees the cyborg as neither essentially subversive or essentially repressive.[73] Moxon's appreciation of the human worker was not necessarily liberating, just as actual print shop practices under the regime of master printers like Moxon's were not without their own hazards. The rules of the chapel were strict and punishment was corporal. Apprentices were tracked into their field at a young age and forced to withstand physically demanding work, long hours, and a curtailment of their personal freedom. At the same time, Moxon's movement from manual labor to manuals on labor elides their work (and pain) and abets a hierarchy that privileges two-dimensional print over somatic instruction—a process that continues today.[74] More subtle forms of repression are also evident: the sexualized machinery relies on and supports a rigid model of heterosexual penetrative sexuality, and despite Moxon's use throughout his text of masculine pronouns for workers, many women were involved in the late seventeenth-century business of print, women whom Moxon effectively erases from the scene.

The shift from Moxon to Smith, however, marks a move from explicit violence to repressive discourse, from the worker who might, as a result of being punished, "piss Blood, and shortly after dye," to the Cartesian subject who denies corporeality. In the mind-body split, the body is the secondary and feminine term. Before this move, in the seventeenth and early eighteenth centuries, women flourished as print trade workers, a phenomenon I discuss in chapter 4. Smith's masculinization of the print product, however, submits them to a double erasure, both as women and workers. They are relegated instead to the ghetto of sociability and feeling, meant at best, as the italic, to dress up a text, or, as a reader, to consume it passively. Ideologies such as Smith's had material results: the number of women involved in the print trade dwindled in the second half of the eighteenth century.[75]

In examining these printers' manuals, I have tried to show that the medium of print has never been—and was not always thought to be—a pure or neutral form of communication, but one that always conveys and supports a specific ideological regime. I have traced a narrative about the provenance of knowledge, a struggle between intellectuals and professional writers on one side and artisans and workers on the other. I have shown print transform from the work of the body to the carrier of the mind. And despite literary culture's rejection of all things commercial, this chapter illustrates that the rise of authorship went hand in hand with the creation of the print text as commodity. This idea turns our standard teleology—that print culture created proprietary authorship—on its head, as it poses the Author as the creator of print, rather than vice versa. The ideology of authorship deployed for its own benefit an enduring vision of print as fixed, standardized, and invisible. To adopt these notions as an "essential" aspect of the print medium is to accede to this regime.

# 3

# CITIZEN, HERO, OR MIDWIFE? RE-PRESENTING THE BOOKSELLER

*Stationers deal with all those who write Bookes, as Receivers of Stollen Goods do with Thieves: Give them what they please and make no Conscience of cheating them of all, if they do not use the greater Caution in making their Bargaines.*

—SAMUEL BUTLER, *PROSE OBSERVATIONS*, CA. 1670

*[T]here was a necessity for concerting measures to humble the presumption of booksellers, who had, from time immemorial, taken all opportunities to oppress and enslave their authors; not only by limiting men of genius to the wages of journeymen tailors, . . . but also in taking such advantage of their necessities as were inconsistent with justice and humanity.*

—TOBIAS SMOLLETT, *THE ADVENTURES OF PEREGRINE PICKLE*, 1751

The battle between Grub Street writers and booksellers has long been an accepted trope in eighteenth-century studies, emblematized most vividly by the infamous wrangling between Alexander Pope and Edmund Curll. With literary criticism's tradition of celebrating great authors and their works of inspired genius, it is not surprising that scholars have, in general, labeled booksellers as the culpable party. Booksellers, among others in the trade, are charged with creating and maintaining the worst sort of mass literary culture, supporting (if poorly) dissolute scribblers in a craven attempt to pander to their customers, while cheating superior writers out of their copyright, or worse, offering barely disguised, plagiarized versions of their work.[1] The few booksellers who are heralded, such as Robert Dodsley or Jacob Tonson, are figured as exceptional, and usually only in reference to the more worthy writers they assisted. In the moral terms in which this rhetoric is usually couched, the "good" booksellers are ones who understood their secondary role.[2]

This chapter hopes to rescue booksellers from their historic ignominy, though not by merely transposing the debate. Instead, I expose the discourse of the immoral bookseller as part of a larger early eighteenth-century cultural "discussion" interrogating the very nature and purpose of print texts—who should produce them, what they could or should say, and how they should circulate in a capitalist market. While the antagonistic binary of author versus bookseller did sometimes represent a real-life conflict between divergent economic interests, it more importantly personified a nexus of competing ideologies: different ways of imagining the process of textual creation as it evolved from the glimmer of an idea to the solid book in a reader's hands. That the author-centric model became (and remains) dominant is best emblematized by the prototypical Grub Street scene of popular imagination: the starving artist scribbling late into the night for the plump, bourgeois bookseller. And just as this representation flourished, buttressed by the Romantic celebration of the victimized writer now vindicated through the immortality of his art, alternative understandings of text making were erased.

In a biography reclaiming Robert Dodsley's importance to the period, for example, Harry M. Solomon remarks on Alvin Kernan's elision of booksellers, complaining that Kernan "acknowledges that booksellers 'dominated' both printers and writers in the eighteenth century but transfers that power to an abstraction called 'print,' thereby reducing booksellers to mercantile pawns in a technological revolution to which they are oblivious."[3] Kernan's work is, of course, merely representative of a larger trend in the growing subfield of eighteenth-century "print culture studies," which often takes as its point of entry into the business of print the words—and therefore the unacknowledged prejudices, blind spots, and self-promotional strategies—of canonical authors. While the material conditions of print work are explored by self-identified "book historians" or bibliographers, who produce crucial empirical information on production records and other archival materials, their work often lacks the context of larger cultural issues, the discursive environment in which the trade participated. In this chapter my analysis bridges this gap by reinstalling as an essential component of the literary culture of this period the contested discourse of booksellers, situated in the broader field of the cultural production of print. I look at their descriptions of publishing ventures not as neutral windows onto the world of the trade but as assertions of a particular view of what the print trade was or should be. Such a recovery reveals that "Grub Street" was indeed a zone of representational conflict, a discursive and economic terrain, constructed differently at various times, shaped by the often competing interests of the many parties involved.[4]

Here, I focus on three central and representative figures: Francis Kirkman (1632–80), John Dunton (1659–1732), and Robert Dodsley (1703–64), whose writing in published and private texts marks significant ideological points across the often tumultuous print market of the late seventeenth- and early eighteenth centuries. Their desire to print their lives in the first place does not mark these three unusual: the number of biographies, autobiographies, and memoirs of print workers written from the late seventeenth century through the eighteenth century makes it clear that booksellers thought of themselves as important public figures even before the "lives and works" of authors commanded readers' attention.[5] Carefully analyzing these, instead of dismissing them as vanity productions, allows us to better understand how booksellers themselves viewed their contributions to print culture. The text work of these three is especially noteworthy, though, in that it reveals significant changes in the self-representations of booksellers that help us to understand the transformation in their roles and responsibilities as the print trade developed from a government-regulated, yet loosely defined, enterprise, producing a chimera of tracts and tales, to a staid and efficient market-regulated business, promoting taste and genteel authorship to a large middle-class readership.

## From Rights to Copy to Author's Rights

Before discussing these specific booksellers, though, it might be useful to review the tangled history of writers and print workers in this period and the laws and conventions that governed them. The standard narrative of the rise of the author in England shows how, through a variety of intertwined discourses in the realm of aesthetics, economics, politics, and the law, the modern author emerged as a proprietor of his original works.[6] Before the early eighteenth century, however, the dominant constructions of authorship were not associated with concepts of ownership and originality. Whether one sees the early modern author as a master craftsman, a manuscript-sharing coterie poet, an inherent collaborator, a performance-oriented eschewer of print, or constructed through the anonymous scraps and tidbits of commonplace books, it is clear that the notion of the public (published) writer existed alongside and was formulated within and against complementary, if complexly articulated, views on the roles, rights, and responsibilities of the members of the book trade during this period.[7] If writers were not often considered owners of their works, neither exactly were printers or booksellers. In 1557 the guild of Stationers was granted a royal charter giving them corporate legal status. One of the most important provisions of their charter required them to install a mechanism guaranteeing prepublication licensing, a de facto censorship meant to screen out the most scandalous and heretical books. The company was also granted the right to control, through its apprenticeship programs, who and how many entered the trade. Most important to our purposes, though, their charter established the means to regulate competition between company members by granting and monitoring "rights to copy." These rights, a privilege of membership, were understood as the right *to copy* a tangible manuscript or print text, but while rights could be sold, bequeathed, or divided, they were not in any sense *proprietary* rights. Furthermore, the right to copy had nothing to do with writers, who were not invited to become members of the prestigious Stationers' Company. Once a writer sold his manuscript, a ware like any other, to a printer or publisher, he was rarely involved in the process of bringing it to the public.

Nonetheless, changes that began to occur in the seventeenth-century print trade did affect conceptions of authorship. When sixteenth- and early seventeenth-century Stationers registered their copies, the rhetoric of the entry reflected the member's *license* to print. By the late seventeenth century, however, the form of the entry emphasized the member's *proprietorship*. Mark Rose stresses that the underlying legal basis was still the same—the right to copy "was a grant from the company to the member"—but that this change does reflect the introduction of the ideology of possessive individualism into the discourse of the trade.[8] Ideas such as this, consolidated by Locke at the end of the century, as well as "the general emphasis on liberty and property in public discourse after the 1688 revolution," may have been responsible for Daniel Defoe's 1704 call for a parliamentary law that would protect authorial property rights: "[E]very Author being oblig'd to set his Name to the Book he writes," he asserts in *Essay on the Regulation of the Press*, "has, by this Law, an undoubted exclusive Right to the Property of it."[9] This point was also echoed in several subsequent *Tatler* articles by Joseph Addison. Rose claims that these sorts of statements represent the growing interest, since Locke, in property as the keystone to a well-governed society and that such views were sympathetically received. Indeed, it was this burgeoning discourse, he relates, that influenced the London Stationers to adopt a strategy using authorial rights to protect their own interests. However, I later in this chapter call into question the source of the Stationers' rhetoric, arguing, in my analysis of Dunton especially, that ideas such as those of Defoe and Addison were just one sort of view being expressed in the early eighteenth century and are not necessarily indicative of the trade's understanding of a writer's relationship to his work.

These questions of ownership were expressed in the context of the general turmoil in the print trade after the Licensing Act lapsed in 1695. The 1662 Licensing Act had taken away the Stationers' Company's ability to control and regulate its trade directly, and its nonrenewal meant that rights to copy were no longer explicitly granted through any governing body. Though the trade lacked the authority it once had, however, it did continue to grow. While literacy rates are difficult to trace and thus cannot be relied on as an indicator of change, there is clear evidence that demand for printed materials was on the rise.[10] Because there was no centralized power to enforce company traditions in this time of rapid expansion, practices such as unauthorized printing proliferated. Newer businesses, marketing cheap copies of popular and lucrative sixteenth- and seventeenth-century texts, ignored the so-called rights to copy that individual Stationers had inherited along with their established businesses; the nonrenewal of the Licensing Act had removed any explicit legal means of preventing them from doing so. The print trade therefore turned to Parliament to regulate this potential chaos, petitioning it, as Adrian Johns notes, "some fifteen times between 1695 and 1714," in the hopes that it might "provide some statutory protection for what was increasingly being called the 'the property in the copy.'"[11]

The resulting Statute of Anne, also known as the "Copyright Act," was enacted in 1709 and went into force on the "Tenth Day of April, One thousand seven hundred and ten."[12] Titled "An Act for the Encouragement of Learning, by vesting the Copies of Printed Books in the Authors or purchasers of such Copies, during the Times therein mentioned," the act might be considered a classic example of unintended consequences, especially in terms of its representational effects. The bill the Stationers had advocated was, of course, one that worked in the interest of their trade; the ability of writers to support themselves financially was not their most important consideration. Similarly, when Parliament responded by reducing the terms of protection suggested by the trade, it did so *not* to protect writers from Stationers' appropriating their rights but to encourage economic growth by limiting the trade's monopoly. The resulting statute granted rights to copy (in the most material sense) to an author *or his assignee* for a period of fourteen years. Of course, in order to get published a writer had to sell this right. The new statute thus used the idea of author's rights as a smoke screen, protecting the interests of booksellers but not calling attention to the added control this would allow them.

Rose believes the concept of "author's rights," once introduced, was hard to ignore. One goal of this chapter, however, is to present a more complicated and detailed picture of the development of authorship in relation to other parts of the trade—to show, indeed, that there were flourishing alternatives to the proprietary author. In fact, much of what we consider to be characteristic of authors—their habits of mind as well as their legal claims—was already part of the discourse of bookselling, based in the bookseller's material relationship to the commodity of print. Thus I disagree with Rose's assertion that Stationers "saw in [Defoe's] call for a law to protect literary authorial property a *new strategy* for pursuing their interests."[13] Rose has the influence backward—Defoe's comments could have existed only in the context of *trade* politics. Booksellers would have seen in his words a *familiar* strategy. Ironically, in adopting this strategy, in constructing the author in his own image and for his own interests, the bookseller wrote himself out of literary history.

## What Is a Bookseller?

Early modern booksellers were almost always Stationers and as such had privileged access to the rights to copy discussed above. Indeed, in the seventeenth century, it was mostly booksellers who owned these lucrative properties, and they grew in power and prestige within the Stationers' Company, while the early modern prominence of printers waned. As the holder of these rights, booksellers functioned much more in the role of modern-day publishers than merely retailers. In fact, with the assistance of family members, and often working in partnership with wives, they juggled a multitude of tasks: they negotiated with writers, managed employees and/or apprentices, hired printers, collaborated with other booksellers on large projects, and encouraged puffery or bought advertising to promote their works. At times they gathered subscribers to underwrite projects, or forged connections with aristocratic patrons, whose sponsorship minimized booksellers' financial risk.[14] They also supervised distribution and retailing to local shops, stalls, and mercuries as well as to provincial networks, while at the same time selling print texts and sometimes other wares in their own shops. Even in this last function, they held remarkable power, creating literary taste by guiding their customers' choices. Specific bookshops carrying large amounts of pamphlet literature rivaled coffee shops as meeting places for political activists, while those specializing in plays or poetry might serve as ersatz literary salons, and those catering to scientific interests became valuable gathering spots for natural historians.

Despite the variety of activities in which booksellers engaged, keeping the engine of print culture humming, historic attention has been paid mostly to their purchasing of texts (and concomitant right to copy) from writers. This was often the least of their duties. Instead, many conceptualized projects themselves, merely hiring or commissioning writers to work as directed, if not writing their own texts. Several constructed editions of collected works whose right to copy they owned (or not), or served as editors of newspapers or periodicals, the content of which they often controlled.[15] It is thus crucial to realize how involved booksellers were in every aspect of printmaking, including those tasks deemed "creative" or "intellectual." As Johns explains,

> In managing publications, Stationers, and often booksellers in particular, controlled events. The practices and representations of their domains affected every character and every leaf of their products. Isolating a consistent, identifiable, and immutable element attributable to the individual author would be virtually impossible in these circumstances. Attributing authorship was thus intensely problematic for both contemporary and future readers. A priori, virtually any element in a work might or might not be the Stationers' responsibility, in virtually any field of writing.[16]

Such a realization helps undermine the priority given to authors in literary histories. Textual production may be best viewed as a collaborative partnership, in which "intellectual" and "imaginative" tasks could segue seamlessly into production schedules and business decisions.

Of course, stories of authors' texts being altered or their poems butchered by wayward Stationers are legion, but the complaints that have been preserved in literary history belong almost solely to canonized authors, often of high social status—because those are the voices that have been accepted as authorities.[17] Many writers, of course, never complained, or thought to mention that such alterations were problematic; their silence is not written into our histories. In fact, such revision, as we saw in the previous chapter, was once a normative practice. Such practices reflect and represent a common attitude among booksellers in the late seventeenth and early eighteenth centuries, that professional writers were only minor contributors to work of the trade. Indeed, central to the ideology of the bookseller, revealed in the texts of Kirkman and Dunton, is the premise that booksellers themselves are the creative protagonists of print. As I will show, it took the rise of the author, and the discursive removal of published writing from the realm of labor and economics, to eclipse this role.

## Of Luck and Lucre: Kirkman's Commodified Print

Francis Kirkman, notorious as the publisher and coauthor of the bestselling *The English Rogue* series, was a rogue bookseller in his own right, entering the trade through a circuitous and nontraditional route. While he has been called one of the "great[est] scamps in . . . bookselling," John Feather describes him as one of the most important literary booksellers of the reign of Charles II, notable for collecting and reprinting sixteenth- and early seventeenth-century plays, helping to create reader demand for entertaining narrative prose fiction, and for opening the first commercial circulating library.[18] What I focus on in this section, however, is the way he positions himself in his autobiographical writing as simultaneously a fabricator of engaging tales *and* a producer of potentially lucrative commodities, not only embracing both roles, but seeing little difference between them.

In relating aspects of his tumultuous life in *The Unlucky Citizen* (1673), Kirkman traces the roots of his (ad)ventures in print to a youthful passion for reading.[19] Since this activity was not encouraged or supported by his practical father, Kirkman describes how he resorted to literally begging, borrowing, and even stealing books to support his habit of consuming fiction, especially heroic French romances. From the beginning, then, the materiality of texts featured prominently in his representations of them: books are something one needs to possess in order to enjoy. At first his entertaining pursuit seemed unrelated to, even at odds with, his early apprenticeship as a scrivener, in the business of notarizing documents and lending money. It was while thus employed, however, that he began his first professional foray into the print culture of the period. Watching a shop in which little commerce transpired, Kirkman renewed his interest in the romances and tales of knight errantry that had captivated him as a youth. These flights of imagination were thus contextualized in his training as a scrivener in which notarized deeds and wills explicitly linked text with cash and where fictional narratives—spun by his dishonest master to snare customers—generated income.

Kirkman relates two parallel narratives of artifice in the scrivener's office. In one, a case of blatant fraud, Kirkman's master lures and strings along a would-be customer by promising to supply funds he cannot in actuality provide. Kirkman himself is the inadvertent instigator of the second. He places his collected romances on a shelf in the scrivener's office, forming a small library that adds to the prestige of the scrivener's business—if only through misapprehension:

They that came into our Shop, might by the outside of the Books, imagine that we were well furnished with Law Books according to our practice, but if they had searched their inside, they would have found their mistake, when in stead of *Statutes at large*, and *Cooks Reports*, they should see *Amadis de Gaul*, and *Orlando Furioso*, and instead of *Brooks Abridgement*, and some such old Law Books, they would have found the *Mirrour of Knighthood*, they would have been much mistaken when instead of Gown-men pleading at the Bar, they found Sword-men fighting at the barriers. (*UC*, 174)

In both cases, a fiction shapes perceptions to financial advantage; it is notable, however, that in Kirkman's case the fiction has a concrete embodiment in real-life books. This foreshadows his own later career: as he develops his own desire to write, he does not divorce it from his material conditions, nor does he view his connection with commerce as debasing his work.

At the same time, Kirkman also claims an apprenticeship of sorts in the reading of romances, describing a program of self-education that resulted in his first appearance in print, a translation of the sixth part of *Amadis de Gaul*. This publication, he believes, produced an important social benefit: he notes that "[I] did resolve to do the same kindness to others as had been done for me, and as I thought would be of publick good: I did not think it fit that since I had a Talent, to lay it up in a Napkin, but to put it to the best use I could" (*UC*, 174). It is clearly a passionate reader or writer who sees "publick good" in relating another episode in the adventures of a knight, but Kirkman seems to take seriously the fact he is making an important contribution to a continuing literary tradition. He also sees himself as an artistic producer, believing that translators should be freely generative in their approach to texts, not merely literal. This goes beyond the inevitable differences between languages: he asserts that translators should have the "knowledge to add where the Author wants matter, or to lessen what he abounds."[20] He even takes a generative approach to his own tongue, claiming that "I had (like other conceited Translators and Authors) coyned several new English Words" (*UC*, 180–81). While he eventually became a bookseller in his own small shop, he went on to pen (singly and in collaboration) parts of

*The English Rogue* series, which has been termed "experimental fiction," as well as the generically distinctive *The Unlucky Citizen*.[21]

Despite Kirkman's inventive approach to textual production and his own obvious interest in writing, however, market considerations were ultimately more important than attributes inhering in the text itself, such as originality, authenticity, or claims of authorship. In fact, he is clear and unapologetic about his interest in "the great profit I should gain" by appearing in print (*UC*, 174). This material and financial emphasis is consistent throughout *The Unlucky Citizen* and many of his other texts, in which he relates acts of writing, or even reading, to those of buying and selling. In the prefaces to the several editions of *The English Rogue*, for example, he describes a similar rationale, noting in 1668 that he is "desirous it should sell, for to that end in part was it written and Printed," and in 1672 that the "first and chiefest" reason he wrote the second part "was to gain ready money."[22] He also emphasizes the profit that will come to the other booksellers who will sell his text.[23] He is equally considerate of his readers, noting of a collection of plays, that "besides those who read these sorts of Books for their pleasure, there are some who do it for profit, such as are young Players, Fidlers, & c."; explaining to the readers of part 2 of *The English Rogue* that he wrote the preface so "that you should have all possible content for your money"; and wishing for the readers of *The Unlucky Citizen* that "the buying of this book will be a happy purchase" (*UC*, n.p.).[24] To Kirkman, then, text is always transaction; creativity is always commercial. In his representation of the book world, there is no contradiction, or even tension, between these terms.

Indeed, the narrative energy underlying *The Unlucky Citizen* is the desire for release from debt.[25] The quest for this unattainable quiescent state fuels both the plot—how he was so unlucky to fall into debt—and the extratextual motivation for writing: if the book sells, he can reclaim his economic equilibrium. His "unluckiness" is, in fact, only financial, for despite his despair and depression over his financial state, he is in good health, and he describes no great personal tragedies or losses, even through the Plague and the Great Fire. However, as he baldly states at one point, "I wanted nothing but the principal verb, *money*" (*UC*, 132). And if "money" here is a verb, books are both its subject and object— material products of paper and ink, the exchange of which is central for the plot to proceed. An example of this dynamic frames *The Unlucky Citizen*: Kirkman's prefatory letter to the reader explains that the book's late publication and large number of errata are due to the fact that the unfinished sheets were seized when a judgment was issued against his *printer's* goods by one of the printer's creditors. Kirkman was forced to pay to redeem his sheets, exacerbating his financial woes. Then, while he was waiting to send them to another printer, Kirkman himself was arrested and imprisoned for his own debts. Thus, even before their existence as a book, Kirkman's pages were circulating as part of a larger system of economic exchange, circumstances that serve only to highlight their ultimate purpose, to become, as Kirkman terms them, a "happy purchase" (*UC*, n.p.).

In his many self-conscious pieces on his published works, in fact, he never refers to the *intellectual* labor involved in writing, but only to the financial calculations and concrete processes necessary for getting into *print*. This is because, to Kirkman, the commercial basis of the trade does more than merely help create or transact print products; it also informs the meaning of the words themselves and the identities of those who write them. He explains that "having already been in Print, in writing somewhat of this Nature, I was the less concerned at the common Vogue of the people; neither did I much value it, so as I might gain by them, and that so considerable, that I might have occasion to unsay what I now write, and tearm my self the *Lucky Citizen*: In hopes whereof . . . I once again put Pen to Paper" (*UC*, 7). He is confident that what he writes will be desired by readers, but that is significant to him only insofar as their taste supports his own desire for economic gain. Though he does elsewhere pay the usual lip service to the lessons readers can gain from his misfortunes (such as learning to avoid debt), it seems that for Kirkman, words do their truly important work only as objects in a system of trade. In fact, this passage implies that the exchange value of Kirkman's words, a commodity constructed through the physical processes of pen and press, trumps their textual meaning, or symbolic exchange value: through the sale of the book, the word "unlucky" morphs into the lucrative "lucky," transforming the discursive identity of Kirkman himself.

Kirkman stresses the economic element of the text trades so often that it becomes thematic. His disclosures of his financial interests should not be read, however, as either refreshingly sincere or quaintly naive. I believe, instead, that such rhetoric represents a strategic lure to a class of readers whose interests are also explicitly commercial—the urban tradesmen of London. He explains in the preface to *The Unlucky Citizen* that

> I have calculated the discourse for the Meridian of this City, chiefly for City Readers. I would not have the Town or County wits to meddle with it. It is of a strain much too low for them, neither does it concern them, I do not profess my self to be guilty of much wit at the best much less when I was at the lowest condition: I had little to heighten my fancy, for in four months together ... I drank but one glass of wine: therefore it is not suitable to those sparkling fancyes, which are everyday heightened with the delicacies of high feeding and large drinking; it is only fit for such whose wit are of the same assize with my own, and yet I despair not of having enow, such as are Citizens Sons, Citizens servants, or Citizens themselves: it is useful for, and of like use it may be for the honest Country-man. (*UC*, n.p.)

Here Kirkman constructs boundaries of taste, for rich food and wit against plain food and (financially) useful prose, aligning himself with the middling sorts—artisans, less affluent merchants and retailers, and literate servants—eager, he obviously believes, to read about one of their own.[26] A citizen was, ipso facto, a freeman of a livery company, a political identity defined by its trade alliance.[27] It is these readers, who understand the urban economic environment, the necessity of commerce, and the importance of solvency, that he hopes to attract with the language of lucre. And so he positions himself in the opening chapter of *The Unlucky Citizen*, in which he explains his book's title, claiming,

> I apply [the word *Unlucky*] to the Word *Citizen*, because such an one I am, being so born and bred; And as he is reckoned to be a *right Gentleman*, that is so by three Discents, so I by that Rule may reckon my self to be a *right Citizen*; and most, if not all the Misfortunes that have happened to me, were in or near the *City* ... : And therefore the Scene lying there, and my Quality being such, I may not unfitly tearm it Citizen. (*UC*, 2)

Such an assertion, coupled with his relentless use of the language of commerce, suggests that Kirkman capitalized on the fluid identities made available by print, purposefully representing himself as an economic man.[28]

Nonetheless, Kirkman's rawness of rhetoric, his undisguised allegiance to the material conditions of writing, not concealed by manners or a call to morals, was repugnant to many of his later readers, trained by eighteenth-century writers from Pope to Wordsworth that getting and spending were incompatible with tasteful authorship. As Brean Hammond notes, those writers who "most artfully concealed the profit motive," appearing to transcend material production, are the ones who form our current canon: "[T]he 'self-crowned laureates' of the period have had their ideological victories . . . accepted as objective verdicts of an unerring literary taste."[29] Of course, this victory of artistic transcendence over coarse materiality also implies a losing side of this struggle. Thus, views by writer-booksellers such as Kirkman, constructing an idea of creative works as intrinsically intertwined with pecuniary motivations, were historically dismissed as distasteful. Even his chief bibliographer, Strickland Gibson, comments on the "general indication of vulgarity" apparent in Kirkman's engraved portrait.[30] Kirkman is easily cast as the antihero of print culture, a proto–Grub Street villain or clown, one who is always already debased by the market. Such labeling, however, anachronistically capitulates to the eighteenth-century ideology of art rising triumphantly, unhindered by economics. Instead, Kirkman shows himself buying, selling, *and* creating. He comfortably represents himself as simultaneously a fabricator of imaginative narratives *and* a purveyor of these in a commercial system of exchange, constructing a view of print as a commodity that exists in harmony with the pleasurable text.

## *Economic Originality: John Dunton's Print Projects*

The rhetoric and self-representations of John Dunton provide an even more complex understanding of the role of the bookseller. His 1705 *The Life and Errors of John Dunton Citizen of London with the Lives and Characters of More than a Thousand Contemporary Divines and Other Persons of Literary Eminence*, a sort of "value-added" autobiography of

an entire social scene—like Kirkman's, written while deeply in debt—
presents an especially detailed picture of his business dealings and his
attitudes toward the various participants in his trade. *Life and Errors*,
however, is an at least superficially odd text, for, much like James Watson's contemporary *The History of the Art of Printing* (1713), it is a life
story that includes the highly personal—diatribes against former friends
who deserted him in his time of financial need, and emotional blackmail
directed at his estranged second wife, who refused to pay off his debts—
alongside more distanced descriptions of his day-to-day activities as a
bookseller. As a literary "work" it is considered a failure and has been
called "one of the queerest books ever written" and "embarrassingly
naïve . . . a whining, rambling, incoherent flood of words."[31] J. Paul
Hunter, although he considers many of the works by Dunton to be
precursors to the novel, describes it as "halting," "silly," "crude," in bad
taste, and even "ludicrous."[32] It is precisely Dunton's odd juxtaposi-
tions, however, that provide us with a fascinating and new version of the
early eighteenth-century print trade. The aspects that escape generic
convention—the places that seem most "incoherent" or odd to us—are
the parts of the text that require the closest analysis. Here we see an
eighteenth-century print culture that is "ludicrous" only because it is not
what we have been trained to expect.

Writing from within the trade, Dunton, like Kirkman, is particularly
interested in the material aspects of the making of books. In fact, Dunton casts his entire life in typographic terms. In the prefatory poem that
opens his text, "The Author's Speaking Picture," he plays with the convention that usually placed a picture of the writer opposite the title page,
claiming that printed words offer a more accurate version of authors
than a pictorial likeness:

> Fain would the Graver here my Picture place,
> But I myself have drawn my truer face:
> Reader, behold my Visage in my Book;
> My true idea most exactly took.
>
> . . . . . . . . . . . . . . . . . . . .
> My Book's my Picture; there's my living face;
> And speaking tears the image of my case.

> . . . . . . . . . . . . . . . . . . .
> You, whose great Characters I here present,
> Be witness that Dunton does repent,
> And here does stand in sheets for punishment.
>
> . . . . . . . . . . . . . . . . . . .
> But for those Errors I do here confess,
> I would so mend and alter all the Press,
>
> . . . . . . . . . . . . . . . . . . .
> Thus does my Speaking Picture conquer Death.
> 'Twas but a dead face, Art could here bequeath,
> Look on the following Leaves and see me breathe.[33]

Dunton not only substitutes a print poem for a picture but suggests that a published book stands in for his entire life. The image of a "speaking picture" may seem to draw from a discourse of orality, but Dunton's use of printing terminology stresses his allegiance to a more concrete realm: the speech of his typographical "picture" is the silent voice of his book. Thus his "very soul" is made up of the tangible elements of print: he lives and breathes in the leaves, would amend the press to correct his mistakes, and stands repentant in "sheets," a double entendre suggesting both a sinner's lowly garb and loose pages in a print shop. The pun here suggests other puns: "the image of [his] case" can be seen as not only the specifics of his life but also the case of letters compositors worked with; the "great Characters" who fill his text are both the people he describes in his text and the individual letters and symbols that make up those descriptions. By calling attention to the solid materiality of language—constructed of cast letters and pressed paper—as constitutive of identity, Dunton privileges typography (and hence typographers, printers, sellers, etc.) over more abstract individualistic notions of authorial personality suggested by an engraved likeness.[34]

Another prefatory poem, by Richard Friend, continues the analogy:

> The Press grows *honest*; and, in spite of fate
> Now teems a *Birth* that is legitimate:
>
> . . . . . . . . . . . . . . . . . . .
> Thy forty years did *print* thee full of crimes,
> But . . . Repentance cleanses all thy lines,

> . . . . . . . . . . . . . . . . . . . .
> Thou'st read both men and books, thou hast a key
> To each man's breast, which is thy *Library*. . . .
> (*LE*, ix-x)

Here we see not only a man *in* print, as in Dunton's poem, but a man *made* through printing—the press gives birth to him, then prints his fate. It is perhaps inevitable, therefore, that many men would make up a library. The analogy appears a few times throughout the main text. "Were I to correct the *Errata of my short life*," Dunton explains at one point, "I would quite alter the press" (*LE*, 158). Other examples are less explicit. He lists the books he has printed alongside and in the same style as the lists of his friends and acquaintances, as if these characters and his print products were equivalent units. He also repents his errors in printing in the broader context of repenting his sins in general (*LE*, 159). Although the spiritual autobiography has been viewed as a predecessor to the novel's insistence on interiority as a primary characteristic of narrative fiction, here we have a form of confession that resolutely insists on the material.

In his own life in/of print, Dunton casts himself as hero. Another opening poem, by Samuel Warper, written on the occasion of Dunton's return from his travels to the American Colonies and Europe, compares him to Ulysses and describes his business trip as an epic adventure complete with a visit to the Underworld:

> But ah! Thou empty teazing name, farewell,
> That charms the ship, and down it sinks to Hell;
> And wilt thou then thy third last Ramble make
> To the dark confines of the Stygian Lake?
> Be n't Earth and Heaven enough, that thou must go
> To view the Kingdoms of the World below?
> Both of thy pockets and thyself take care,
> For shoals of Booksellers will scrape acquaintance there.
> (*LE*, vi)

Here in Hell Dunton meets a stock type in anti–Grub Street rhetoric, the dishonest bookseller (a type against which, presumably, he is being contrasted). The odd conjunction of classical allusion and a contemporary and familiar joke about the ethics of booksellers, however, is not just an example of a bad poet's stylistic inconsistency. The juxtaposition of heroic narrative and trade tale marks much of Dunton's text.

Despite these classical allusions, though, the master plot of *Life and Errors* is Dunton's spiritual journey, the ostensible motivation for writing his life at all. Indeed, the confession of his errors provides the structure for the first part of his work, which is made up of alternating chapters, first describing "stages" of his life, then correcting them with "an idea of a new life," detailing examples of what he should have done instead. It is telling, however, that while he is eager to revise what he did as a child and young man (the narrative of which is divided into three short stages), when he begins to recount his professional career in stage 4 (which is three times as long as the previous three stages and "new lives" put together), he seems almost to abandon the repentance theme.[35] His business life, it seems, is beyond regret.[36]

The central elements of his life story are contained in this large section, and mostly concern, as the inclusion of Warper's poem in the preface might indicate, his extended expedition, for business reasons, to North America. Here, he vacillates between describing his life as an adventure, with himself as the chief protagonist on a journey both epic and spiritual, and giving frank descriptions of his various "ventures," that is, his business schemes. Indeed, throughout much of the narrative the latter drives the former. As much as Dunton represents himself as a classical and spiritual hero, then, it is clear that his adventures are ultimately motivated by his financial "ventures," his term for his economic undertakings. His business dealings—not a heroic challenge or an epic battle—force him to leave his beloved wife and undertake this perilous journey in the first place. He describes his meetings with wholesalers, his purchases of warehouses, and his troubles with an apprentice with the same enthusiasm that marks the more traditional aspects of his travelogue/spiritual narrative. The epic or spiritual hero is a capitalist, and the epic or spiritual journey, a business trip. Of course, the spiritual autobiography, though still rarely published, was a genre growing more popular, at least in the private realm. Dunton could have guessed that a confession, combining gossip and voyeurism with morality, might be easily marketable, bringing him the financial remuneration he desperately needed. This is not to deny Dunton's spiritual mission, but to insist that it was not incompatible with economic goals.[37] Dunton, bookseller and writer, printer and penitent, forges a sturdy link between the ethereal concerns of the spirit and the worldly interests of trade.

Just as in Kirkman's text, then, the context of commerce does not for Dunton taint the public good he can undertake in his role. Dunton takes pride, for example, in the intellectual abilities required to thrive in this trade, believing that bookselling is an appropriate trade for the well-educated and intellectually interested man. He explains that his father, a learned minister, chose bookselling for his son because it was an honorable trade in which he could serve as "a friend of Learning" (*LE*, 39). Dunton regrets that as a child he was not a better student, for, "had I taken other measures, my Shop might have been a Library, and my mind the richer, and the better furnished of the two" (*LE*, 39). However, it was in fact his apprenticeship in this field that provided his enthusiasm, bringing him to "love Books to the same excess that I hated them before" (*LE*, 43). Dunton insists that a scholarly bookseller can run a scholarly operation and that the ideal shopkeeper should be a moral and learned guide for his customers.

This vision of the bookseller as the arbiter of morality and higher knowledge stands in contrast to Dunton's view of the writer's role. In fact, he consistently denigrates writers throughout his text. Discussing "Hackney Authors," for example, he asserts that

> their great concern lay more in how much a Sheet, than in any generous respect they bore to the Commonwealth of Learning; and, indeed, the Learning itself of these Gentlemen lies very often in as little room as their Honesty; though they will pretend to have studied you [*sic*] six or seven years in the Bodleian Library, to have turned over the Fathers, and to have read and digested the whole compass both of Human and Ecclesiastic History—when, alas! They have never been able to understand a single page of Saint Cyprian, and cannot tell you whether the Fathers lived before or after Christ. (*LE*, 61–62)

Writers, in Dunton's view, are at best fakes, not to be relied on for any sort of spiritual wisdom or moral erudition. He further criticizes the dishonesty of writers, representing them as parasites feeding off of the work of others and contrasting them with upright, virtuous booksellers:

> A man should be well furnished with an honest policy, if he intends to set ont [*sic*] in the world now-a-days. And this is no less necessary in a Bookseller than in any other Tradesman; for in that way there are plots and counterplots, and a whole army of Hackney Authors that keep their grinders moving by the travail of their pens. These Gormandizers will eat you the very life out of a Copy so soon as it ever appears; for as the times go, Original and Abridgement are almost reckoned as necessary as Man and Wife; so that I am really afraid that a Bookseller with a good conscience will shortly grow some strange thing in the earth. (*LE*, 52)

The language of conspiracy, warfare, and death is marked: plotting armies of teeth-gnashing writers kill and devour print texts. Playing with the common motif of the writer as father of his text, Dunton here figures an unnatural husbandry that produces only the stunted or monstrous. Of importance here is that we see Dunton's denigration of "Hackneys" *not* as arguments against writers in general—though he is clearly negative, he does list exceptions—but as a strategy for highlighting the importance of booksellers.[38] To Dunton, it is he and his fellow shopkeepers who are the moral and learned agents of the trade.

In the process of casting writers as degenerates and booksellers as spiritual heroes, Dunton endows himself and his fellow tradesmen with another characteristic usually thought of as pertaining only to authors: originality. This aspect of *Life and Errors* is worth examining closely, for it complicates the anti–Grub Street rhetoric in which his distaste for writers seems to participate. According to Dunton, a published text belongs to the bookseller, not just because he has it printed, imprints it with his name, sells it in his shop, and registers it with the Stationers' Company (though all these reasons may be criteria enough), but often because he thought up the idea for it in the first place. Thus Dunton can say of a fellow bookseller: "His talent lies at Projection. . . . He is usually fortunate in what he goes upon. He is a man of good sense; for I have known him lay the first rudiments and sinews of a design with great judgement, and always according to the Rules of Art or Interest" (*LE*, 209). Throughout *Life and Errors*, Dunton calls his own texts and those sponsored by others "projects," often using the term as a gerund, "projecting," or in its infinitive form, "to project." These verbals connote an ongoing state, the work of the past reaping the benefits of the future. We might compare this term to the more familiar, static term, *literary work*, which conveys a frozen, timeless object that erases from its history all evidence of the mental and physical work involved in its creation. Dunton, though, did not subscribe to the idea that great art is immortal. He quips:

> Books have their time of life as well as we;
> They live by Chance, but die by Destiny.
> Our fate is less severe, in this alone
> That Books no resurrection have, we hope for one.
> (*LE*, 63)

To Dunton, a book's life is its brief existence on the market; whether it lived or died depends on a bookseller's talent to forecast market demand—the "chance" that readers might like it. The bookseller's job was to supervise the work of his project from its origins in rough idea through to its final form as a commodity on store shelves, awaiting its readers.

Thus Dunton's use of the term "interest" in the above description of his bookseller friend who designed "according to the rules of Art or Interest" is also significant. In this context, the term most obviously refers to a reader's first and continued attraction to the text—his or her interest in it. *Interest* in this period, however, was also commonly used to express someone's financial concern or involvement. To a bookseller, these definitions were one in the same, for he had an economic interest in ensuring that readers were interested in the texts he sold. Artistic "design" could thus never be considered separately from economic outlay: art, in the end, mattered only insomuch as it garnered sales. The job of the successful bookseller was to create projects that would almost literally "capture" an audience. In the eighteenth century, "design," after all, could mean an idea, an aesthetic pattern, or a plot to ensnare or entrap (Lovelace "has designs" upon Clarissa, for example). In this passage, all three definitions seem to be deployed at once. The bookseller invents ideas for projects and manages their evolution, dictating everything from the writing style to typographical layout—all in order to attract a reader. The "rules of art" he refers to apply to the art of mastering this process.

In this context, it makes sense that, when Dunton lists and describes the numerous booksellers among his acquaintance, he always includes the most important works they sponsored and sold, never bothering to mention who may have actually written these texts. He does the same with his own list of "projects." Any writer involved was merely a hireling not worthy of notice.[39] (He does make exceptions in the rare cases in which the writer is well known enough—whether for literary or other reasons—that his name itself is a selling point.) Further, it is the booksellers themselves who must assume ultimate authority for the language of their texts. For example, while regretting his selling of some books larded with "profane expressions" (*LE*, 201), Dunton protests, "I am heartily sorry I had any concern in them: but the Author sent the Copy to the press as he wrote it off, and in regard I had no suspicion of him, I did not peruse the Letters till it was past time to alter them" (201). While Dunton blames the writer, the writer is not ultimately the responsible party; any public condemnation will be directed at Dunton, who has the final obligation of "perusing" and censoring. Dunton clearly believes the writer has no right to have printed what *he* may want, but, as an employee, has only the duty to be above suspicion in fulfilling the desires of the bookseller.

This notion of the bookseller's dominance in the creation of projects of interest helps us to understand Dunton's comments on his own work. Again and again through his text he goes out of his way to insist on its originality. In his introductory letter "To The Impartial Readers" (*LE*, xi), Dunton claims that his *Life and Errors* is an "Original Project" (xv), "pure Novelty" (xvi), and "wholly new" (xv). He elaborates:

> [I]f, after all I can say, my Ideal Life must pass for a maggot [i. e., false wit], I must own it my own pure maggot; the natural issue of my brain pan, bred and born there, and only there.... [T]he History of my Life and Errors is ... wholly gathered from my own breast, neither is my Idea of a New Life stolen from anything else but my own thoughts of becoming a New Man. (*LE*, xvi)

To the modern reader, there seems to be a contradiction in this passage: Dunton stresses both that this work came entirely and only from his own mind *and* that it is a "history"—one would assume a true story—of his own life. For Dunton, though, *originality* and *imagination* (that which inspires fiction and poetry) were not terms that were inexorably linked, as they became a century or so later. His terms "new" and "novelty" provide a clue to the bookseller's use of "originality," as does another passage in which he apologizes for repeating some of the same word patterns in descriptions of the many personages he enumerates: "My Thousand Characters are entirely new, except Nine that I formerly published; and having written those before with my own hand, I was loth to be at the pains of writing again the same characters, having done it as well as I could before" (*LE*, xviii). Again, he is discussing his representation of real people, not referring to "characters" in the sense of imaginary, fictional devices. What he does apologize for, however, is the fact that their descriptions have been *published* before, that they are not new to *print*. To Dunton, this is when ideas count—there is no sense that they matter much before being printed (as a life outside print does not), except inasmuch as they will be used for later print projects. His is a concrete, not an abstract or intangible, originality. His ideas may have emerged from his brain, but they are embodied through the work of his hand, which stands in for all the work a bookseller oversees that brings words to life: the inscribing of language in ink, the pressing of letters onto a page, and the stitching of those pages into a book.

A more dialectic approach to the discourse of the print trade thus helps us catch a glimpse of what is hidden in many standard histories of eighteenth-century authorship. "New" and "novelty" are booksellers terms, not linked with intrinsic, individualized notions of authorial genius. Yet they are connected with Dunton's use of the term "originality," a concept that later became the cornerstone of proprietary authorship. Dunton's *Life and Errors* is a new (or original) product, never seen before on other booksellers' shelves. The idea for it, too, is new but matters only because it is part of his investment. "Originality," therefore, is used to mark the boundaries of a print commodity for which one expected the rewards of good sales. We might see in Dunton's rhetoric of projection, though, the beginnings of the concept of the text as abstract, for "project," though dynamic, encompasses a spectrum of work that includes mental inception and insists on novelty as a demand of the market. This linkage between "new" and "idea" would later be removed from the realm of material print products and become important in later authorship debates. In Dunton, though, this is not yet the dominant reason for claims of originality. While I do not want to create a history of origins, date the emergence of an *ur*-originality, or claim that one party "owned" the phrase, what we can infer from Dunton's rhetoric is that *originality* was in a fact a vexed term, with multiple parties attempting to define it in their own terms.

We can conclude, therefore, that booksellers also hold claim to the various discourses that created authors; the language and the value system of the print trade run through the central terms that brought them into existence. As my reading of Dunton has shown, booksellers could claim that they were the ones "encouraging learning" (as the title of the Statute of Anne promotes) and often the ones creating original projects worthy of protection. Dunton's physically embodied notion of originality as "new to print" is mirrored in the act's literal, material meaning of rights to copy. The Statute of Anne, then, can be seen not as the birthplace of authors but as one of the Stationers' last consolidations of their rhetorical and legal power. Nonetheless, while the booksellers may have been rewarded most tangibly and immediately by the act, they won the battle only at the expense of the war, as the resulting discourse of proprietary authorship provided writers more long-term cultural capital. And essential to the construction of the burgeoning ideology of authorship was a circulation of the figure of the Grub Street bookseller as a greedy, churlish boor, whose claim to a financial interest in creative work was exploitative at best, a transgression of the natural mind-body hierarchy at worst. Thus by the twentieth century, a tradesman's insistence that his economic, material, and technological concerns were part of a creative and spiritual journey could be seen only as "ludicrous."

## Robert Dodsley: Constructing an Author's Bookseller

As the idea of the author as a natural genius grew in popularity, representations of the commercially creative bookseller waned and print workers were evicted from understandings of the creation of texts. Clifford Siskin points to the economic contraction in book production from the 1720s through the 1740s as a time when the periodical press flourished, claiming "the product of its critical efforts was new forms of professional behavior embodied in the Author."[40] This is also part of the larger eighteenth-century project fostering polite discourse and disinterestedness. Early expressions of this system of thought mark as inferior anyone with intellectual or literary pretensions who also explicitly or purposefully works within the context of a market economy. True authorship, by definition, was not besmirched by the commercial.[41] Oddities like Kirkman and Dunton were thus relegated to the ranks of the eccentric, bizarre, or even unacceptable, and their works were ignored.

Such a viewpoint could not fail to reverberate into the trade itself. As the contempt for the commercialization of publishing, emblematized most notoriously by Pope, became the dominant discourse, booksellers themselves, at the center of the tainted financial nexus, reinvented themselves. Just as ideology ostracizes some representations, it signals others as worthy of attention and praise. Robert Dodsley was (and is) heralded as the "good bookseller," one who understood the proper delegation of intellectual and commercial work. His persona is representative, however, of a larger trend. By the second third of the century, the literary-print marketplace had consolidated into fewer large concerns. At the same time, as bookselling simultaneously became more capital-intensive and potentially lucrative, it was influenced less by the Stationers' Company, with its rigid guild structure mapping traditional job routes from apprentice to master. In a more stable political climate, print was also less dangerous; the popularity of sermons and novels made it a respectable medium. Booksellers carefully and consciously constructed an image of propriety that reflected well on the texts they sold.[42] It is thus not a stretch to believe they would participate in other discourses of middle-class propriety, such as financial disinterest, as well. At the same time, they were also commercially motivated tradesmen who recognized the marketing potential of popular notions such as "natural genius."

Robert Dodsley ran a successful business, although it is hard to find detailed references to this fact in biographies. He also blurred author-bookseller boundaries even more than Kirkman and Dunton, being well known and respected as a popular playwright, a published poet, an editor of influential anthologies of English poetry, the author of a much imitated textbook, and the sponsor of Samuel Johnson's *Dictionary*. Nonetheless, his early self-representations are frequently self-effacing and any articulation of the creative aspects of publishing is muted. Later, even as his business and cultural sway grew, he downplayed his commercial interests. In public discourse, he ignored the concrete aspects of bookmaking, discussing literary effect and rhetorical tropes instead of letter, print, or page.

The earlier dynamic, in which he assumed a position of subordinate to the great authors around him, was built in the foundations of Dodsley's career. His story is famous: working as a footman, he was encouraged in his early poetic impulses by an employer who recognized how his talent could be used to capitalize on the trend for "untutored genius" signaled by the success of Stephen Duck[43] It was Pope himself, however, who liberated Dodsley from aristocratic patronage. Infamous for demanding unprecedented levels of authorial control and financial remuneration (despite his interest in disinterestedness), Pope had set up his own printers and booksellers, reversing the conventional author-bookseller relationship of the established trade. Dodsley served as an unofficial apprentice for one of these, Lawton Giliver, who would subsequently publish Dodsley's first work. Later, Pope provided financial assistance in setting up Dodsley's own shop. While the role of independent tradesman was clearly a socioeconomic promotion for Dodsley, he still seems to have retained his servant's habits, feeling uncomfortable with his cultural "betters" whom he had once served at his master's table. The fact that he never joined the Stationers' Company, relying on Pope's influential friends instead of traditional trade relations (he rarely collaborated with other booksellers, although this was a common practice at the time), further circumscribed his self-positioning and his representation of the role of the bookseller—especially vis-à-vis that of the author.

This deference to those he published affected how writers viewed him, as is revealed in his correspondence of the 1740s and 1750s. Many, for example, asked that Pope's protégé, Joseph Spence, edit their manuscripts, evidently seeing such intellectual work as outside the domain of a tradesman.[44] Others credited the judgment of their friends as more discerning than Dodsley's; one wrote, for example, upon sending in a religious history for purview, that "I doubt not of their favorable Acceptance, having had the approbation of several of my learned Acquaintance."[45] They also felt free (and encouraged by Dodsley) to dictate titles; specify material details such as bindings, page size, or typography; demand specific publication dates; and otherwise meddle in business details most commonly outside a writer's purview.[46] Dodsley's usual practice, perhaps learned from Pope's demands, was to return copy to authors to correct, amend, or update themselves—sometimes even at financial risk to himself.[47] While this delegation of duties seems normal, even "natural" today, it was not always so, as we have seen in discussions of the practices described by Moxon and Dunton. Dodsley, then, can be seen as strategically casting himself as one whose role was to serve the needs of writers—and the requirements of their writing.[48]

In the next decade or so, though, after his business had grown in prestige and his confidence had increased, Dodsley wrote less often of trade issues. Instead, it is writing itself—usually his own—that becomes the frequent topic of many later letters. Unlike Kirkman's and Dunton's representations of texts, however, Dodsley's written word is curiously divorced from any aspect of its physicality. In writing on writing, he rarely concerns himself with the materiality of text making, ignoring issues of typography, press, page, market demand, or distribution. Clearly, as a successful publisher and book*seller*, one known to be "conscientious about all the physical attributes of a book," he was daily immersed in the concrete details of turning ideas into commercial products.[49] However, his public writings betray little of this. For example, although he had clear financial incentives in the publication of his *A Collection of Poems by Several Hands* (1748), which was first produced as an inexpensive edition of works the copyrights of which he already owned, he advertises it as "sanctioned by men of discernment, learning and taste"—motivations that refer to an authority outside his own and pointedly transcend the economic realm.[50] Indeed, in the following years, in his letters to fellow authors and friends, he is more often concerned with their approbation of his writing, in the most ephemeral sense of the word: suggestions for revisions, characterization, effects, and so forth. Much of his surviving correspondence of the 1750s, for example, centers on prepublication and preperformance versions of his play, *Cleone*.[51] This textual circulation is notable in that, in its inattention to print (although that may have been the end result), and its dependence on the patronage of those in positions to help him, it reflects earlier and persisting scribal or coterie practices of manuscript circulation, the ethos of which was often anti-trade.[52]

This abstraction of writing from its physical incarnation is even expressed, ironically enough, in his letters to the president of the Society for the Encouragement of Arts, Manufactures and Commerce, a group focusing (despite its misleading name) mostly on the development of industry.[53] Despite the organization's obvious trade bias, Dodsley encourages the society to issue a reward whenever "any Person of real Abilities, true Genius or useful Knowledge, shall produce to the Public, any extraordinary Work, in Literature and the polite Arts, any improvement in Mechanics, or any useful Discovery in the Science."[54] While the last categories were well within the organization's purview, what is notable is not just that Dodsley wants to add literature but that he wants to reward the *writing* of the industrial arts, not just its concrete manifestation in trade. To this end, he also suggests, in the same letter, that the group's title be changed to "The British Society for the Encouragement of *Letters*, Arts, and Manufactures" (my emphasis). Similarly, in a later letter, he urges the society to "promote the Knowledge of our own Language in its several Branches of Reading, Speaking, & writing it, with Elegance & propriety."[55] He does not, notably, refer to the means of production that enable the wide circulation of that language and that provide his own living—his representation of writing, even in a letter to a group whose interest was in rewarding artisanal and mechanic efforts, elides its physical and commercial grounding.

In this context it should be remembered that Dodsley was (and is) known for his support of writers: despite his own prodigious abilities as a poet, playwright, editor, project sponsor, and businessman, he proudly extolled his reputation as the "Muse's Midwife."[56] Clearly, he was invested in maintaining and promoting an author's point of view and belief system and in promoting a reputation—good for accruing that cultural capital that led to economic gain—of being aligned with writers. In fact, as the publisher of Edward Young's *Conjectures on Original Composition*, he would have been well acquainted with the new ideals of authorship and creativity circulating at midcentury.[57] Young advocated originality as organic growth, "a vegetable nature; . . . ris[ing] spontaneously from the vital root of genius." This he opposed to "imitations," which he denigrates as a "sort of manufacture wrought up by those mechanics, art and labor"; he speaks elsewhere of the "invaders of the press."[58] Such newly circulating notions placed Dodsley—whose very livelihood, in fact, utilized "mechanics" to sell the "vital root of genius"— in a place marked by intersecting yet contradictory ideologies. Ironically, it was perhaps a wise business decision to cede to representations that muted the physical and commercial at the behest of this new definition of worthy writing as emerging naturally from the brain of the genius. It may also be, however, that Dodsley, who was an aspiring writer before he was a bookseller, did feel more comfortable with such views, a belief in which he could use to place himself, despite his humble origins, within a group of men once seen as his social betters. Indeed, reviews of *Cleone* focus on his "natural capacity, unimproved by scholastic erudition," and compare him to Shakespeare.[59] Nonetheless, whether strategically or unconsciously, Dodsley does seem to position himself more and more often as a subject of and to the expanding discourse of authorship. His success in constructing this identity for himself can be judged by the inscription on his tombstone, penned by close friend Joseph Spence, heralding Dodsley as someone "who, as an Author, raised himself / much above what cou'd have been expected / from one in his rank of life / and without much learned Education."[60] While it is notable that, even after a lifetime of middle-class comfort and association with the upper echelons, Dodsley's lowly origins are not forgotten, what is most striking appears only in its absence: there is no mention of the profession in which he labored so industriously in order to "rise." In the polite discourse of eulogy, bookselling, with its associations of money and manufacture, is erased. It is only as an Author that Dodsley is publicly acknowledged.[61]

## THE SELLING OF AUTHORSHIP
### AND THE AUTHORING OF BOOKSELLERS

Dodsley's self-positioning can be seen as part of a larger cultural shift, described by James Raven as a widespread suspicion of, even hostility toward, overt economic activity that flourished in the second half of the eighteenth century.[62] This could not help but have specific effects on the literary marketplace during a period when, as Raven notes, the Free

Debating Society of Birmingham posed the question in 1774, "Why is Trade and Commerce in a manner become incompatible with polite literature?"[63] As "taste" became a product in itself, the producers of this ideology by necessity had to conceal its manufactured origins. That booksellers themselves, at the center of the text-commerce nexus, could play a creative and constructive role in this process was an idea both feared and disdained: as one *Monthly Review* essay sniped in 1766, "We seem to live in an era when retailers of every kind of ware aspire to be the original manufacturers, and particularly in literature."[64] As we have seen, however, the idea that one who sold books might also make text was not a new trend. Nonetheless, in a period that witnessed increased literary production as well as intensified marketing and advertising for these products, such control over discourse must have seemed especially threatening.[65]

If, as I discussed earlier, booksellers created authors, then mid- and late-century authors, in turn, constructed the greedy bookseller as the dark Other of literature. Certainly, the vision of the venal and conniving Grub Street bookseller as the enemy of a clean and contained print owes an ironic legacy to the unabashedly economic self-constructions such as Kirkman's and Dunton's. Yet the later socio-literary context of the image of the bookseller's investment in trade changed the representation's meaning, so that after the mid-eighteenth century, most commentators can describe these two only as bizarre or degraded and their attitudes as embarrassing. This later reconstruction of the "bad bookseller" is rooted in Dodsley's celebrated era of authorship and burgeoning notions of the natural genius, when the "good" publisher was recast as a grateful and supportive amanuensis. Such a revision is also related to the century's middle-class project of the novelization of discourse and the construction of the polite. Usually, this is seen as a usurpation of aristocratic production values, the victory of the print market over patronage and scribal publishing. In my overview of these three booksellers, however, I hope to point to another realm that was expropriated, the writing of the mechanic class of citizens, artisans, and small retailers, those who saw trade as a heroic venture instead of an embarrassment—and were placed in a position to circulate these values. My interest lies in the ways in which what Paula McDowell has called "new bourgeois models for discursive behavior" ensured that discussions of the material and the commercial could not be contained in a sanitized print culture.[66] Further developments in the "disciplining" of writing secured its status as an almost purely intellectual activity.[67] Representations of texts produced by the hand of workers and in their interests became encroachments to be derided or ridiculed; later, such representations faded as they were ignored and no longer circulated. This act of erasure itself was made invisible as the ideology became commonsense.

My goal, then, is not to admit booksellers into an exalted pantheon of "true" authors, though I do wish to claim them as the creative agents they saw themselves. Those involved in the mechanistic or financial aspects of the book trades did not merely transparently reproduce eighteenth-century culture in print; they helped to construct it, at every level. Nor do I wish to celebrate these booksellers' financial interests as the best, "right," or only way to approach the work of writing, though I do call attention to the ways in which their unwillingness to mystify that aspect of textual production later marked them as transgressive. Instead, my attempt to recover this alternative discourse of text creation, one that reveals the material and economic basis of texts, highlights the contested nature of "the rise of the author" and the eighteenth-century project of artistic disinterest—and casts doubt on the inevitability of both.

# 4

# *From Authorized Print to Authoritative Author: The Regulated Trade*

*Dispersing seditious books is near a-kin to raising tumults; they are as like as brother and sister: raising tumults is more masculine; printing and dispersing books is the feminine part of every rebellion.*

—SERJEANT MORTON AT THE TRIAL OF THOMAS BREWSTER, 1663

*It is a general prejudice, and has been propagated for these sixteen hundred years, that arts and sciences cannot flourish under an absolute government; and that genius must necessarily be cramped where freedom is restrained. This sounds plausible, but is false in fact. . . . [W]hy the despotism of government should cramp the genius of a mathematician, an astronomer, a poet, or an orator, I confess I could never discover. It may indeed deprive the poet or orator of the liberty of treating of certain subjects in the manner they would wish, but it leaves them subjects enough to exert genius upon, if they have it. Can an author with reason complain that he is cramped and shackled, if he is not at liberty to publish blasphemy, bawdry, or sedition?*

—LORD CHESTERFIELD, 1749

In the foundational article "What Is an Author," Michel Foucault claims of a book or text with an author that its

> status as property is historically secondary to the penal code controlling its appropriation. Speeches and books were assigned real authors . . . only when the author became subject to punish-

ment and to the extent that his discourse was considered transgressive. In our culture . . . discourse was not essentially a thing,
a product, or a possession, but an action situated in a bipolar
field of sacred and profane, lawful and unlawful, religious and
blasphemous. It was a gesture charged with risks long before it
became a possession caught in a circuit of property values.[1]

While historians of the French book trade have, following Foucault,
historicized the emergence of the author in relation to his responsibility
for potentially seditious texts, the relationship between authorship and
censorship has been largely ignored by critics concerned with the professionalization of the author and the rise of the novel in England.[2]
They seem to have succumbed to the notion, promulgated by Lord
Chesterfield, that genius exists separately from, and is not influenced by,
any government efforts to repress the wayward writer. This is partly due
to a misunderstanding of the nature of censorship and its targets in the
second half of the seventeenth century. Susan Stewart, for example, in
discussing the English treason cases of the period, asserts that "before
the development of concepts of original genius and intellectual property, all thoughts were potentially held in common, . . . and it was those
who disseminated ideas who reaped any rewards or punishments
prompted by such ideas."[3] The disseminators of sedition Stewart refers
to were, of course, booksellers, publishers, and hawkers—a group Stewart, in this comment, makes sharply distinct from authors, who, she
seems to imply, were ignored by government agents.

Nonetheless, the author as an accountable agent *did* emerge in
England—albeit as an entity intrinsically *connected to* printers, publishers, and others legally responsible for texts: writers, in the eyes of the
law, were just one of many print workers. My previous chapters have
discussed alternatives to the regime of original authorship that emerged
from the rhetoric of master printers and booksellers, wherein the text
work of the print insists on its own creative contribution. This chapter
also offers a challenge to the standard notion of the author as a singular
proprietor by focusing on earlier—and markedly different—discourses
of authorship and responsibility. Emerging from the realm of licensing
and seditious libel is a view of the authorized circulation of print texts
that highlights their material nature as tangible products made by a num-

ber of responsible agents—many (and sometimes any) of whom were considered appropriate "subjects of punishments." As the period evolved, however, legal responsibility, best emblematized by the imprimatur of the licenser, blurred into more abstract and interiorized notions of decorous propriety, best represented by the moral and moralizing female author. Thus this chapter illustrates the ways in which eighteenth-century English censorship, rather than being purely repressive, worked to produce a specific form of discourse. I refer here to more than the obvious notion that government censors favored pro-monarchy and standard religious tracts and silenced political critics and sectarians. Rather, I believe that even texts outside the usual purview of censorship, such as literary entertainment and edification, were shaped by the changing norms of textual regulation. I focus particularly on women in the print trades, a group who by definition could not be proprietors, whether as printers or authors, and a group whose importance has been largely ignored in both publishing and literary history. It is their jobs on the front lines of dangerous textuality—and their struggles with and manipulation of the constraints governing the print trade—that helped bring about the epitome of eighteenth-century textuality, the "feminized" novel.[4]

## POWER AND/IN PRINT

Foucault concludes "What Is an Author?" with a look toward the future. In a culture without authors, he reflects, questions such as "who is the real author?" might be replaced with questions about discourse: "where does it come from; how is it circulated; who controls it?"[5] In late seventeenth- and early eighteenth-century England, however, *both* sets of questions were posed by the government. In 1662, in response to fear of a seemingly uncontrolled increase in print production, especially of political books, pamphlets, and broadsides commenting on the Stuart Restoration, Parliament passed the Licensing Act, or the "Act for preventing the frequent Abuses in printing seditious, treasonable, and unlicensed Books and Pamphlets, and for regulating of Printing and printing Presses."[6] This act restricted printing to twenty printers, all of whom were required to be members of the Stationers' Company. Although sixteenth- and early seventeenth-century printers, as I discussed in chapter 2, had been able to regulate themselves through the company, Restoration Stationers were no longer allowed to monitor their own activities, considered too financially interested and too Presbyterian to be entrusted with this duty. Instead, the act prohibited the printing of any book or pamphlet unless "it shall be first lawfully licensed and authorized to be printed by such a person and persons only as shall be constituted and appointed to license the same."[7] This licensing was certified with the imprimatur of the licenser, and printers too were required to put their names on their products before dissemination. Thus authorized print declared who controlled the discourse—the licenser—as well as where it came from—whose printing house—as it circulated. As a provision of the Licensing Act, however, printers were also compelled to learn the name of the author so that they could divulge it on demand. The author as a source was as important to the authorities as the printer or publisher as disseminator: a common warrant might enable its bearer to "seize all seditious books and libels and to apprehend the authors, contrivers, printers, publishers and dispersers of them, and bring them . . . to be proceeded against according to law."[8] This warrant is representative of the larger discourse of licensing, however, in that it holds authors and printers (who might together be termed "producers") to be *equally* responsible as the many disseminators of these texts.

The Licensing Act lapsed in 1695, a date often considered to mark the beginning of freedom of the press in England. Of course, the act did not lapse, however, because the government was liberal and philosophically committed to this freedom. Various forms of licensing and other regulating mechanisms were suggested in Parliament up through 1712.[9] Rather, the government was overwhelmed: licensing was inefficient and ineffective. Illegal presses still flourished. Even the first Surveyor of the Press, the notoriously ruthless Roger L'Estrange, much despised by the Stationers, could not keep the press in control in times of political upheaval, such as the Exclusion Crisis of 1679–81. Furthermore, by 1695, the government had polarized into two parties, Whig and Tory, both of which relied on printed material to garner support and besmirch the opposition. Thus, as Alan Downie has noted, "the necessity of government control was replaced by an arrangement which exploited the advantages government possessed to subsidize printed propaganda."[10] The government could use the press more easily than it could stop it, so explicit licensing was traded for the more pointed use of seditious libel and treason laws already in existence.

Despite the prevalence of these laws (which I discuss in more detail below), the standard narrative of freedom of the press in this period has legal control and censorship (repression) vanquished by argument and debate (liberation). Foucault reminds us, however, that an analysis of power "must not assume that the sovereignty of the state, the form of the law, or the over-all unity of domination are given at the outset; rather, these are only the terminal forms power takes."[11] Power is ratified, becomes culturally acceptable, long before it becomes law. Its terminal expression is merely the result of an ideological contest later suppressed. In this period what the plethora of pamphlet literature explicitly addressing the issues of licensing and the press tells us is that the opposition was never Law versus Print, with the Law first dominating then Print eventually asserting its natural tendency to achieve democratic reform—a view still with us in such aphorisms as "information wants to be free." Instead, throughout the late seventeenth-century period of licensing, a variety of social forces struggled for control, an encounter that always already manifested itself *within the boundaries of print*. Thus power always circulated through print; print itself could never be an agent in opposition to the Law-outside-print.[12]

Several pamphlets by Roger L'Estrange supply particularly striking evidence of the nature of the print-versus-print debate. As Surveyor of the Press, a government agent, he would seem a prototypical representative of the Law. Yet his two best-known pamphlets, *Truth and Loyalty Vindicated, From the Reproches and Clamours of Mr. Edward Bagshaw. Together with a Further Discovery of the* LIBELLER *"Himself," and his "Seditious Confederates"* (1662) and *Considerations and Proposals In Order to the Regulation of the Press: Together with Diverse "Instances of Treasonous" and "Seditious Pamphlets," Proving the "Necessity" thereof* (1663), challenge this view. These consist of reports on the problem of sedition and his recommendations for controlling it. The first tract is addressed to "the Right Honorable the Lords of His Majesties Most Honorable Privy Council," and the second, to both "the Kings Most Excellent Majesty" and "the Right Honorable the Lords, And To the Honorable the Commons Assembled in Parliament." Yet these are not, of course, private letters or court documents but *published* (and therefore public) texts, meant for a large general audience beyond the government. L'Estrange explains his purpose in writing these pamphlets in *Truth and Loyalty*:

> Freedom of the Press, had so manifest an Influence upon the minds of the People, that in a short time, That Unanimous Proneness of Affection, which upon the Kings Restauration was most remarquably evident in the Generality of the Nation, was so far alter'd, and wrought upon, by means of these poysonous Discourses that the Presbyterian Cause was grown to be the Common Argument of Publique Meetings, and the Power of the Two Houses *Co-ordinate* with his Majesty not obscurely defended. Finding so many Bitter and Infectious Writings to escape, not only *unpunished*, but *unanswered*, to the dayly *Encouragement* of the *Faction*, and the *Scandal* of the *Government*: I reckon'd it my Duty (since no on else would meddle) to supply the Place of a Better Defendent.[13]

An interesting circulation of discourse is evident here: although seditious texts infect or poison *oral* culture—"Publique Meetings"—the antidote lies only in more public *texts*. Print must be fought with print.

Like much of the text-work rhetoric of this period that I have previously explored, print was considered by L'Estrange to be of a most concrete nature: he not only takes on his enemies in their own medium, but he deploys the most material aspects of print, such as font and page layout, to make his points.[14] *Truth and Loyalty* refutes Edward Bagshaw's accusation that L'Estrange was a spy for Cromwell and illustrates the seditious nature of Bagshaw's writing in general. In constructing his argument, L'Estrange literally sets up a battle of text countering text—he excerpts the "Rhetorical Libell" of Bagshaw "Word for Word" (*Truth*, preface, n.p.) or paragraph by paragraph, inserting his own counterinterpretation at each significant point. L'Estrange creates not merely an opposition of ideas, however, but an opposition that takes place at the level of typography: Bagshaw's excerpts are not only shorter than L'Estrange's explanations, but they are physically smaller, dwarfed by L'Estrange's more authoritative, larger print. Bagshaw's words are primarily in italics, while L'Estrange's are in a clearer and bolder roman (see fig. 8). For the king's words, the staunch Loyalist uses gothic, a type

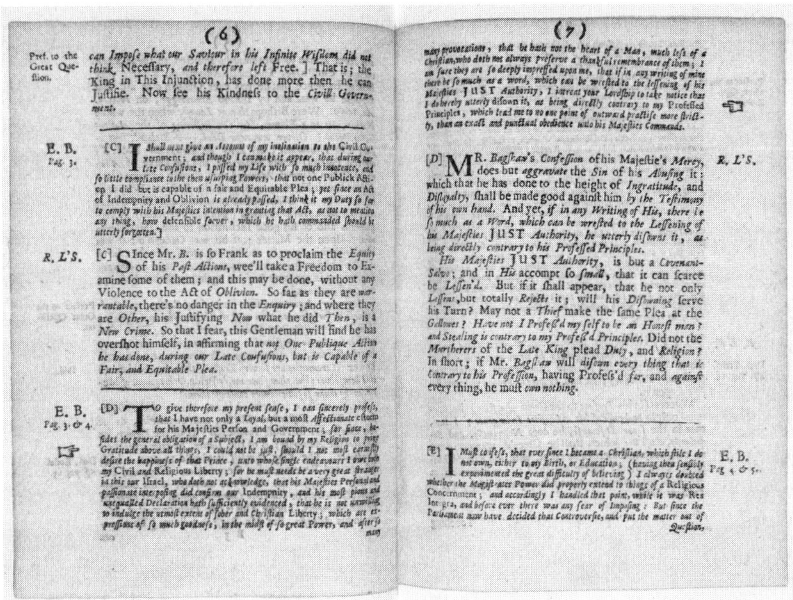

*Fig. 8: L'Estrange's use of the italic and roman type. (Roger L'Estrange,* Truth and Loyalty Vindicated From the Reproches and Clamours of Mr Edward Bagshaw, *printed for H. Brome and A. Seil, London, 1662. Reprinted by permission of the Syndics of the Cambridge University Library.)*

that eventually comes to stand for authority itself. At first, L'Estrange deploys the gothic only for direct quotations of the king's proclamations. Then, when summarizing these declarations, he intersperses his more ordinary type with a gothic representation of the king's ideas:

> His Majesty, in his Declaration from *Breda*, Grants a Free and General Pardon to all that shall lay hold upon that Grace and Favour, and by any Publique Act Declare their doing so, and Return to the Loyalty and Obedience of Good Subjects: … Which *Loyalty* is to be *Manifested, by* not Persevering in Guilt for the Future, and by not Opposing the quiet, and happiness of their Country, in the Restoration both of King, Peers, and People, to their Just, Antient and Fundamental Rights. (*Truth*, 22)

Eventually, however, the king's authority becomes, more broadly, the Law, and the gothic type becomes a rhetorical device that he employs to emphasize authoritatively the legalistic elements of his text:

> Now the Question is, first, *whether Those that* **Persevere in their Guilt,** *and* **oppose** *the Restoration of the King to any of his* **Just, Antient,** *and* **Fundamental Rights** are not by This *Limiting Condition excepted* from *Pardon*? (*Truth*, 22; see fig. 9)

Libel is thus countered by a *typographical* embodiment of the king himself, expressed through the king's agent L'Estrange.[15]

If the sheer size and weight of L'Estrange's material words are not enough to make his point, he also uses page layout to recast Bagshaw's words. In a section enumerating Bagshaw's political resolutions, he quotes Bagshaw, apparently verbatim, and then "clarifies" these words in a summarizing marginal note adjacent to the text. Though small in size, and literally "marginal," these notes clearly reflect a pedagogical authority, as is indicated by L'Estrange's use of them elsewhere in the text to refer back to other, better-known, writers' ideas. Buttressed by this sense of the scholarly, his marginal notes supply the "correct" reading of Bagshaw, one that points up more directly the libelous nature of his passages. For example, when Bagshaw avers that "the real Sovereignty *here amongst us, was on* King, Lords, *and* Commons," L'Estrange reads this as "The King of *England* no Monarch" (*Truth*, 20). Bagshaw's "*If a* Prince *be so long* Out, *that the* Nation *cannot withstand without* another: Providence *has* dispossess'd *the* former, *and we are to make a* new Choyce" becomes, in L'Estrange's margin, "*Oliver* Chosen by *Providence*" (*Truth*, 19). Similarly, L'Estrange translates "*If the* King *raise Warr against such a* Parliament *upon their* Declaration *of the* Dangers *of the* Common-wealth, *the* People *are to take it as raised against the* Commonwealth" into the straightforwardly treasonous "the *People* judges of the *King*" (*Truth*, 20; see fig. 10). My point here is not that L'Estrange's commentary is incorrect or at best reductive (which may be true) but that he uses the *physical space* of the page to shore up his argument. Other particularly offensive passages need no extra words to explain their treasonous nature, but are marked merely by the typographical

*Time,* pretend to any favour from the Act of *Pardon* ; but That will not much avail Mr. *Bagshaw,* who by *Justifying Now,* what he *Did Then,* does it *over again,* and stands accomptable for the same Fault upon another Score.

But methinks the Case is not here, whether *This Pamphlet,* but whether or no the very *Authour* of it be *Pardon'd ?* and This Question (if any there be) arises from the very Letter both of his Majesties *Declaration from Breda ;* and of the *Act it self.*

Decl. from Breda.

His Majesty, in his Declaration from *Breda,* **Grants a Free and General Pardon to all that shall lay hold upon that Grace and Favour, and by any Publique Act Declare their doing so, and Return to the** Loyalty, and Obedience of Good Subjects : ( *Exceptis Excipiendis* ). Which *Loyalty* is to be *Manifested,* by **not Persevering in Guilt for the Future, and by not Opposing the quiet, and happiness of their Country, in the Restoration both of King, Peers, and People, to their Just, Antient, and Fundamental Rights ;** Here's the *Promise* and *Condition* of the Pardon : *Persuant* to which *Promise,* and *Correspondent* to which *Condition ,* the following Pardon is said expresly to be *Enacted,* i. e. [**In Performance of his Royal and Gracious Word signified by His Letters to the several Houses of Parliament now Assembled, and His Declarations in that behalf Published.**]

Act of Pardon.

Now the Question is, first, *Whether Those that* **Persevere in their Guilt,** *and* **oppose** *the Restoration of the King to any of his* **Just, Antient,** *and* **Fundamental Rights** are not by This *Limiting Condition excepted* from *Pardon ?* And the next Question is,

*Whether His Majesties Supreme Authority in Causes Ecclesiastical, be not One of His* **Just, Antient,** *and* **Fundamental** *Rights ?* If so: *Whoever Persists to oppose the Prerogative Royal in This Particular, has no Right or Title to the Intent or Benefit of the Act of Indempnity.*

The Extent of his Majesties Power as to the matter in Question, may be seen in King *James* his *Ratification* of The

Canons

---

*FIG. 9: L'Estrange utilizes* Gothic *to represent the king's ideas. (Roger L'Estrange,* Truth and Loyalty Vindicated From the Reproches and Clamours of Mr Edward Bagshaw, *printed for H. Brome and A. Seil, London, 1662. Reprinted by permission of the Syndics of the Cambridge University Library.)*

symbol of a pointing hand in the margin, standing in for a judge's literal finger of guilt.[16] The manipulation of the space of the page reinforces his textual points. In a graphic sense, his notes stand out clearly, which, despite their relegation to the margins, gives them a central position—one can imagine readers skimming through L'Estrange's condensation and ignoring the more densely printed work of Bagshaw. Ideologically, his strategy also has the effect of suggesting a moral purity to his words, which resist the contamination of Bagshaw's paragraphs. Thus, in fighting sedition, L'Estrange deploys the entire arsenal of a printer's weapons—type font and size, symbols, and page layout—to assert the government's righteous opinion. Sedition is to be fought within the boundaries of the print page because, after all, it is there—at least as far as L'Estrange is concerned—that it is committed.

Given his understanding of print as a tangible medium that he—with the help of his printer, one assumes—was able to manipulate toward his discursive ends, we might expect L'Estrange to hold a similarly concretized attitude toward the production of sedition. Indeed, material pages are understood by L'Estrange to be material *products*—his view of seditious tracts as financial investments is evident throughout his work. Thus he excuses those who act "rather upon Necessity than Malice" (*Truth*, 57), recommends that fines be made more than profits, and suggests that the government buy out the machinery of printers willing to take up another trade. L'Estrange, in fact, envisioned a long line of responsible agents, from makers to distributors, who benefited financially from seditious texts; he believed that many branches of the print trade were fed by this lucrative market. In *Considerations and Proposals in Order to the Regulation of the Press* (1663), for example, L'Estrange casts a wide net:

> The Instruments of setting the work afoot are These. The *Adviser, Author, Compiler, Writer, Corrector*, and the Persons *for* whom, and *by* whom; that is say, the *Stationer* (commonly), and the *Printer*. To which may be Added, the *Letter-Founders*, and the *Smiths*, and the *Joyners*, that work upon the Presses.
>
> The usual *Agents* for Publishing, are the *Printers* themselves, *Stitchers, Binders, Stationers, Hawkers, Mercury-women, Pedlars, Ballad-Singers, Posts, Carryers, Hackney-Coach-men, Boat-men, and Mariners.*[17]

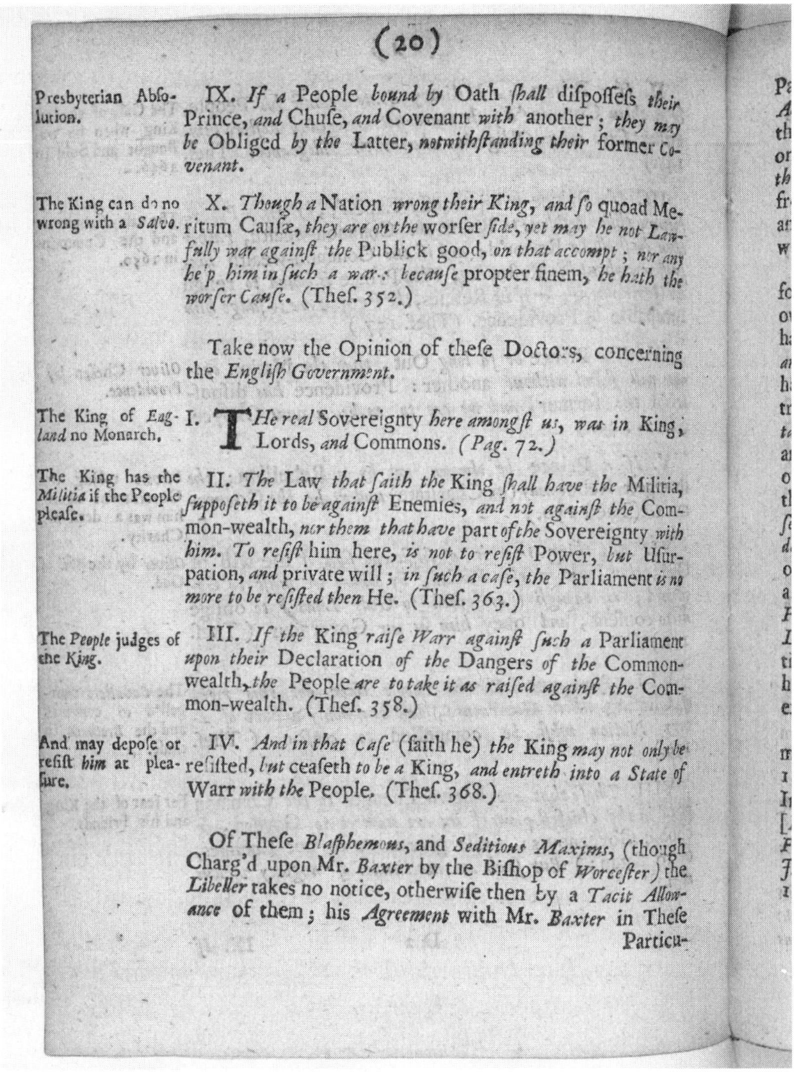

(20)

Presbyterian Abso-  IX. *If a* People *bound by* Oath *shall* dispossess *their*
lution.  Prince, *and* Chuse, *and* Covenant *with* another; *they may*
*be* Obliged *by the* Latter, *notwithstanding their* former Co-
*venant.*

The King can do no  X. *Though a* Nation *wrong their King, and so* quoad Me-
wrong with a *Salvo.* ritum Causæ, *they are on the* worser *side, yet may he not Law-*
*fully war against the* Publick good, *on that accompt; nor any*
*help him in such a war, because* propter finem, *he hath the*
*worser Cause.* (Thes. 352.)

Take now the Opinion of these Doctors, concerning
the *English Government.*

The King of Eng-  I.  **T**He real Sovereignty *here amongst us, was* in King,
land no Monarch,  Lords, *and* Commons. *(Pag. 72.)*

The King has the  II. *The* Law *that saith the* King *shall have the* Militia,
Militia if the People  *supposeth it to be against* Enemies, *and not against the* Com-
please.  mon-wealth, *nor them that have* part *of the* Sovereignty *with*
*him. To resist him here, is not to resist* Power, *but* Usurpation, *and* private will; *in such a case, the* Parliament *is no*
*more to be resisted then* He. (Thes. 363.)

The *People* judges of  III. *If the* King *raise* Warr *against such a* Parliament
the King.  *upon their* Declaration *of the* Dangers *of the* Common-
wealth, *the* People *are to take it as raised against the* Common-wealth. (Thes. 358.)

And may depose or  IV. *And in that* Case (saith he) *the* King *may not only be*
resist *him* at plea-  resisted, *but* ceaseth *to be a* King, *and entreth into a State of*
sure.  Warr *with the* People. (Thes. 368.)

Of These *Blasphemous,* and *Seditious Maxims,* (though
Charg'd upon Mr. *Baxter* by the Bishop of *Worcester)* the
*Libeller* takes no notice, otherwise then by a *Tacit Allow-*
*ance* of them; his *Agreement* with Mr. *Baxter* in These
Particu-

FIG. *10: L'Estrange deploys the space of the margins to physically construct his arguments. (Roger
L'Estrange,* Truth and Loyalty Vindicated From the Reproches and Clamours of Mr Edward
Bagshaw, *printed for H. Brome and A. Seil, London, 1662. Reprinted by permission of the Syndics
of the Cambridge University Library.)*

It is clear in this passage that almost anyone who touched a text on its way to a reader, even the most remote rural reader, is considered responsible for its distribution. The libelous book taints all, from those who built the press on which it was printed, to those who stitched the print pages together. Authors are not exempt from this contamination: it is not *only* disseminators who can be prosecuted. Instead, authors are understood as *part of* this chain of dissemination—they are neither solely to blame nor free from responsibility. Thus writers were not considered a separate category of producers but were part of a larger group of working contributors that together make the seditious print product.[18]

Other parts of *Considerations and Proposals*, however, have been singled out in recent criticism to illustrate that the Restoration government was mostly interested in authors as the ultimate and originary source of sedition. Harold Weber points to the following passage as proof that L'Estrange possessed a "desire to combat the protean and diffused power of the press by assigning to the author an originary responsibility and power":[19]

> Touching the *Adviser, Author, Compiler, Writer* and *Corrector*, their Practices are hard to be Retriv'd, unless the One Discover the Other.
>
> This Discovery may be procur'd partly by a *Penalty* upon *refusing* to *Discover*, and partly by a *Reward*, to the *Discoverer*; but let both the *Penalty*, and the *Reward* be *Considerable* and *Certain*: and let the *Obligation* of *Discovery* run quite Through, from the *first Mover* of the Mischief, to the *Last Disperser* of it. That is to say; *If any unlawful Book shall be found in the Possession of any of the* Agents, *or* Instruments *aforesaid, let the* Person *in whose possession it is* found, *be Reputed, and Punished as the Author of the said Book, unless he* Produce *the Person, or Persons, from whom he Receiv'd it.* (*Considerations*, 2)

It is true that L'Estrange does point to the author as the place where the chain of responsibility stops, but this alone does not seem to validate an understanding of the author as "originary." First, he is not in a special category, but is mentioned only in conjunction with other print workers, such as the adviser, compiler, or corrector. Further, his splitting of the duties of the adviser, author, and writer in the first sentence suggests L'Estrange had discrete notions of these roles, which certainly complicates an easy understanding of responsible authorship. He seems to imagine that a seditious, idea-generating instigator—one who "gives rise to or causes an action, event, circumstance"[20]—might work in conjunction with political collaborators ("advisers") in addition to those who are merely wordsmiths on a final product. Finally, in focusing on this passage, Weber ignores the context of the entire tract, which takes on each category of the trade separately and presents ways to stop each group. Writers and their cohorts are only one among many to be controlled, and all, the pamphlet seems to imply, are interchangeable. The linkage L'Estrange makes in his passage, the chain of punishment, thus does not seem to be put in effect to catch the author specifically; rather, it seems to be set up to punish as many connected individuals as possible— he is satisfied as long as each worker turns in the person who touched the text before him. L'Estrange does, in the conclusion of the pamphlet, comment that "for the *Authors*, nothing can be too *Severe*, that stands with *Humanity*, and *Conscience*. . . .'[T]is the Way to cut off the *Fountain* of our Troubles," but even here he lumps them together with other "*Grand Delinquents* . . . the *Authors* or *Compilers*, (which I reckon as all One) the *Printers*, and *Stationers*" (*Considerations*, 32). Indeed, he devotes much more space to discussions of the last two.

This is not to say that officials were not at all interested in those who wrote the text, only that the belief system underlying censorship and putting it into practice was not always internally consistent, but complex and contradictory. Indeed, in a discussion of L'Estrange, Joseph Loewenstein notes that it may be the "range of polemical services that authorial property could perform" that eventually "secured it legal reification."[21] For example, a 1679 proclamation creates a chain of responsibility similar to L'Estrange's. It offers a forty-pound reward to anyone revealing the author or printer of a seditious work, and, more significantly, pardons hawkers, booksellers, or printers who will "Discover and make known the Authors thereof."[22] Similarly, one of the censorship bills proposed after the lapse of the Licensing Act in 1695, for example, suggested that "anyone whose name appeared in an imprint would be as answerable *as if he were the author* of the book" (my emphasis).[23] At the same time that this statement assumes a broad range of participants who *can* be held responsible, such as the printers or publishers named on the title page, it also does seem to assert that the author is the primary agent. Lord Chief Justice Scroggs certainly believed so when he commented in a 1680 libel trial that, although "it is hard to find the author [and] not hard to find the printer, . . . one author found is better than twenty printers found."[24] Despite this commentary, though, workers in the print trades were the most prosecuted in such trials and the most notorious flouters of government regulations. In trials, booksellers and publishers were often answerable for the actions of servants, shop workers, and family members, implying that the Stationer held ultimate responsibility. This suggests that the discourse of holding authors as primarily "subject to punishment" was not yet dominant, but existed alongside the more common notion that distributors and other contributors were the accountable parties.

Within the print trade itself, ironically, the latter view seems to have been privileged, perhaps because, in the practices of some booksellers, authors were unnecessary. John Feather notes, for example, that a "stock excuse" on the part of booksellers who sponsored newspapers was that an offending article had merely been copied from another newspaper.[25] A strategy like this simultaneously relieved the copier of responsibility and rendered any hired writers politically negligible. In fact, the suggestion that published print was, as a literary common, available to all, fundamentally obscures the notion of an originary source. Indeed, writers were discursively "erased" by the trade in many ways. Some booksellers invented magical or mysterious origins for their texts: one claimed when pressed that a "masked woman" had left libelous books in his shop.[26] Another testified in 1714 that

> it is a very usual thing for persons to leave books & papers at his house and at the houses of other publishers, and a long time after to call for the value thereof, without making themselves known to the said publishers, and if the Government makes enquiry concerning the authors of any books or papers so left, in order to bring them to punishment, it often happens that nobody comes to make any demand for the value of the said books.[27]

Others were more explicit about the role they would play in rendering these writers invisible. Isaac Fell, a mid-eighteenth-century bookseller, went so far as to sign the following affidavit before the Lord Mayor: "I. F. of Pater-noster Row, London, bookseller, maketh oath, and saith, he will not at any time whatever, declare the name of any person or persons who shall send any papers for the Middlesex Journal, or any other periodical publication in which he shall be concerned, without the express consent and direction of the author of such paper, and that he will not make any discovery by which any of his authors or employers can be found out."[28] It was also not uncommon for printers and booksellers to hire writers—either through discrete third parties or through their network of alliances within the trade—whose identities remained unknown to them.

Such obfuscating maneuvers were not just politically motivated, though—they point as well to the economic implications of anonymous authorship for the book trade. Since the chain of responsibility ended with him, these practices did increase the liability of the bookseller, but they also extended his control over his investment, especially in an economic and legal climate in which views on intellectual property were changing. Daniel Defoe's first proposal that the trade consider authors' rights (in his 1704 *Essay on the Regulation of the Press*), for example, linked property to responsibility, and a bookseller might have preferred to keep property even if it meant more responsibility. Economic interest thus led to removing writers from the scene of sedition: in a petition to the Commons in 1713, Stationers discouraged a ruling that would require all published texts to state the author's name. Such a gesture may have served incidentally to safeguard writers, but, more importantly, it represented the protection of and investment in future profits. Sedition was a popular commodity, a fact that L'Estrange laments and the *Grub Street Journal* celebrates: a 1731 edition acknowledges that the pillory as punishment "is so universally esteemed, that he, who has had the honour to mount that rostrum, is always looked upon amongst [the trade], as a graduate of his profession."[29]

Henry Fielding satirizes this idea in *The Author's Farce* (1729) in a conversation between a "scribbler," Scarecrow, and a bookseller, Bookweight:

SCARECROW. Sir, I have brought you a libel against the ministry.
BOOKWEIGHT. Sir, I shall not take anything against them; —for
I have two in the press already. [*Aside.*]
SCARECROW. Then, sir, I have an apology in defence of them.
BOOKWEIGHT. That I shall not meddle with neither; they don't
sell so well.[30]

Fielding's mockery of what he saw as unscrupulous booksellers reflects a reality: the most successful members of the trade could more easily risk fines and dodge prosecution than strapped writers usually could and could continue to run their business from jail. Most of those arrested were, in any case, bailed out and were not brought to court unless the attorney general thought there was a good chance of success. Because of the overwhelming amount of print licensors had to screen, their difficulty in finding good informers, the bureaucracy of the courts, and the amount of evidence necessary, few in the print trade were ever prosecuted. Nonetheless, the whole process was, for the suspect, expensive and time-consuming, so a nervous writer might be more eager to sell his libelous wares where he knew he was protected. Thus while these claims may be seen as working in the best interest in writers by minimizing their importance in the discourse of regulation, they also constructed writers as legal nonentities. For much of the trade, and, indeed, in the many practices of the law, writers only existed in connection with and as an aspect of the larger print community.

## THE FEMININE IMPRINT OF SEDITION

Since, in the day-to-day workings of the law, writers were only a fraction of the larger target of government regulation, other members of the print trade had to develop strategies through which to protect themselves from prosecution. They were united in despising informants, for example, and would refuse to work with anyone in the trade suspected of cooperating with the government. The usual course was to admit to nothing—though it was certainly best if one could avoid suspicion completely. One way of doing so is described by Fielding in *The Author's Farce*. Here, Bookweight the Bookseller proclaims that "the study of bookselling is as difficult as the law," since both require "many tricks."

He notes, for example, "[S]ometimes we give a foreign name to our own labours, and sometimes we put our names to the labour of others. Then as the lawyers have John-a-Nokes and Tom-a-Stiles, so we have Messieurs More near St. Paul's, and Smith near the Royal Exchange."[31] Fielding's jibe at the masquerades of booksellers purports to satirically reveal the truth about the trade, but disguises a large and important part of it. True, using a name other than one's own in the imprint of controversial texts was, in actuality, an important tactic used by booksellers to escape government notice both before and after the lapse of the Licensing Act. This name, however, rarely belonged to a fictional or anonymous character like "John-a-Nokes," the eighteenth-century's John Doe, and Fielding's examples of John, Tom, and "Messieurs More" are also misleading. In common practice, the name on potentially libelous literature was often the name of a woman.

In order to understand the role women played in bearing the burden of imprint for potentially seditious documents, it is necessary to review the structure and terminology of the trade in general during this period. As my last chapter showed, in the early part of the century, booksellers played the role we call "publisher" today: they were the chief organizers and financiers of projects, investing enough capital to pay writers, hire printers, and oversee distribution. They were thus, through the ownership of copyright, the ones realizing any profits from their venture. The books, pamphlets, journals, or other printed objects that resulted from this process might be sold solely through the bookseller's own shop, or they might also appear in other bookstores. Only the largest cities, however, supported bookstores that sold only books; it was also common to find music texts at a musical instrument maker's, naval books at a navigation supply shop, cookery books at a china shop, and a variety of texts at stationery shops and general stores in provincial towns. Distribution was a complex job, so, as Michael Treadwell details, successful booksellers usually delegated this task to those print workers called "trade publishers."[32] This was true especially when the printed material was, like most potentially seditious works, of an ephemeral nature, the type that garnered high sales quickly, but just as quickly became dated.

The trade publisher usually ran his or her own shop, located near Stationer's Hall at the center of the trade, but also worked closely with both mercuries, who set up small shops or stalls of pamphlets, newspapers, and a few quick-selling books in population centers such as the Royal Exchange and Temple Bar, and hawkers, who strolled the city crying their printed wares. The names of trade publishers and a few mercuries, while sometimes given on the title page with an accurate "sold by," also appeared in imprints under such misleading rubrics as "printed for" or "printed and sold by," as if they controlled the project. Despite such labeling, however, the textual property—the copyright— did not belong to the trade publisher. The fact that these distributors did not own what they put their names to was indeed enough of a defining feature of their role that a dictionary entry of 1740 states that and not much else: the publisher is "among the *Booksellers*, . . . one that has his name put at the bottom of pamphlets, news-papers, &c. tho' the property is in another person, to whom he is accountable for the sale."[33]

Of course, many people in the eighteenth century did not own property, but it is the *defining* characteristic of only a few, especially in an era that took pride in an ostensible social mobility. One group that fits this property-less categorization, however, is women. Given their alienated relationship to property in this period, it is not perhaps coincidence then that so many names in imprints belong to women, who constituted a substantial number of the few trade publishers and comprised the majority of mercuries and hawkers. As trade publishers, women worked alone or in conjunction with husbands, but even in the latter case their contributions were often public enough that wives' names appear in imprints along with or separately from husbands'. Treadwell's important recovery of the names and function of eighteenth-century publishers does not explicitly thematize gender, but his findings supply us with some useful figures. In 1700, publishers Richard and Abigail (also known as Anne) Baldwin appear in forty-five imprints; John Nutt, who was aided by his wife, Elizabeth, who took over after his death, appears in forty-six.[34] No other publishers appear regularly at all that year.[35] By contrast, the name of a typical copyright-owning bookseller, Walter Kettilby, appears in only twenty-two. Out of the publishers Treadwell lists as active from 1714 to 1717, two out of five are women. Mary Cooper was perhaps the most prolific of all: in the early 1740s she is named in two-thirds of all known publishers' imprints; after her husband's death in 1743 she sold more than one hundred titles a year. More precise figures may never be established, but there seems to be no argument that women constituted a significant part of the publishing trade.

Recent work has, in fact, begun to uncover their contribution to the print trade in general.[36] Women worked in family businesses as well as on their own, a reality that contradicts the ideal of domestic femininity (a problem I discuss below). In fact, the subtitle of *Advice to the Women and Maidens of London* (1678) states that women should "apply themselves to the right understanding and practice of the method of keeping books and accompts, whereby either single or married, they may know their estates, carry on their trades, and avoid the danger of a helpless or forlorn condition, incident to widows."[37] Workingwomen were, of course, rare in the upper middle classes and aristocracy, so when a businessman became prosperous, he would often, in aping his superiors, relegate his onetime business partner to a merely ornamental status. Among the working classes, though, a woman had to do much more than just manage a household. Despite coverture laws, a London custom from the Middle Ages let women trade as individuals, converting the wife of a freeman "from the servile status of *feme covert* into *'feme sole merchant'* with the legal rights of an independent trader."[38] This applied only to women who practiced a trade separately from their husbands; if they worked together, he was the legal owner and responsible agent. Another ancient custom allowed the widow of a freeman to become a freewoman, with the right to take apprentices and hold stock in the company. Many Stationers' widows followed this route. Even if they remarried, their rights were not alienated but shared with their new husband.

C. J. Mitchell reports women serving as Printer to the City of London and Printer to the City of Dublin, the King's Printer and Printer to the General Assembly in Scotland. Less prestigiously, women worked in pressrooms, typesetting (their small fingers supposedly made them particularly adept compositors), pulling the press, and removing printed sheets. The folding and stitching of sheets and binding of books were all common work for women. Some made paper and others sold it in stationer shops. Margaret Hunt states that between 1701 and 1740, "more than thirty newspapers show a woman as either publisher, printer, editor or major distributor."[39] Unfortunately, Mitchell's otherwise wide-ranging survey of women in the book trades does not discuss trade publishers as such (he may include them with mercuries), and it is difficult to determine whether his estimate, that 6–11 percent of book trade businesses were owned by women, includes this group. If his numbers are close to being accurate for the trade overall, it is clear from even these rough figures that publishing contained a higher percentage of women than was average for the print trade in general.[40]

Trade publishers also worked closely with the other women-centered occupations in the trade, supplying mercuries with materials, who in turn supplied hawkers, though both trade publishers and mercuries also sold directly to the public.[41] Fewer figures are available for the mercuries as a group because they rarely appear in imprints, with the notable exceptions of Anne Dodd and Elizabeth Nutt, who appear frequently. An entry in Thomas Mortimer's *A new and complete dictionary of trade and commerce* (1766) notes of mercuries that "this business is principally carried on by women."[42] Other contemporary sources call them, succinctly, "mercury-women," and, indeed, being a mercury seems to have been considered "women's work" in the same way that so-called pink-collar or service-sector jobs are today. Treadwell and others have noted the difficulty in distinguishing publishers from mercuries, and admit there does seem to be little difference between them, but they do not seem to notice that the problematic cases concern mostly women. John Dunton, for example, in his 1705 *Life and Errors*, lists a Mrs. Baldwin— presumably the Abigail Baldwin I earlier described as a prolific publisher— in a group of "Honest (Mercurial) Women" (*LE*, 236). It could be that women publishers were often called mercuries since the latter was more popularly associated with women (like women doctors until recently assumed to be nurses). Hawkers, occupying perhaps the lowliest echelon of the book trade, were also almost always women. Though hawkers do not appear in imprints at all, they did, as we see below, bear responsibility for works in other ways.[43]

The jobs of trade publisher, mercury, and hawker were, however, more than just *occupied* by women. I believe that this aspect of the print trade in general—the work of distribution—was indeed *gendered* "feminine," marking even the men in these jobs as marginal and of low status. Treadwell, for example, concludes that "publishing seems to have been an appropriate occupation for a bankrupt bookseller . . . or a poor widow," that is, the economically disenfranchised and those with little social mobility.[44] Feminizing features also include the fact that publishers, like mercuries and hawkers, required little immediate start-up capital and little if any formal or technical education. Their work did require a certain level of functional literacy and numeracy, but a bookseller might happily assume that the trade publisher or mercury he hired had only just enough reading ability to manage title pages and enough math skills to keep accounts. Trade publishers did not necessarily need to be able to read the books they put their name on, a point I return to, and hawkers often signed only with a mark. Trade publishers, mercuries, and hawkers did not have to enter their field as apprentices, and they rarely took apprentices. This also feminized their positions at a time when the high-status jobs within the trade were still entered (although this was gradually beginning to change) through rigidly structured apprenticeship programs, which occasionally included girls (mostly from families in the trade), but were by and large dominated by boys—even the few female masters rarely took on girls. Furthermore, although there were exceptions like Mary Cooper, who became wealthy publishing popular titles, the jobs in the distribution end of the trade were also the least lucrative. Trade publishers and mercuries were perhaps most feminized, however, by the fact that, as I indicated earlier, they rarely owned what they labeled as theirs. This alone is what truly separates booksellers from publishers: both owned shops and sold books, and both were named in imprints, but only the former regularly owned and registered the copyrights to and thus realized the profits from the texts they imprinted. Very few women ever became copyrighting booksellers.[45]

Thus, an ideological tautology structured these jobs. The reasons they are marked "feminine"—their low status, their alienation from property—are the same reasons that opened them to women; the fact that the jobs were filled with women, no matter how industrious or successful, insured that these jobs remained marginal. In a revealing anecdote, Dunton, himself frequently plagued by financial setbacks and the scorn of colleagues, mocks the pretensions of a publisher who attempted to transcend his domain. He comments sarcastically that Richard Baldwin's "fame for Publishing spread so fast, he grew too *Big* to handle his *small Tools.* . . . [H]aving got Acquaintance with Persons of Quality he [took] a Shop in *Fleet-street*, but *Dick soaring out of his Element*, he had the Honour of being a Bookseller but Few Months" (*LE*, 259–60). The derision Dunton heaps on this effeminate man of "small tools," however, contrasts the approval he gives Baldwin's wife, a mercury or publisher herself, who fills her doubly—and properly—feminine role well as "help-meet" (*LE*, 260) to her misguided husband.

To further understand the role of the feminization of this part of the trade, we must also understand how and when it developed and the uses to which it was put. According to Treadwell, publishers provided services for three groups. The first were self-publishing writers, who could not get a bookseller to underwrite their project. The second were printers who seldom owned copyright, having been shut out of the struggle for dominance in the trade by booksellers, a phenomenon I discussed in chapter 3. Both of these groups, like publishers themselves, existed on the relative economic margins and perhaps were therefore themselves feminized. The third group, however, was powerful—and hoped to protect that power. The separate function of publishing seems to have emerged around 1680, when the increased printing of pamphlets following the Popish Plot and Exclusion Crisis converged with the first (temporary) lapsing of the Licensing Act in 1679. At this time, Treadwell believes, "while a growing number of . . . booksellers were as ready as ever to satisfy a hungry market with an unprecedented outpouring of political literature, they were less ready than ever before to put their names to what they issued."[46] In other words, publishers were virtually invented to take responsibility for the words a writer wrote, a printer printed, and a bookseller owned.

The Licensing Act lapsed for good in 1695. Prepublication censorship, however, was replaced in the next few decades by a vigilant enforcement of the libel and sedition laws within common law, which were made even stronger in the eighteenth century: any criticism of the government (true or false) was considered libelous, and no mention was allowed to be made of Parliamentary proceedings or members' names at all.[47] The trade was further regulated by the Stamp Act of 1712, which required a name and address to appear on every printed newspaper or pamphlet and demanded that these texts be brought to the Stamp Office to be registered—a task that fell under the purview of the publisher.[48] Throughout this period of stricter government control, booksellers hired publishers mostly to distribute controversial texts–not only did these, being topical, require the quick turnover that publishers, working with mercuries and hawkers, could supply, but they were dangerous to keep around one's shop or printing house.[49] The popularity of these texts meant that it was a rare bookseller who would eschew the opportunity to profit from them. Those, however, who could afford to employ others to label the text as "theirs" and to sell it on their premises, did so. The poorer members of the trade had no choice. They made their living by giving their names to texts no one else wished to officially own, claiming property that could never be theirs. Indeed, Adrian Johns notes that it was precisely the liminal status of mercuries that made them so useful: "[M]ercuries could take peculiar advantage of their conventional invisibility amid patriarchal domains that in fact depended on them."[50] Despite this "invisibility," however, mercuries, along with trade publishers and hawkers, were arrested and brought to trial more frequently than more privileged members of the trade. Not even a warrant was necessary to seize mercuries, who might be committed to Bridewell as vagrants for ten days on the order of a justice of peace.[51]

## *Trading (on) the Feminine*

When the government imposed strict if indefinite regulations on this burgeoning industry—indefinite because what was seditious was open, in many cases, to an interpretation made by an individual judge—the trade reacted by creating its own self-regulating mechanism to circumvent the law. In doing so, I maintain, it consequently borrowed from new notions of middle-class femininity circulating at the time—notions largely promulgated through print. This is not to say that (male) booksellers consciously created (female) publishers in order to subvert the law, but rather that in reaction to changes within the law, power in the trade was redistributed along lines of gender already marked by the dominant culture. I use *gender* here much as Joan Scott does, that is, as "a primary field within which or by means of which power is articulated." Understood in this way, gender "provides a way to decode meaning and to understand the complex connections among various forms of human interaction."[52] An examination of the uses of gender helps us understand a complicated trade practice: the feminizing of certain parts of the trade, which allows property in words to be divorced from the responsibility for them. Thus the *gendered* response to censorship after the lapse of licensing strengthened the separation between the discourses of print regulation and of print property despite the concurrent development of intellectual property laws and the rhetoric of author's rights.

I do not wish to argue that the dynamic of publishing was as simple as the higher status or "masculine" members of the trade scapegoating or taking advantage of marginalized "feminine" victims. To see Abigail Baldwin, Mary Copper, Anne Dodd, and Elizabeth Nutt along with their lesser-known female and feminized male colleagues as victims not only does them a grave disservice but is historically inaccurate.[53] Furthermore, an insistence on "victimization" vastly oversimplifies the workings of this ideology of gender, the complexity and apparent contradiction inherent in having women take political blame in the middle of a century that strove to depoliticize them, a century that spawned the middle-class project of making the feminine private and the masculine public. It is useful to remember, of course, that the public/private distinction often operated more in theory than in practice, despite the fact that the upper echelons of the business (perhaps represented emblematically by Samuel Richardson) were striving not only to be middle class but to create the middle class, both in their lives as industrious tradespeople and through the texts that they created and disseminated.[54] The family-based businesses of the print trade certainly did not fit this rule, for the place of work was often also the family residence, and husbands, wives, children, and servants/employees worked side by side.[55] We cannot, therefore, separate eighteenth-century "family values" from "trade values"—the two domains interacted and affected each other, especially at a time when, as Johns says, the good name of a Stationer's home, "as the archetypal site of morality and patriarchal authority," guaranteed "standards of reliability and sobriety in the exercise of [his] craft."[56]

Seeing the larger realm of the print trade as a metaphorical household, with proper roles for both husband and wife, allows us to understand textual regulation and responsible circulation in a new light. As the upper echelon of the trade became more respectable (as it consolidated more wealth), it increasingly reproduced the rising middle-class value system to ensure propriety. The middle-class domestic woman of this period was charged with managing her husband's private household, especially, as Nancy Armstrong has shown, its internal spiritual, emotional, and ultimately textual domains. Likewise, publishers and mercuries, although more "mechanick" than "middling," were named in imprints as the agents responsible for virtuous textual circulation, a practice that placed them in the wifely role of managing the public household of print. Despite their actual lack of political authority, or more accurately, because of it, the women (and the feminized men) of the trade were charged with supervising, and being held accountable for, the potentially unruly world of words. Thus the ideology of middle-class domestic femininity, when applied to the trade, reveals a contradiction in its own mechanisms, or the limits to its power: the gendered role played by this part of the trade gave women responsibility as it simultaneously took it away. When the interests of trade and gender converged, the paradox produced an anomaly. An ideological blind spot created by this overlap allowed these women to be held accountable for the excesses of the trade precisely because they could not be understood, within the standard notions of domestic femininity embraced by the middle class, as responsible public agents. That is, within the print trade, where propriety, as Johns points out, was crucial in maintaining the respectability—and, therefore, the authority—of the printed word, the femininity of the lower echelons of the trade worked discursively—often, as we will see, with real-life legal effects—to erase the taint of sedition from the household of print.

It was precisely this peculiar positioning that these women could use to their advantage; or, rather, their manipulations of the conventions imposed on them produced a contradictory form of femininity. Anne Dodd, for example, in a letter written from prison to the Duke of Newcastle, begs for clemency by stressing her downtrodden, feminine role. She writes on May 26, 1731:

> I most humbly beg leave to trouble your grace with these few
> lines. I have been left an afflicted widow with a Large Young
> family some years, whose only support has been selling news
> papers; which, with as much pains as my own Ill State of Health
> would admit of, has by the Assistance of Heaven, just enabled
> me to Feed my Self and helpless Children. I need not Acquaint
> your Grace that this Business sometimes Compells me to sell
> Papers that give Offence, but I must beg Leave to Declare Sin-
> cerely 'tis Greatly Against my Inclination when they are so, and

> that what papers I sell in Just Praise of Our Happy Govern-
> ment far exceeds the Others in Numbers. Hard case! That I
> must either Offend where I am shure I would not, or else Starve
> my Poor Babes. I am to be Tried next Tuesday for selling a
> Craftsman, a paper that I neither Read nor Understand. I
> Beseech you let my Children plead with your Grace to put a
> stop to the proceedings. . . . Your Grace's Known Character is,
> To Do Good, and to shew Mercy, and where can that goodness
> and that Mercy, be Better shewn, than by helping the Father-
> less and Widow[ed.] [I]f I have offended, tis an ignorant
> offence and [I know] the Distressed have always the surest
> Title to your Grace's Protection.[57]

Of course, any prisoner writing to a social superior to beg for clemency might grovel, but I believe that Dodd's position as a woman allows her a certain freedom to exploit what were usually the constraints of femininity. She can tap into discourses of pathos and sentimentality, appearing helpless rather than actively evil, wronged rather than wronging. She represents herself primarily as a mother, not a worker, a nod to the ideology of middle-class feminine respectability. She stresses her position as a widow—not only a woman beset by financial difficulties, but a woman with no husband to guide her and supervise the family's political role. The paper she sold, she explains, she "neither Read[s] nor Understand[s]," suggesting not only her appropriate ignorance of politics but also her perhaps understandable lack of reading comprehension skills in general. Paula McDowell argues that workingwomen were distanced from the norms of middle-class femininity, identifying more with fellow workers than with an all-encompassing "category of 'women.'"[58] While I believe that is likely, I think McDowell underestimates the extent to which women in these situations *performed* gender, manipulating the dominant culture's expectations of gendered behavior. It has always been in the interest of those occupying the lower rungs of social hierarchies to know exactly what the hegemonic values are, and often to adopt their form, even if they do not subscribe to them internally.[59] In the case of these workers, their jobs required them to be crafty, that is, to craft a persona that could protect their livelihoods and save their lives. It is not clear whether the Duke of Newcastle found Dodd's performance believable—the script of gender does not always follow logically to its obvious conclusion—but by the next year she was back at work selling controversial tracts once more.

Dodd's strategy was not unique. Women skilled enough to run successful businesses became amazingly incompetent upon questioning. Catherine Nutt admitted to selling the *Daily Press*, but "could not be certain" that she had sold the issue in question.[60] Jane Curtis pleaded in court, in reference to her alleged selling of a libelous pamphlet, that "I was ignorant in the matter, and knew no such thing, my Lord, my Husband . . . was in the Country a hundred miles off of me."[61] Elizabeth Calvert claimed, in a petition for release from prison, that she did "not know . . . the cause of her commitment" and begged mercy for her children and her own ill health. She even justifies her destruction of damning evidence by implying she acted only in accordance with the feminine virtues of obedience, thrift, and ignorance of the workings of the Law: "[W]hen my husband was in prison And had there Continued about a week he Gave me order to Gett up all the sheets of wast what ever together which Mr. Lay Strange had taken part of And Safely Secure them and Carry them into his Honor if Required In obedience to wch I presently went home And did as Commanded . . . wch not being demanded I sold for Wast Paper." She concludes by asking the court officers "to pity my Condition as a woman."[62]

Calvert's letter, Maureen Bell notes, is also representative of a number of testimonies that refer to an absent husband. A widow like Dodd might exploit the pathos of her situation, but legally she was responsible for her own actions. A married woman, however, was expected to obey her husband's orders, as Calvert stresses she was doing. Bell explains that the legal principle of coverture "protected a wife even when her husband was absent. . . . In most cases under criminal law the wife was understood to be acting under the command of her husband and could not therefore be prosecuted."[63] In other words, a married woman could not legally be a criminal. Ignorance was not the only guarantee of innocence, however. These women had recourse as well to the binary ideology of natural feminine virtue: if they were not sexually voracious slatterns—and their rhetoric emphasizing their willingness to meekly obey their husbands must have countered this, because such a construction is never suggested—they must be, by default, morally upright. If they refused to speak in court, they were only following their culture's dictates against women's public speech. Government officials were so stymied by the success of these strategies that they occasionally invented evidence that a woman's husband was dead, so that they could try her as an independent legal agent.

It is important to remember, however, that many women were punished, for the Law can choose to ignore its own contradictions, or cast women departing from the norms of femininity as monsters who must be disciplined back into their proper roles. When this happened, these women, like most of the men in the trade, usually chose to accept punishment—often brief imprisonment—rather than turn in the suppliers of their seditious texts. If they had revealed their sources, they would be banished from the trade forever, which meant, of course, an end to their livelihood. The few men who did turn in printers, booksellers, or authors had to be given other jobs—usually fairly menial—by the government. The government may have been less willing to do this for women, or there may have been fewer jobs suitable for women within the government bureaucracy. More likely, a woman's family network and upbringing in the trade ensured her loyalty to them. In any case, when we look at women's resistance to government pressure, I think we should avoid the temptation to turn them into pure political subversives critiquing a repressive government. While we can still admire the courage and determination of these women, I believe we should understand that much of what they did they did because of cultural convention—this was the role most commonly relegated to women in the print trade. At the bottom of the hierarchy, economically as well as sexually, they had little choice. They could flourish in their positions because of the way the structure of their trade intersected with the demands of middle-class femininity. They may not have chosen to adopt the "feminine" identity as their own, but they could slip it on when circumstances made it necessary.

In the latter half of the century, publishers begin to disappear as their function became less important to a trade printing in a more politically stable environment. Treadwell believes that many were siphoned into newspaper publishing, which emerged as a separate activity and profession, while others, in a more politically stable climate, were able to make enough money to invest in copyrights and become booksellers in their own right. The decrease in publishers, however, parallels another trend: the number of women in every aspect of the print trade was dwindling.[64] This reflects, of course, what was happening in many trades by midcentury: professionalization and acceptance as a respectable, middle-class trade meant the sacrifice of women's careers. In the print trade specifically, however, I believe that the use of the ideology of domestic femininity made the gap between the theory and reality of women's lives too obvious. Women frequently imprisoned for selling controversial literature challenged too profoundly the feminine discourses they had used to their advantage.[65]

What I have tried to do in this section is to recover the remains of a lost battle, to re-create a struggle later masked by the workings of the dominant discourse of domestic femininity. The unique positioning of publishers, mercuries, and to some extent hawkers reveals that ideology is never monolithic, but can be used against itself, its own weaknesses exploited. This challenges us as critics to look beyond upper-middle-class constructions of gender, not to the "reality" underneath, but to alternative versions and strategies that also were available for use. "Gender" has seemed a fairly stable category for eighteenth-century studies; class less so. The intersection of the two within trade practices confounds notions of a simple, all-encompassing, stereotypical femininity. It shows that, rather than having recourse to only two stable binary constructions of femininity, workingwomen possessed an agency that allowed them, albeit not freely, to negotiate between them. The seditious women of the print trade were not considered anomalies or monsters—not even the government construed them as such—but were respected members of the trade. Publishers and mercuries positioned themselves in an ideological contradiction, teetering between public and private notions of femininity and among discursive constructions of virtue, ignorance, and legal responsibility. This position may actually have been enabling to these women, allowing them a categorical "space" in which both to manipulate and stretch the dominant norms of gender. E. P. Thompson has described the way in which class struggle produces class.[66] It is possible that the struggle of these women to work and escape punishment produced new versions of a "trade gender."

## Author-ized Virtue in Print

Although we cannot celebrate the fact that women publishers and mercuries could be incarcerated for activities in which they may have been economically pressured to participate, we can see that their role could be empowering. At the most practical level, their businesses benefited from the free advertising; as I noted earlier, a publisher harassed by the law could count on increased revenues as buyers rushed to discover what was so upsetting the government. More importantly, however, these women were positioned, even if only in a fictional ruse, as textual agents, with the authority and responsibility for the safe circulation of the printed word. With only their names on the imprint, they literally embossed the text with their presence, announcing themselves—and, by extension, potentially all women—as active producers in an important trade. Indeed, their role as producers would have long-lasting effects, for as their presence and utility in the construction and circulation of texts waned, another group of women rose to replace them: women writers. In this final section I hope to show how censorship worked to produce the authorized feminine story—a modest, regulated print product.

The first half of this chapter revealed the ways in which the discourse of press regulation connected material print producers to text writers. I believe this link continued to operate throughout the early eighteenth century, despite the emergence of a discourse of proprietary authorship. I have shown in each chapter that this discourse did not maintain a teleologically neat ascent, but was complicated by notions of *material* ownership promulgated by printers and booksellers. In this chapter, I have argued for another notion complicating the "rise" of the author, that of the regulated "authority"—not always an actual writer—as opposed to proprietary author. The resulting regulated text developed out of the intersection of gender with material production.

My examination of John Smith's *Printer's Grammar* in chapter 2 illustrated the way in which the authority of print was buttressed by its connection to an authoritatively masculine font, thought to reveal transparently the (male) author behind the words. Nonetheless, critics such as Jane Spencer, Cheryl Turner, and Janet Todd, among others, have theorized that cultural attitudes regarding women as morally superior allowed women writers to become immensely popular in the second half of the century.[67] The novel as a particularly feminine form of writing was so established by midcentury that the anonymous signature "by a Lady" was often almost enough to secure a book a place in this expanding market niche. Even men disguised themselves as such to garner better sales.[68] The eighteenth-century feminization of discourse meant that "a woman writer was expected not simply to express her sex, but also call attention to her femininity, her delicacy and sensitivity."[69] Thus Richardson, in writing to a female friend in 1746, could rhapsodize that "the ladies who love the pen are qualified by genius and imagination to excell in the beauties of this sort of writing: —and that *bashfulness, or diffidence of a person's own merits, are but other words for undoubted worthiness*; and that such a lady cannot set pen to paper but a beauty must follow it; yet herself the last person that knows it" (emphasis added).[70] Although Richardson uses the terms "genius and imagination," terms used elsewhere to naturalize the proprietary claims to authorship, it is clear that to him it is specifically feminine virtues such as bashfulness and diffidence that actually make a woman's writing worthy. Indeed, most rhapsodies in the popular press celebrated women's chastity and modesty, "conflating . . . literary & feminine virtues."[71] Thus by 1775, a *Gentleman's Magazine* article could, in creating a lineage of renowned women writers, blandly assert that they "are all sentimental—have all supported the cause of virtue."[72]

The problem with this understanding of female authorship is that it sees femininity as preexisting outside literary discourse and merely being reflected in works by and reviews of women writers. It also begs the question of why virtuous femininity necessarily became a written and published femininity. This gap in feminist literary history is worrisome in that it seems to imply that women possessed some natural, inner need to write, a need that expressed itself naturally through publication of the implicitly moral form of the novel.[73] Nancy Armstrong supplies a partial corrective to this by revealing the ways in which desire for a specifically feminine "individual" who controlled a text-based realm of morality was shaped by and through domestic fiction as a form of middle-class power consolidation. Despite her use of parafictional material such as conduct books, however, she only marshals as evidence a set of canonical novels that she admits were conceived of as such in the nineteenth century.[74] She does not address these books as anything but *textual* agents, ignoring the discourses of authorship that enabled their circulation and avoiding any discussion of them as concrete commodities. Looking at women's fiction as part of a larger print market, and at women writers as part of a larger group of print workers, however, allows female textuality to be seen in the context of a very specific political and economic environment.

Catherine Gallagher's study of the empowering of women writers in a culture of feminized discourse is notable in that she does examine some broader legal considerations, focusing specifically on proprietary authorship and women writers' feelings of dispossession. The Statute of Anne, she explains, "initiated the idea that texts, as opposed to manuscripts, were exchangeable commodities belonging ultimately to their authors by virtue of being 'the product of their learning and labour.'" She further argues that this seemingly "natural" ownership privileged novels in particular, "for if the story itself and the vehicle of its language, if both 'idea' and 'expression' were invented, authorship became uncontestable." Since, in Gallagher's view, fiction writers were the inherent owners of property that was purely intellectual and so solely theirs, they resented their copyrights being sold to booksellers. This resentment, she claims, became in itself a condition of authorship. In this dynamic, women writers, especially married women writers (though single women were always potentially married women), could flourish. Because they could never legally own their property in the first place, they were doubly dispossessed or what Gallagher calls "Nobodies"—and so were the ultimate authors.[75]

As compelling and neatly argued as it is, however, Gallagher's account of women's authorship presents an incomplete picture, downplaying, despite her use of the Statute of Anne, the day-to-day dynamics of the entire literary marketplace of the early to mid-eighteenth century and the writer's place within it. For example, her theory relies on the commonplace notion of the text as intangible, the belief that "the text's 'materiality' . . . is only tenuously connected to its value, either its exchange value qua text (an entity different from a book, which is only an instance of a text) or its more elusive 'literary' value. If we speak of the 'use value' of a text, moreover, we certainly cannot equate that with the paper, print, binding, and so forth, that make up the books."[76] Throughout this study, however, I have shown that the producers of "the paper, print, binding, and so forth" were indeed held to be responsible contributors *alongside* writers—and that the legal realm, despite the increasing weight given to notions of intangible intellectual property, still focused on the concrete aspects of print culture. My focus on the regulatory discourse of textual production that privileged the *material* print commodity and *all* its producers shows, I believe, that a simplistic understanding of proprietorship as the sole discourse of authorship in this period is at best anachronistic. Before the institutionalization of the intellectual property regime in late eighteenth-century courts of law and aesthetic discourses, other ways of understanding the place of the writer circulated in the public imagination. Thus relying on an ahistorical construction of an author's "work," Gallagher erases the contribution of print workers—those who made "the paper, print, binding, and so forth"—not realizing that the value of a book was once seen as inhering in these material elements as well as in the less tangible contribution of the writer. In fact, even the Statute of Anne, used by Gallagher to anchor her notion of immateriality, was supported by Stationers because it worked in the interest of their own trade—the ability of writers to support themselves financially was not their most important consideration. Similarly, when Parliament responded by reducing the terms of protection suggested by the trade, it did so not to protect writers from Stationers' appropriating their rights but to encourage economic growth by limiting trade monopolies. The resulting 1710 Statute of Anne granted rights to copy, in the most literal sense of the word, to an author *or his assignee* for a period of fourteen years. Of course, in order to get published, most writers had to sell this right to those undertaking the capital risk of printing and disseminating. Therefore, "the leading booksellers who owned copies or shares in them continued to operate after 10 April 1710 in much the same way they had before that date."[77] Because the Statute of Anne did not, then, immediately privilege authors as owners, the selling of texts would not have automatically signaled dispossession.

Gallagher's theory is helpful, however, in that it calls attention to the specifically nonproprietary nature of female authorship. Like their counterparts in the print trade, women writers rarely owned copyright—it was denied to both groups by the laws concerning their sex and by the conventions of their shared trade. It is a mistake, though, to assume that proprietorship was the only influence on feminine authorship—other forms of regulation also had strong effects. If we are to see writers as many of their contemporaries did, as merely a part of a larger print market, we can also understand how changes in the trade itself produced new forms of writing. As licensing lost efficacy and eventually officially lapsed, mercuries and publishers rose to become the new agents of textual responsibility. I believe it was the precedent set by the women workers of the print trade that allowed women writers to become agents of moral authority, the virtuous wives in the house of fiction.

I have noted that women writers seemed to increase in number at the same time the number of women in other areas of the trade declined. Even though mercuries were sometimes able to use the norms of a virtuous, passive femininity to shield themselves from criminal litigation, the type of texts they were associated with (ballads, political tracts, and scandalous and anonymous literary texts), combined with their frequent brushes with the law, may ultimately have tainted their reputations. Also, as domestic femininity consolidated itself as a primarily (upper-) middle-class characteristic (a development Armstrong traces), based on women's role as primarily household supervisors, the ideology may no longer have had the flexibility to include women whose work deconstructed binaries of both private/public, home/work, and crime/virtue. As these trade women were evacuated from the scene of middle-class femininity, though, what lingered was a sense of a feminine responsibility for the "virtuous" (i.e., regulated, contained) circulation of texts. The balancing act of female and feminized publishers and mercuries— working as independent businesswomen yet claiming to possess a prototypically feminine ignorance of their own activities—perhaps allowed women writers also to bridge the gap between private sentiments and their public distribution. Janet Todd's description of the midcentury woman writer sounds strikingly like the mercury, if one substitutes "selling" for "writing": "[S]he had to be virtuous and domestic, writing either from financial necessity, unsupported by the proper guardians of femininity such as husband or father."[78] Even the woman author's justifications of her writing—celebrated writers often claimed errant or absent husbands, had imaginably starving children, but were nonetheless always models of propriety—mirror those used by mercuries in their legal battles in court. For example, in Catherine Ingrassia's discussion of Eliza Haywood's manipulation of her cultural position, she notes that Haywood "highlights her position as widow in an appeal for increased sympathy" and calls on her unfortunate marriage and the claims of her young children. Ingrassia notes that "in doing so, she converts possibly negative categories (woman and writer) into valorizing markers in an effort to tap into another type of gendered currency."[79] What is notable in this "gendered currency" is the disavowal of the male model of disinterest circulating at the same time: feminine authorship is authorized precisely through its affiliation with "necessity" and the economic conditions—and payoff—implied by that. In this, they seem more connected to a material trade than their brother writers found it expedient to suggest of themselves. They also paralleled the mercuries in the success of their strategies: just as mercuries dodged imprisonment, the woman writer's rationale for publishing was found acceptable in the court of public opinion. By 1773 the *Monthly Review* could claim of novel writing that "this branch of the literary *trade* appears now, to be almost entirely engrossed by the Ladies."[80]

In the end, though, this popularity, based on an understanding of the material demands of text work, undertaken by the financially needy, may have ultimately helped marginalize women writers as Romantic constructions of authorship flourished. Much work has been done on the eviction of women from the nineteenth-century canon, their earthbound feminine bodies making them ineligible for the unsullied realm of the (male) mind.[81] "The scribbling women," as Hawthorne infamously called them, however, are also marked by their very mediation—the instrument of scribbling. The "scribbler" pens, if poorly, while the genius poet somehow spontaneously pours himself into (an invisible) writing. Her dependence on a writing machine affiliates her with "mechanick" trade and sets her on the wrong side of the industrial/organic binary that the early nineteenth century used to categorize written production.

I have shown that the regulation of the press connected writers to other members of the broader trade. By looking at women writers as part of a larger group of specifically female print workers, we may began to understand why they were authorized to write at all—and why, a half century later, their authorization was revoked. For several decades before the midcentury moral woman set pen to paper, a virtuously needy femininity had been an integral part of the print trade. The discursive manipulations of mercuries and trade publishers as they negotiated the terrain of legal responsibility and material punishment reproduced a form of gender based on ignorance of the political realm of print. It is this construction of print gender based on a naïveté about public power that allowed the properly domestic woman access to this trade; the middle-class woman writer became "author-ized" because the trade had created a space for the female producer of public print to exist. Such a theory does not contradict Gallagher's notion of the "Nobody," but it does complicate it. The first "nobody" was a likewise liminal, but very real, female body, subject to punishment. The story this body created in her own defense ultimately worked against her, erasing her from the history of female textual production. We should remember, then, that while an ideological door opened, albeit briefly, for one group of women, it closed for another. When we celebrate the rise of the woman author in the eighteenth century, we also need to credit her lower-class, usually invisible, predecessors.

# 5

# THE PRINTER AS AUTHOR: SAMUEL RICHARDSON, INTELLECTUAL PROPERTY, AND THE FEMININE TEXT

*I being his favorite . . . he calls upon me continually, to read to him when he is grave. . . ; and so I have frequently become sad to make him cheerful, and happy when I could do it at any rate. For once, in a pet, he flung a book at my head, because I had not attended him for two hours, and he would not bear to be slighted by little bastards, that was his word, that were fathered upon him for his vexation! O these men! Fathers or husbands, much alike! the one tyrannical, the other insolent: so, that between one and t'other, a poor girl has nothing for it, but a few weeks' courtship, and perhaps a first month's brid-alry, if that: and then she is as much a slave to her husband, as she was a vassal to her father. . . .*

—SAMUEL RICHARDSON, THE CONTINUATION OF *PAMELA*, 1741

The last three chapters have explored the role of printers, booksellers, and other print workers in the late seventeenth and early eighteenth centuries, illustrating the ways in which reading the rhetoric of the trade forces us to examine more critically our anachronistic notions of the intangibility of literary work. Those within the print trade should be understood as they often viewed themselves, as significant *creative* agents in the physical production of material commodities *and* their affiliated values—at least as important as, often even more important than, the writers of text. Nonetheless, as each of the previous chapters indicates, by the mid-eighteenth century the project of erasing these print workers' contributions and the material basis of print itself, in favor of a disinterested author, was well under way. This chapter is an attempt to trace the shift in cultural emphasis from print worker to author by focusing on one individual who, at the same time and often in contradictory ways, encapsulated both roles. I examine some of the ways in which Samuel Richardson's work as a printer fundamentally shaped his understanding of, indeed his construction of, his status as a writer and the ways in which his ideological concerns as a novelist writing for and about women affected his views on the nature of the print product. Perhaps because he holds a unique place in publishing history as a man who was both a successful commercial printer and a popular and beloved novelist, he is the ideal representative of the contradictory and often internally inconsistent discourse surrounding the issues of authorship and intellectual property.

Many aspects of Richardson's career and life indicate that he saw his own works *both* as a mixture of moral lesson and sentimental entertainment *and* as commodities, to be bought, sold, traded, and regulated. In short, Richardson's role as producer of both the imaginative text and the physical book allowed him to see the two sides of that paradoxical, if not oxymoronic, abstraction, "intellectual property." I thus look at his work as what Wendy Wall has termed a "textual commodity," that is, "an object that marks a juncture between the material and the symbolic, the historical and the textual."[1] In this chapter, I focus mostly on a series of events in his busy life that seems significantly to link Richardson the printer to Richardson the novelist and helps us realize that these were not separate careers, or even vocation and avocation, but inextricably linked ideologies and material practices. From this individual case study I hope to draw some conclusions about changes in the larger cultural scene that resulted in authors being understood as the natural and inalienable owners of their texts. I thus show, as I did in my last chapters, that the "rise" of proprietary authorship was not a smooth or uncontested one.

To say that Richardson was deeply concerned with the materiality of texts is to state the obvious: he was first and always a printer. He was fifty years old and had been practicing his trade for twenty-five years (post-apprenticeship) before he published his first novel. He was extremely successful in his business and admired by his peers; he was chosen for important government printing jobs and for several offices in the Company of Stationers.[2] I think it is fair to say then, that his life as a printer—his worldview for two-thirds of his life—could not help but structure his relationship to anything textual.[3] The obvious, however, is often the easiest to ignore. "Richardson the printer" has received little critical attention since William Sale's 1950 biographical study, *Samuel Richardson: Master Printer*.[4] Instead, the focus has been primarily on the sexual politics of Richardson's novels.[5] My chapter proposes to link these two strands of criticism by examining Richardson's novels and other writings as his "text work," that is, as objects marking a merger between concrete print and discursive construction, simultaneously commodities and ideological tools. I argue that to Richardson, creator of the popular and beloved heroines in distress, Pamela and Clarissa, and the feminized hero, Sir Charles Grandison, intellectual property was always already *gendered* property, linked intimately to the rules of sexual propriety and proper feminine behavior. I do this by focusing on a series of public and private discursive events—letter writing, advertising, and, eventually, the writing of the continuation of *Pamela*—that took place shortly after the publication of Richardson's first novel in the fall of 1740.

## *Sir Charles Grandison: A Printer's Property*

First, though, it will be helpful to look at another incident in Richardson's life, one that highlights his complicated views on intellectual property. Although it took place twelve years after the *Pamela* debates that provide the focus for this chapter, it reveals that, even toward the end of his career, Richardson's views could never be slotted as those belonging firmly to either printer or author. Richardson's battle with the Irish "pirates" over the unauthorized publication of *Sir Charles Grandison* is notorious. William Warner believes that this episode in Richardson's history represents his metamorphosis from "self-effacing writer" working "within the belly of the book trade" into "ambitious author" serving as a "vocal public advocate for the position that a book was the property of its author."[6] In other words, he claims that we can see, in the events of 1753, a definitive move on Richardson's part from writer/printer to author/owner.

I argue, however, that the issues raised in this case do not warrant such a straightforward narrative. The story is simple enough, though it does suggest problems of nationalism and colonialism beyond my purview here. While Richardson was still in the process of printing *Sir Charles Grandison* for English release, he began negotiations with an Irish bookseller, George Faulkner, for the rights to publish there. Before these plans could be completed, though, other Irish booksellers bribed Richardson's workers for copies and illegally printed and sold the novel there. English law at this time did not extend copyright protection to Ireland, though it did forbid, in the Import of Books Act of 1739, the importing into England of any book printed there within twenty years of the date of imprint. This protected English booksellers only from having to compete with cheaper foreign editions of their works in England itself. Because Richardson had no legal recourse to prevent the dissemination of the unauthorized copies of *Grandison* throughout Ireland, Faulkner, of course, declined to continue what would presumably be an unprofitable venture.

Thwarted by the law, Richardson, attempting to persuade the Irish public to boycott the Irish edition, wrote, printed, and distributed throughout London and Dublin a pamphlet titled summarily "The Case of *Samuel Richardson*, of *London*, Printer; With Regard to the Invasion of his Property in the History of Sir Charles Grandison, Before Publication, By certain Booksellers in *Dublin*" (1753). This publication is usually used to cement Richardson's allegiance to notions of organic authorship that served as the underpinning to authors' rights. It is true that this tract does call on, as Warner attests, the notions of proprietary authorship that had been circulating since Defoe and had been becoming more common in the twenty years preceding Richardson's case. Warner correctly argues that "Richardson articulates piracy with moral laxity and crime, and aligns authorized authorial publication with probity and virtue."[7] In making a moral case for more stringent forms of protection for all, through publicly protesting the outrages inflicted on himself, Richardson points to the ways in which this particular "invasion" is particularly scandalous: "[N]ever was Work more the Property of any Man, than *this* is his. . . . He borrows not from any Author." He concludes by linking a claim of originality with a claim for inherent proprietorship in a call for legal recourse:

> After all, if there is no Law to right the Editor and sole Propri-
> etor of this new Work (*New* in every Sense of the Word), he
> must acquiesce; but with this Hope, that, from so flagrant an
> Attempt, a Law may one Day be thought necessary, in order to
> secure to Authors the Benefit of their own Labours.... At
> present, the *English Writers* may be said ... to live in an Age of
> *Liberty*, but not of *Property*.[8]

The rhetoric of "newness" combined with a desire to secure property through legal means (one assumes through stricter copyright protection) can be seen as partaking of the discourse of proprietary authorship. Even beyond that, it seems to point toward the future notion of Romantic authorship, which based its claims for an inherent property right in the unique and original nature of the literary work.[9]

Such teleological prognostications, however, aid us little in an attempt to understand Richardson's writing in 1753, when a full expression of Romantic genius was still half a century ahead. If we read Richardson's pamphlet more completely, looking for more than merely the phrases signaling his eager participation in the burgeoning regime of Romantic authorship, we will find that much, perhaps most, of the rhetoric is that belonging to a printer. This is, after all, how he names himself in his title: "*Samuel* Richardson, of *London*, Printer." In fact, he never labels himself "author," but still retains the fiction throughout that he is the *editor* of the novel, a mere compiler rather than the creative source. Rather than see this as perhaps a tiresome continuation of a transparently fictional device, I propose that we take his self-labeling, with all that it implies *and* disowns, seriously. His positioning as one who compiles the texts of others, rather than meta-physically creating them in an intangible, intellectual process, can be seen in the rhetoric of materiality that pervades this tract. He begins with a narrative of events that explains how this "invasion" came about. We see from this that the "invasion" is a literal event—the Irish booksellers are not copying a published text but physically stealing, by means of Richardson's own workers, material pages. His recitation of events brings the reader, not into the scene of imagination and abstract creation, but into gritty workrooms and warehouses. Referring to himself in the third person, he describes the precautions he took after hearing that an Irish bookseller was boasting of the ease with which he could take print sheets from any "Printing-house" in London:

> He gave a strict Charge, before he put the Piece to Press, to all his Workmen and Servants, as well as in PRINT . . . , as by Word of Mouth, to be on their Guard against any out-door Attacks. This was the Substance of the printed Caution which he gave to his Workmen, on this Occasion: "A Bookseller of *Dublin* has assured me, That he could get the Sheets of any Book from any Printing-house in *London*, before Publication. I hope I can depend upon the Care and Circumspection of my Friends, Compositors and Pressmen, that no Sheets of the Piece I am now putting to Press be carried out of the House. . . . Let no stranger be admitted into any of the Work-rooms. Once more, I hope I may rely on the Integrity and Care of all my Workmen—And let all the Proofs, Revises, &c. be given to Mr. Tewley" (his Foreman) "to take care of." . . . Yet, to be still more secure . . . he ordered the Sheets, as they were printed off, to be deposited in a *separate* Warehouse. . . . Having Three Printing-houses, he had them composed, and wrought, by different Workmen, and at his different Houses; and took such other Precautions, that the Person to whose Trust he committed them, being frequently questioned by him as to the Safety of the Work from Pirates, *as* frequently assured him, That it was impossible the Copy of any complete Volume could be come at.[10]

Richardson's use of the term "pirates" here thus has less to do with the "theft" of *intellectual* property than it does of real, *tangible* property. This is not a "novel," but a set of sheets, proofs, and revises, manipulated by compositors and other workmen, being put to press and stored, like any other product, in warehouses. In this depiction, "piracy" is an apt analogy, for the text here is conceived as a concrete treasure, guarded by brave (and hopefully honest) workmen, who might themselves be in danger of "attacks."

Interestingly, despite the value given to the "Sheets" and so forth, there is no indication that they contain a special or unique "work" and will be stolen only because of this abstract value. Instead, they merely represent the current project, the printer's latest product. Even when Richardson does refer specifically to *Sir Charles Grandison*, he describes it in the most material terms as "Three Sheets of each of the Twelves Edition, and One of the Octavo."[11] Thus when Richardson says that "never was Work more the Property of any Man, than *this* is his," there is no reason to assume he speaks of a *literary* work; his previous rhetoric leads us to understand that he may mean a work *product*. It is true that he does refer briefly to the writing of the novel when he avers that none of it is borrowed and that it is a new work, but he also in the same passage, explaining why the work is more his property than anyone else's, refers again to its physicality: "The Paper, the Printing, entirely at his own Expence, to a very large Amount, Returns of which he cannot see in several Months."[12] *Sir Charles Grandison*, throughout most of this pamphlet, is thus represented, like most of John Dunton's projects, as the financial investment of a capitalist in a new product, in addition to an organic, imaginative expression. Indeed, the pamphlet contains so much of the rhetoric of materiality that it seems as if the few references to proprietary authorship are deployed on behalf of the proprietary capitalist printer.

Richardson's description of the theft as physical is highlighted by another, very different, version of the same events that was printed in the *Gray's Inn Journal* approximately a month after Richardson's pamphlet appeared. Referring to the Dublin booksellers, the writer exhorts,

> They should all be expelled from the Republick of Letters, as literary Goths and Vandals, who are ready to invade the property of every man of genius.... I am sorry that the Laws of the Land have not sufficiently secured to Authors the property of their Works....
>
> ... Pity, indeed, it is, that some single and exemplary punishment cannot be inflicted upon the encouragers of this vile treachery, as well as upon the perpetrators, who ought to be condemned as the discouragers of public instruction and oppressors of genius, and the invaders of the Republick of Literature.[13]

Even though both Richardson and this writer call for stricter laws to protect writers, here, the "invasion" is figured as one perpetrated not only against one man but also against an abstract idea of "genius" and the entire imaginative realm of Literature itself. The *Gray's Inn* version sets up an idealized republic of authors, in which "Goths and Vandals"—foreigners in this rarified land—commit a crime not against a writer's financial interest but against an intangible notion of public good. The "crime scene" is imagination, not a warehouse where actual sheets are stolen. This is not to say, however, that Richardson posits his material view *against* this sort of rhetoric. Rather, we see in Richardson's protest a tension between two coexisting and contradictory discursive models of ownership and theft.

This case may shed light on Richardson's conception of himself as a writer throughout his career. Understanding his values as a printer may help us understand what has often been seen as his peculiar compositional habits. Because he relied so much on the advice of friends, his style has been termed "consultatory";[14] I think it is not too much of a stretch to call it collaborative. His first writing assignment, or so he claimed in later relations of his life, was to serve as what we would now call a "ghostwriter": as a young boy, he composed love letters for his female neighbors, working with their ideas and sentiments and presumably merging them with his own to produce the finished letter.[15] He was not embarrassed by this beginning, but created from it a career narrative, representing this type of writing as leading seamlessly into one of his early print projects, the letter-writing guide, *Familiar Letters*, which he in turn indicated was a source for *Pamela* and his later epistolary novels. He erases all sorts of distinctions in the story of his evolution: the pen from print, the conduct manual from the novel. He also leaves out a variety of writing projects that he undertook as a printer: indexes, abstracts, advertisements, abridgements, revisions, compilations, dedications, introductions, and a conduct manual for apprentices. He also printed several newspapers, and T. C. Duncan Eaves and Ben Kimpel claim that available evidence suggests "a greater influence [on the content of these] than a modern printer would have"—though this sort of influence over content was, in fact, normative at the time.[16] Much like Robert Dodsley, though, he may have avoided emphasizing the material aspects of his life as his fame as a writer grew. Nonetheless, his routine as a printer, working collaboratively with other writers and with other print workers, seems to have guided him even as his fame as a novelist increased his choice of partners. He never gave up working closely with others: the fact that he allowed Aaron Hill, Edward Young, Catherine Talbot, and other members of his letter-writing coterie to read his manuscripts and influence his final published versions is well known. In fact, he read published criticism of his novels and took notice of both complaints and compliments from friends as well as strangers. He often ignored advice, but he also often heeded it and never seems to have been offended to receive it. When rejecting others' ideas, he would merely explain why he chose not to modify a certain passage or scene, but he did not seem to feel that he had to guard his intellectual territory from marauders.

My point in this section has not been to deny Richardson all claims to proprietary or original authorship—to do so would be as anachronistic as the slotting of him as a proto-Romantic. I want to stress, however, how much of the discourse of authorship in this period relies on intertwined and multiple explanations of the work of writing and print. Richardson's self-representation bears traces of his life in trade *and* the growing emphasis on abstraction that was beginning to categorize literary production. Nonetheless, once we free ourselves from locating all references to proprietary authorship on a trajectory to the modern author's final consolidation in the Romantics, we can see that much of this "confusion" is the result not just of competing discourses but of the influence of discursive constructions that lie, seemingly, outside the boundaries of the literary market.

## PAMELA IN PRINT: FATHERING THE FEMININE TEXT

If, on the *intellectual* side of "intellectual property," Richardson was able to see writing as an open, fluid, even collaborative, process, the *property* aspects of his texts he seemed to view as much more rigidly fixed. He may have let others influence his written text, but, as we have seen, he did not appreciate print pages, his capital investment, being literally stolen by others who would then benefit financially. Solid as he may have seen them, however, he knew that print pages could not be separated from their textual content, and vice versa. Like most respectable printers, Richardson had a high regard for the aesthetics of the page, down to the appearance of individual letters. Writing to Johannes Stinstra in 1755 about a mutual acquaintance, a letter founder seeking employment, he comments:

> Let me observe for the Sake of this worthy Gentleman, that in
> his Text Romyn, the Capital Letters are thought rather too
> large for the rest, and too gross; the small [w ha]s also been
> objected to, as not open or free enough; such a one as this w,
> being preferred to W, as in the specimen. The capital in ye Text
> Cursyf are also thought to be too full and black. But on the
> whole, both that and the Gar[a]mound are very pretty Letters.
> (Editor's brackets)[17]

In chapter 2 I illustrated the ways in which "accidentals" such as font are
ideologically weighted, but Richardson does not give us enough matter
in this passage to analyze, and few records of Richardson's printing
practices have been located or published. We can, however, link this care
for material detail to his characters' correspondence. Lennard Davis, for
example, claims that "the feel and shape of the text becomes itself the
object of scrutiny. This characteristic becomes most obvious in the
notion that a character's writing style, his or her orthography . . . , the
turn of phrase and so on becomes the marks or signs that reveal personality, inclination, and intent."[18] This typographical consciousness, an
awareness of the ways in which the micro-details of physical form and
textual content interact, is further elaborated in Richardson's continuation of *Pamela*, in which bad spelling is a sign of a debased nature and
good handwriting an indication of a moral character. It is probably best
epitomized, though, in Clarissa's "mad letters," in which Richardson
employs erratic, off-center typesetting to indicate her disturbed state.

Richardson's work as a printer also provided him with an insider's
view of the economic basis of the literary market. This is especially obvious in his treatment of the newly written *Pamela*. I do not deny that
Richardson hoped, as he claimed, that the novel *Pamela* would serve as
a moral agent, a source of entertaining instruction, a good influence on
the potentially corruptible youth of the day. Richardson also seemed
to realize, however, that in order for the discursive, ideological *Pamela* to
do its work, the physical *Pamela*—the book itself—had to make its way
into readers' hands. In short, it had to be sold. Of course, no one knew
this better than a printer, especially one who also occasionally functioned as a bookseller, that is, sponsoring projects and registering copyright in them in his own name. Thus Richardson, a shrewd and successful

businessman as well as a moralist, had no hesitation in treating his moral and didactic novel as a commodity, that is, as a product on the market.[19]

Richardson claimed that only four people had read *Pamela* before it was published. Nonetheless, knowing how well both moral tracts and the salacious *roman* were selling, he must have suspected that he had a potential best seller on his hands, for the novel was launched into the world in a sort of eighteenth-century equivalent of a media blitz.[20] While it is not clear that Richardson himself always purposely manipulated this campaign, his position within the network of print culture certainly allowed him greater access to market resources than many other writers of this period had. For example, three weeks before the novel was available to the public, the *Weekly Miscellany*, a religious periodical edited by the clergyman William Webster, printed an anonymous letter to the author of *Pamela* praising it highly for its morality. This preview praise was not necessarily disinterested: Richardson had printed the *Miscellany* for Webster in the 1730s, and Webster still owed him ninety pounds for this project. Richardson forgave this debt sometime after 1740. Another contact from the trade wrote a laudatory preface for *Pamela* shortly after Richardson printed a translation for him. Because the novel was disguised as authentic letters, Richardson, as "editor," was even able to write his own laudatory preface. He thus definitely understood the importance of praise in promoting the novel; in fact, this preface was later printed, testimonial fashion, in the *Weekly Miscellany*.

This is not to take away from the novel's real popularity—once the *Pamela* phenomenon caught on, it operated to a large extent under its own steam, meshing perfectly with the cultural climate of the mid-eighteenth century.[21] It was probably Richardson's friends and colleagues in the business of printing, publishing, bookselling, and newspaper editing, however, who allowed, or at least helped, *Pamela* to garner such attention from the beginning. Some kind of notice—the lines begin to blur between ads, puffs, excerpts, reviews, letters to the editor, and news about the book's popularity—appeared at least once more in the *Weekly Miscellany*, as well as in the *Gentleman's Magazine*, the *Daily Advertiser*, the *Daily Gazetteer*, the *London Evening-Post*, and even in the academic journal *History of the Works of the Learned* throughout the winter and spring of 1740–41. Even Richardson's most legendary praise—the recommendation of *Pamela* by a parson from his pulpit—may have been an example of Richardson's shrewd machinations. The fact that Richardson subsequently took over a bad debt owed by the minister, as biographer Alan McKillop relates, suggests that this mention should be viewed as advertising in addition to moral commentary. Even if Richardson had not planned or purchased the minister's comments in advance, he certainly took advantage of them, never failing to mention them when relating the history of his publications.

It seems, then, that Richardson was not as artless as his famous heroine—which is perhaps why the insightful *Shamela*-type interpretations of his novel irritated him so much. Like Fielding's Shamela, Richardson knew (at least on some level) that morality could be used as a marketing tool, to use an anachronistic if not inaccurate term. He understood his middle-class "target audience," the guilty and conflicted pleasure they took in reading novels. A sexy, voyeuristic novel touted as "instructive literature" was guaranteed to sell. At the same time, Richardson probably was sincere in his belief that his novel was instructive and could contribute to the making of a moral culture. To Richardson, like many of his middle-class contemporaries, moral tenets and religious beliefs were not in conflict with the practices of commodity capitalism.

In the end, of course, Richardson's "PR" campaign was a success. In fact, it may have been too successful. By the summer of 1741, other entrepreneurs were busy capitalizing on the *Pamela* phenomenon.[22] At first, Richardson did not worry. There is no evidence that he was offended by the *Pamela* fan, prints and paintings, waxworks, poems, a French translation, the performance and publication of a play, and an opera. Nor does he protest two books about fallen women both titled *Anti-Pamela*; in fact, his brother-in-law printed one of them. None of these spin-offs, evidently, infringed on Richardson's sense of his intellectual property rights, although he of course received no payments for the use of the Pamela name or idea. We should recall here that this never could have been a legal issue for Richardson: at this time copyright law did not protect an author's rights in a character or idea, only the exact text as originally printed.[23] As I have earlier described, the 1710 Statute of Anne protected rights to copy in a very physical sense; it did not cover a more abstract understanding of creative work. Of course, Richardson had been angered at what he called "that vile Pamphlet *Shamela*," not because

Fielding stole his idea, but because he so sharply criticized the novel. Indeed, Richardson, at least at the beginning, seems to have been quite content to let the buzz about *Pamela* continue to boost the novel's sales. He printed five editions within the novel's first year alone, and it continued to be a best seller for years.

Finally, though, Richardson reacted to what he considered an improper advance upon his *Pamela*, that is, *Pamela* the book as printer's property, Pamela the virtuous young (fictional) woman, and the story "Pamela" as instructional narrative, none of which can be considered separately from the others. On May 7, 1741, he ran ads in several papers for the fourth edition of the novel, announcing at the same time his dismay at recently learning of a plan for what we might call an "unauthorized" sequel to his novel. "Certain Booksellers having in the Press a spurious Continuation of these Two Volumes," he proclaimed, "the Author thinks it necessary to declare, that the same is carrying on *against* his Consent, and without any other Knowledge of the Story than what they are able to collect from the two Volumes already printed: And that he is already continuing the Work himself, from Materials, that, perhaps, but for such a notorious Invasion of his Plan, he should not have published."[24] Nonetheless, despite Richardson's public protests and a later, private, conference with the bookseller sponsoring the project, *Pamela's Conduct in High Life* was released by the end of the month. Richardson again appeared in public to protest, advertising against this "Imposition on the Public" and reminding readers that his authentic continuation would be available soon. This was merely the beginning of a long and often ugly campaign between Richardson and his so-called authentic sequel and the counternarrative of Pamela's life by the writers Richardson dubbed the "High Life Men." (Interestingly, by using the plural term "High Life *Men*," Richardson labels the work as a collaborative production. In actuality, Richard Chandler, a bookseller, employed John Kelly to write the continuation. Richardson's term, and the fact that his battle was with both parties, is further evidence that he saw textual creation as extending beyond the singular originary source of the author.) The debate subsided only when Richardson's version of the *Pamela* continuation appeared that fall. In the meantime, however, it is not completely clear why Richardson cared so much about the High Life novel. Why was this "sequel" an infringement when other spin-offs and uses of the Pamela name were not? Most likely, new Pamela stories would inspire new readers to buy the original text—readers, it should be pointed out, who frequently invented new works from what was understood as the community property of literary characters.[25] As Warner points out, the "media culture" of this period was an "unenclosed commons" where all could "graze at will." In this context, Richardson's vague gestures toward "the heroine's promising future" actually encouraged the serial publication so popular in this period, while his insistence on anonymity left the lucrative venue open to others.[26] Given that the High Life Men could represent themselves as both legally and ethically justified—they were serving the public's desire for more Pamela—as well as partaking of a common reading and writing practice, Richardson may have been better off letting this aspect of the Pamela craze run its course while he continued to silently reap financial rewards on the original. Silence, however, was not to be his course of action.

Richardson's interest in *Pamela* as a financial investment only in part explains his actions. Certainly when the High Life bookseller had offered, as a compromise, to let Richardson write the sequel for him, Richardson indicated that this would not be his most profitable mode of action, "having a young Family of my own that was intitled to All I could do for them."[27] Richardson had split the profits for the first *Pamela*, selling two-thirds of the copyright to his booksellers for twenty guineas, but he learned from his mistake and registered the copyright for his continuation in his name alone. Still, the profit motive alone does not account for the emotional investment he seemed to have made in this issue—for his furious and obstinate pursuit of his goal to rid the world of this unauthorized Pamela. His usually fine business sense, it seems, was abetted by emotion, and it is not clear that the situation—at least in financial terms—warranted it. Rather than attribute Richardson's fury solely to his concern for his ledgers (which were, after all, in pretty good shape), we must look beyond the "rational," to the ways this incident distressed Richardson's moral economy. It is not that Richardson was morally outraged over the "theft" or "piracy" of what was inherently his intellectual property. Richardson never employs these terms, and, as I have pointed out, contemporary copyright law would not have protected him in this case. We have also seen that his understanding of authorship was much looser than that of later writers and that his version of textual theft was materially based. No proofs or pages were stolen in this case. To discover the causes of his emotional distress, therefore, we will have to look momentarily beyond the walls of his print shop and outside what is usually considered the realm of authorship. In order to begin to sketch out the several, often contradictory, ideologies that intersect in Richardson, we need to turn to his textual output.

The epigraph to this chapter is from what is often referred to as *Pamela II*, that is, the sequel, or in Richardson's words the "continuation," of *Pamela*.[28] Here, Richardson represents one of the many possible functions of a book. Pamela's Lincolnshire friend, Polly Darnford, writes to Pamela that she doubts she will be able to visit the newlyweds soon, for her gouty father, Sir Simon, has been in a miserable mood. As an example of the "peevish" (*P.*, 44) behavior she has been forced to withstand, she offers a description of her enraged father using a book as a weapon. Such a scene stands out in this novel, for it is one of the few that reminds us of the physical violence and mental suffering that threaten women throughout the original *Pamela*. It also neatly encapsulates several of the intertwined themes I explore in this chapter: on the one hand, the solid materiality of the book, and on the other, the authoritative role of the patriarch, the notoriously questionable claim of paternity (a problem blamed on women), the physical vulnerability of women, and their disadvantageous position on the marriage market.[29] If the physical nature of the book seems of an entirely different order than the other themes, which might fall under the rubric of domestic ideology, my point here is that it is not, and was not, for Richardson.

The continuation was apparently categorically different from the other uses of *Pamela*, which had all been derivations or outright copies of Richardson's original story. In this case, the High Life Men were wresting Pamela (the character) out of Richardson's control and creating a new life for her. Ultimately, I will show that Richardson was worried not about physical property per se but about the abduction of a helpless woman, her subsequent loss of reputation, and the shame and dishonor this would bring on her father's—Richardson's—house. It would not have been unusual for Richardson to see himself in the role of textual father. Writers and booksellers had long used the metaphor of paternity to describe their relationship to their text.[30] Indeed, printers and booksellers in the early eighteenth century often deployed the figure of the Author as Father in their legal battles to secure copyright, though the metaphors of paternity and property did not always mix. Mark Rose explains that such usage reflects a "continuation of the patriarchal discourse of traditional society: the author is master and owner of his wife and children as well as of the children of his inventions."[31] He questions, though, the inconsistency in treating text as child: how does one then justify selling the child on the market?

Richard G. Swartz, exploring more thoroughly the cultural roots of this representation, is able to justify this seeming inconsistency by seeing the role of paternity in the eighteenth century as going beyond the mere biological fathering of children. In looking at court cases that conceptualize the author as a needy father who must provide for his family, he traces the metaphor to Locke's emphasis on the paternal duty to provide for future generations. He also looks at other eighteenth-century texts that articulate the role of familial property as a capital asset that embodies the upright middle-class family, providing it with "continuity and 'ethical life.'" Swartz summarizes this middle-class conjunction of morality and economics: "[T]he Father's ability to found an estate becomes a sign of his status and value, and the right to distribute this inheritance becomes a sign not only of the Father's power, but his moral worthiness." This, he explains, extends then to authors as fathers: "The *topos* of patrimonial ambition appears to reconcile the professional author's two contradictory roles as a producer in a system of commodity exchanges *and* as a transcendent source of value and meaning."[32] Richardson, as printer *and* writer, would have felt this contradiction most keenly, and his adoption of the role of father would have resolved some of these tensions. Understanding Richardson the printer as a patriarch defending a moral estate—an estate made of and by books—helps us see the logic behind his behavior in the "High Life" case. For example, his indignant insistence that he had a family to support registers as a matter of both class status and moral honor, as well as a financial concern.

Swartz's explanation still leaves much out, however. Despite the fact that he claims to be considering "the extant to which the rhetoric of authorship supported by the social and legal institutions defining this production is itself shaped by the cultural semiotics of gender," the effects of these semiotics on the gendered subjects of reading and writing is absent from his analysis.[33] He discusses "patriarchy," but only as a monolith, avoiding a discussion of the everyday, prescribed and actual practices of men and women that make up the ideology. Claims that the author is Father, for example, beg the question of the role of women writers in this reproductive dynamic. Furthermore, notions of the father's duty leave out the effects of estate consolidation on mothers and daughters. The continuity of the estate depends, after all, on the virtue of the mother, the trust that the father must have that her children are indeed his. There are also many ways in which the institution of marriage supports the morally inflected financial aspirations of the middle class by providing links with other families of appropriate economic status. The role of the daughter is especially important here, for a girl of questionable virtue will not be as valuable a commodity on the marriage market. These issues of gender have links to authorship as well. If fathers must maintain control over female children in order to ensure their virtue, a similar form of supervision must be necessary in the realm of textual production as well. These complications become especially appropriate in Richardson's novels, which have been shown again and again to be about feminine propriety and sexual politics. The relation between the author as Father and his textual child seems especially important in *Pamela*, which tells the story of a young girl in danger precisely because she is far from her father's house, geographically, economically, and symbolically, and in the hands of another man.

The rhetoric of Richardson's argument with the High Life Men helps us understand his approach to these issues. Richardson, in response to the "spurious Continuation," felt compelled to write his own. He had not originally planned on doing so because, he claimed, sequels never sold as well. He insisted, though, in a letter to his brother-in-law, that this publication was necessary "rather than my Plan should be basely *ravished* out of my hands, and, probably my characters . . . *debased*."[34] In other words, taken out of his control, it was uncertain what mischief Pamela—the novel and the character—could get into or what calamity might befall her. "Ravished" and "debased" are terms that signify in the discourse of gender, together telling a cause-effect narrative of feminine vulnerability (to her own feelings as well as to physical predation), the sexual dangers of the outside world, and the ease in which a women's character is permanently sullied. A woman—even a textual woman evidently—was always potentially at risk in the unchaperoned company of men not of her family. And for a tradesman like Richardson, the decadent high life was an especially perilous place for a naive young woman, even the plucky Pamela. How could he trust an unknown hack and an unscrupulous bookseller with determining her fate within this environment? He told the publisher of *Pamela's Conduct* that he would not have his characters "depreciated and debased, by those who know nothing of the Story, nor the Delicacy required in the Continuation of the Piece."[35] Again, "delicacy" connotes a specifically feminine sensibility; it seems to be Pamela herself who will be injured by the High Life Men's lack of it. It was clear that he could not rely on *these* unworthy men to protect Pamela, whose public anonymity, he indicated, was alone cause for concern: "[W]hen any Person who is above Scandal and scandalous Practices, shall say anything worthy of Notice, and set his Name to what he publishes, he shall receive a proper reply."[36] By not attaching their surnames to the text, the High Life Men signal their lack of status as proper patriarchal guardians over family (i.e., feminine) values.

## THE REWARDS OF VIRTUE: PROPRIETY ON THE MARKET

Richardson's umbrage was not triggered merely by the abstract idea that it was morally correct to provide a proper, virtuous environment for his characters. We have seen that he seldom supported abstract ideologies that did not have a concrete basis. For Richardson the printer, this bottom line was once again financial. This is not to question his commitment to values such as feminine propriety—like most of his class, he saw the financial and the moral as tightly intertwined. In a time when so-called companionate marriages masked what could still be a family's best investment—marrying up—a young woman's bad name could ruin a family's economic future along with its reputation, a concern underlying the plot of *Clarissa*.[37] Fielding cleverly revealed this subtext—or, rather, its inverse, in which "VARTUE" garners status and money—in *Shamela*. That novel enraged Richardson because it so neatly revealed the repressed in his text—as well as in his moral universe. For just as a debased daughter threatened the continuation of the patriarchal estate, an association with a besmirched title could undermine Richardson's careful construction of himself as a moral writer and the revenue that accompanied that fame. (Thus Richardson at one point even suggested to the High Life Men that they give their story another name, so that *his* heroine would not be sullied—they of course refused.) At the same time, he must have realized that, as was the case with Robert Dodsley, the discourse of disinterest meant he suppressed any implications of the financial rewards inherent in (literary) virtue.

After publication of *Pamela's Conduct*, his worst fears confirmed, Richardson's chief complaint in his negative ads was the "lowness" of the life to which his character was subjected. Exactly what scenes Richardson objected to is not completely clear. One passage that he specifically pointed to in several advertisements is one in which Pamela drinks bumpers of wine, then marvels at the fact that her pregnancy keeps her from becoming intoxicated. Richardson warned readers that "the *whole* Volume is written with *equal* Spirit and Propriety."[38] This cavalier attitude to her pregnancy is emblematic, for throughout *Pamela's Conduct* Pamela's role as a mother is downplayed (a point I later return to). One is tempted to believe that Richardson was searching for such examples, however, for in most cases, *Pamela's Conduct* is even more pedantic than Richardson's novel, and Pamela is no less tediously moral in either one. One central difference stands out, however: *Pamela's Conduct* is explicitly commercial in its preface, which describes Pamela's letters as a print product on the market, and in the narrative itself, which examines the exact monetary nature of Pamela's new found wealth. The preface supplies examples of correspondence between two characters, the book's new editor and the current owner of Pamela's continued letters, a Mrs. Brenville, the housekeeper of Jervis's niece. In convincing her to publish the private papers, the editor tells her he has "consulted with a Bookseller. . . . He looked over the Papers you have entrusted into my Hand, said they may make up about thirteen or fourteen Sheets of Print, on the same Letter and the same fixed Paper with the two Volumes already published; and if they were writ with as much Spirit, and the same elegant Ease as those which have appeared . . . he would be a Publisher."[39] Mrs. Brenville agrees to the transaction, adding, "I wish him good Luck in the Sale, may he reap a Profit and Reader's Benefit. . . . I leave you to agree about the Price" (x). Thus what had seemed to Richardson's readers the stirringly authentic, earnest outpourings of a young girl's heart are transformed into "thirteen or fourteen Sheets of Print" that are simultaneously morally beneficial *and* a potentially profitable product.

Of course, Richardson the printer would have himself seen *Pamela* in this way, but the work's appeal as moral instruction in proper bourgeois femininity and as a new sort of fiction offering access to "authentic" feeling, he realized, depended on suppressing its affiliation with crass marketing.

The economic exchange highlighted in the preface of *Pamela's Conduct*, however, merely sets the stage for the commercialism thematized in the letters themselves. Pamela describes the relationship between B—— and her parents, for example, in financial terms, as that of debtor and creditor—this despite the fact that her family is later revealed to be (formerly unbeknownst to Pamela) of noble, if fallen, blood. Despite this lineage and B——'s obvious allegiance to the aristocracy, though, it is clear that this novel is a celebration of middle-class industry—the kind that Richardson himself prized. The novel opens with B—— escorting Pamela around London, giving her a tourist's glimpse of the most important spots. A trip to the Royal Exchange prompts this speech: "I will show you the Props of the Nation, and the Fountains whence flow the publick Treasure, and support the Glory of the *British* Name, . . . which are, in a Word, the Cause of that Plenty we enjoy." (5). These fountains, the generative force of British glory, turn out to be, not statesmen or war heroes, but merchants and traders. He continues his inflated acclamation:

> [They] are the supports . . . of the Country, to whose Industry we owe every Thing we hold dear . . . : nay Liberty itself, the greatest Blessing in it, may be said to be preserved by these; for these have been found of Weight to curb the Ambitious Views of wicked and corrupt Ministers at Home: and these, by their Industry, are our Protection against any Attempts from Abroad, of making us groan under a foreign Yoke. (7)

These accolades, promoting this relentlessly commercial location and the financial ideology that underlies it, do more than merely praise industry for industry's sake: they reveal the *power* held by the capitalist class—the class to which Richardson belonged and whose power he shared. They control politics, both domestic and international.

These passages on this mighty economic force, occurring so early in the letters, suggest that it is this sort of activity that supports Pamela in her prodigious estate. For this novel makes explicitly clear the profit that was reaped by Pamela's morality. Of course, in Richardson's *Pamela, or Virtue Rewarded* it is clear that Pamela's goodness does lead her to a better standard of living. Richardson is vague about the material nature of this opulence, however; in fact, compared to the High Life sequel, he relates few physical descriptions of her elevated station. He presents it mostly as a set of sophisticated manners at which Pamela naturally excels, not an economic condition. Her increased wealth does allow her to increase her charitable activities, but there is otherwise no explicit mention of her increased spending power. She is still clearly a representative of the middle-class thriftiness Richardson extolled. In *Pamela's Conduct*, by contrast, the mansion's decor is outlined with concrete precision, as are sumptuous banquets and enormous quantities of wine. In listing these gains, the novel not only extols conspicuous consumption but also implies that Pamela herself is a participant, a trader in her own right. Just as the imaginary publisher of these letters, referred to in the preface, was able to turn virtuous letters into profit (as did Richardson), so Pamela herself exchanges personal integrity for a lavish upper-class lifestyle.

Another unauthorized continuation, *Pamela in High Life, or Virtue Rewarded*, which appeared soon after *Pamela's Conduct in High Life* but before Richardson's version, carries this idea even further. There is no record of Richardson's feelings about this text, though since it is so similar to *Pamela's Conduct*, we can assume he was not pleased. Taken together, both "spurious Continuations" reveal the strength of this counterdiscourse, spurned by Richardson, and thus serve as a reminder of all that Richardson avoids in his own novels. The emphasis in *Pamela in High Life, or Virtue Rewarded*, like its predecessor, is on the second half of its title. Here, again and again, the novel not only describes the extravagant entertainments that Mr. and Mrs. B—— provide their friends but actually categorizes the amounts and costs of each type of food, from geese to puddings, and beverage, from old wines to exotic liqueurs. We find out the price of everything, from baby clothes, to Pamela's diamonds, to a successful ball, and the exorbitant amounts B—— is willing to pay dressmakers and traveling players. The novel makes clear that the rewards of virtue are indeed lavish and do not come cheaply. B——— justifies this expense with another reference to the power of economic exchange and "trickle-down" consumerism: "If we who have great Estates spend no more than is absolutely necessary, how would the Money circulate, and the labouring and trading part of the Nation be supported? —The Prodigal . . . is of greater Benefit to Trade and Society than the Miser."[40] While this passage is more aristocratic in tone than those in *Pamela's Conduct*, it still highlights the economic underpinnings that support Pamela's new (high) life.

While completely straightforward in tone, and maintaining Pamela's moral character, these sequels must have come too close to Shamela's fantasy for Richardson's comfort. Furthermore, the link between the patriarchal marriage market, through which Pamela brings wealth and privilege to her family, and a young girl's letters, which bring wealth and fame to her publisher, had been too clearly revealed. Richardson thus rushed to counter these debased Pamelas and *Pamela*s with his own, the true daughter, obedient and tractable. In Richardson's version of the continuation, published in December of 1741, he thus did not dare allow Pamela any more reputation-endangering adventures. Instead, despite friends' advice to the contrary, he, in his own words, "only aimed to give the Piece such a Variety, as should be consistent with . . . the general Tenor of a genteel Married Life"; he wanted the sequel to be "rather *useful*, than *diverting*," as a good wife should be.[41] After *Pamela*'s reckless ride on the market and a dangerous flirtation with the Men of the High Life (who may have inspired Richardson's later abductor, Lovelace), Richardson knew that it was necessary in the sequel to stress her moral character and her distance from economic materiality.

What results is a Pamela who cannot truly be termed the heroine of the novel. Instead, she is a passive recipient of action done to her and around her. Critics are united in considering Richardson's continuation an artistic failure, chiefly because it is considered *boring*. James Grantham Turner calls Richardson's dialogue "mincing and turgid," for example, and Terry Castle calls the novel "an assault . . . on plot itself."[42] Rather than apply our standards of artistic merit, however, we need to explore the rationale for this static quality. It is true that plot-wise, little happens. Much of Pamela's letters are devoted to retelling her courtship tale or describing the accolades that continue to be heaped on her. Indeed, one of the persistent features of the novel is precisely the circulation of these letters. Especially in the first half of the novel (before Pamela gives birth), correspondence is rarely only two-way. Letters written by Pamela from the original *Pamela* are passed around again among family members to be reviewed and discussed; Lady Davers takes special pleasure in reading the rape scene to her own circle of friends. Current news is disseminated in the same way: Pamela's parents receive copies of Lady Davers's and Miss Darnford's letters, Miss Darnford gets to peruse those of Lady Davers, and so on. This is not merely a convenient rhetorical device that allows Richardson to keep characters apprised without repeating information, but a theme in itself. As Lady Davers says to Pamela, "You have made us a family of readers and writers" (*P.*, 34). That is, not only is Pamela educating an already existing family, but the act of writing and reading is what creates them as a family. Much has been made of Pamela's incarnation in letters and, more broadly, the cultural transformation of the ideal woman in the eighteenth century from one based in physicality to one based in a textual femininity.[43] Thus the letters passed between the various households—the B——'s, Andrews's, Davers's, and Darnford's—stand in for the exchange of Pamela herself, linking patriarchal families.[44] They also substitute for and thus mask a form of financial circulation, made all too clear in *Pamela's Conduct*: that of *Pamela* on the literary market, an object of exchange between writer and bookseller, bookseller and reader. In this light, the circular paths of Pamela's letters within the novel seem to harken back nostalgically to a form of textual dissemination that bypasses the market, coterie manuscript circulation.[45] While it may seem odd for a successful member of the book trade to engage in such fantasies about market alternatives, Richardson did circulate his own in-process manuscripts in a similar way, among a similar group, a sympathetic "family" of readers and writers.[46]

If the letters circulate in this novel, it is notable how still Pamela herself is. While she does actually change places geographically occasionally, her character remains static, and she does not, in this practically plotless novel, progress through a narrative. The London masquerade, and the almost-affair it engenders between B—— and a countess, is often credited with supplying the only action. Even here, though, Pamela never acts as an agent in her own story. At the masquerade, she is reduced to a mere observer, desperately trying to track B——'s interest in the attractive "nun."[47] The narrative movement seems to follow the circulating B——. His pursuit of and banter with a disguised beauty form the real story that attracts the reader's attention. Who is the mysterious countess? What is B—— saying to her in Italian? What is the nature of their relationship? In the end, Pamela plays no real part even in uncovering the affair, but she hears versions of the story—a love story in which she is not the heroine—from others, including, eventually, B—— and the countess themselves.

Pamela's unwilling participation in the plot of others is emblematized by her pregnancy and labor. Her first contraction occurs in the first letter following the masquerade description, almost as if, as Castle points out, the masquerade brings on her labor. She is morbidly afraid of childbirth, meditating on her possible death in several letters and recoiling repugnantly from any overtures by a midwife to discuss her condition and examine her beforehand. She senses herself becoming increasingly frail, and this physical debility mirrors the mental weakness to which she also attests. The brave and determined young woman who once fought off an aristocratic rapist and actively planned an escape from her kidnapper now only comments that "it shall have to be seen how it will please God to deal with me" (*P.*, 263). (Her attitude contrasts with that of the alter-Pamela of *Pamela in High Life*, who spends only an hour in labor and whose attitude toward childbirth is summed up in the blasé comment, "I breed well with little pain."[48]) It is clear that Pamela does not so much *give* birth (an active verb) as *withstand* it. She is never figured as a *creator* of life, but merely the passive vessel for B——'s own sequel, his son and heir. B—— writes the authorized continuation of his family line on her blank page with his pen/penis. This moment of central *sexual reproduction* can thus be seen as representative of a new understanding of *textual production*. Forgetting the ideology that supported him as a printer, one that prized the physicality of the text, Richardson utilizes the burgeoning discourse that represents the (feminine) page as an invisible and inert holder of the (male) author's will.

Soon after Pamela gives birth, B——'s affair with the countess is resolved—they actually never consummated their mutual interest—and domestic bliss returns. No conflicts emerge to provide anything resembling a plot. Not even a sense of chronology remains—the letters are no longer dated and even seasons are not referred to. The only element marking the passage of time is the birth of more and more babies—

seven in all. These babies are precisely the point: B——, in being made a father, has his authority increased, and Pamela is even more securely ensconced on a *paternal* estate, no longer an independent agent, even within the narrative bearing her name. This is emphasized when, against Pamela's ardent desire to nurse her son, her almost religious belief that this is the moral path of true motherhood, B—— staunchly refuses her request. Her body is to be his alone. Her (textual) virtue is thus physically circumscribed through the control of her material body. By refusing access to her body even to his infant son, B——'s legacy can be safely considered his own. This returns us to the material *Pamela*, the published continuation. With its release, Richardson finally decided to imprint on his character his paternal seal, to clearly mark her—the textual character and the material body of the book—as patriarchal property. For the first time, his name was officially associated with Pamela's with the words "Printed for S. Richardson" on the title page. He also registered his right to copy in his own name alone, evidently unwilling to share his paternal privileges. Presenting an alternate reading of Richardson's response to the Chandler/Kelly sequel, Warner concludes that "Richardson can only defend his commodity adrift on the open market by presenting himself as its 'author.'"[49] However, "printed for" was not commonly used to reference writers. As we have seen in the previous chapters, it was instead usually a rubric used by a bookseller, who may or may not have actually written the text but who did own it as property, or by a trade publisher, who bore responsibility for its circulation. Thus Richardson preserves the illusion of authenticity offered by his editorship while simultaneously deploying a trade convention that grants his authority, ownership, and control.

The story of *Pamela* and its continuation reveal that Richardson was a canny member of the book trade who knew how to manipulate his product to appeal to the largest possible audience. While he did not see his work as a printer at odds with his work as a writer, he did seem ambivalent about how to represent the culture of (gendered) commerce underlying both vocations. We have seen, for example, that even after the publication of his final novel, *Sir Charles Grandison*, another best seller, he had no reservations in proclaiming his vested interests as a printer-writer of a capital investment publicly. Why then, would he take such pains to conceal the involvement of *Pamela* and its continuation in what was after all a literary *market*? Why turn to alternatives to print to describe textual circulation? The difference between the two titles is telling: *Sir Charles Grandison* makes reference to an aristocratic man, one whom we assume to be mature (he has acceded to his title) and well placed; *Pamela*, however, signifies a woman, troublingly un-classed, bearing no paternal name—a woman, by definition, at risk. In Richardson's gendered moral universe, for such a woman, any connections with a realm as public and anonymous as the market could only be damaging.

In order to understand this danger, a brief look at the sexual-textual politics of the larger literary marketplace at this time might be helpful. Peter Stallybrass and Allon White, in their study of the literary uses of transgression in the early eighteenth-century project of creating a reputable profession of authorship, claim that "concomitant with the establishing of the 'refined' public sphere and its distinct notion of professional authorship was a widespread attempt to regulate the body . . . so as to create conditions favorable to the operation of the sphere."[50] In other words, in order to clear a space for a specifically moral form of public writing, the shameful and embarrassing "low-other" had to be removed from the scene of textual production.[51] While Stallybrass and White discuss sexuality, they do not engage in a full-scale analysis of the ways in which gender is articulated within this project. Nancy Armstrong has shown, however, that the body that is evacuated from some of the "purer" realms of literary production, such as conduct literature and domestic fiction, was resolutely a woman's body. This is not surprising, since eighteenth-century women's bodies were often associated with what was considered shameful: a deviant biology, out-of-control sexuality, pornography or libertine literature, and prostitution.[52] Indeed, Stallybrass and White do point to the texts in which whores stand in for the sexual, excremental, and crude, all that stands in the way of the proper enjoyment of literature.[53]

Such a dynamic, of course, affected representations of the woman writer: in the late seventeenth- and early eighteenth-century literary market, she was often described as a public woman, or prostitute—indeed, the term *hack*, referring to the dissolute Grub Street writer, was also slang for *prostitute*.[54] A woman writing for money, without the proper justifications described in chapter 4, could only be doubly a whore. These sexual politics of the literary market effect Richardson's representation of Pamela, for he is introducing not just a woman character into the public sphere but a woman *writer*. That Pamela is the author of her letters is a fiction Richardson supports by calling himself "editor," a guise he maintained throughout his argument with the High Life Men. As a female whose writing is circulating publicly on the market, then, Pamela's reputation is at risk.

By asserting that the letters actually *belong* not to her but to her father, however, Richardson protects her reputation and, by extension, his own family name. As a stand-in for husband or father, in fact, Richardson could say that the letters indeed were legally his. That property in letters belonged to the sender rather than the receiver (even though the receiver held the material text) was established in *Pope v. Curll* in 1741. The ramifications of this can be seen in the novel. No matter to whom she sent her letters, Pamela owned them—just like, as she insists again and again in the first *Pamela*, she owns herself, despite her low status as a servant. While Pamela may not have been the property of B—— when he was merely her master, however, she—or at least all she owns—does become his property upon their marriage.[55] She accedes to this when she hands over her reams of letters to him for his review. Ann Kibbie describes this sudden change in Pamela's status in the original novel:

> While the self-possession that Pamela insists upon in her trials, her claims to the proprietorship of her own person, provides her character with its interest and the novel with its drama, such self-possession would be finally incompatible with the notion of female character expressed in the very marriage that enacts her reward. Pamela's character, therefore, must be revised in the ending of her story. . . . In this way, what happens after the wedding is not so much a *continuation* of the plot as an *undoing* of it. The accession to estate effects the transformation of Pamela herself into B——'s property, a transformation that his assaults on her person could not accomplish.[56]

If the end of the first *Pamela* marks her as patriarchal property, then, its continuation, an examination of "genteel married life," as Richardson put it, consolidates this positioning. As Pamela herself circulates between families in the form of letters, as I indicated earlier, it is B—— who controls this circulation, deciding who gets to read what and when. His property in the Pamela-of-letters is secured by his overseeing this exchange.

Similarly, Richardson stands in for B—— as husband-father, making it clear to the public that he owns her letters (and thus her): in advertising his own continuation, he notes that it derives from materials "which *no other* Person can have."[57] Because he is still maintaining his pose as Editor, his claim is not that no other *creator* can understand Pamela, or that he owns rights to the original and unique fictional character (a creative work) because he created her. Instead, his claim to access, in light of his other comments and the succeeding continuation itself, seems based on his *paternal* property rights. Here, however, paternity does not seem to imply a (pro)creative birth, but the structural relationship of proprietorship between husband/father and wife/daughter. The fact that Richardson cements this relationship between B—— and Pamela in the continuation reflects his own feeling regarding the circulation of the textual Pamela. Just as Pamela could not be forever resistant to B——'s advances on her person, a (feminine) text on the market cannot maintain independence or self-possession. To be free on the market means to be open to male tampering: Pamela withstands a near rape in Richardson's first novel; she is mocked as a scheming hussy in *Shamela*; she is abducted and transformed by the High Life Men. The properly moral feminine text, if it was to be marketed—as Richardson the printer knew it had to be despite his nostalgic yearnings for private family circulation—must therefore be clearly marked as patriarchal property. Richardson thus adopts the role of the proprietor, *not* to protect that which is unique and original and so inherently his property, but only in order to control the propriety of his texts. Again, the printer Richardson deploys what might seem like the language of abstract authorship only to protect his investment in the cultural capital inherent in the persona of the moral print worker, in the contradictory position of circulating virtuous femininity in a financial market.

In the end, I believe, the story of Pamela as both moral heroine and marketable book reveals more clearly the relationship between authorship and *authority*—authority over textual meaning as well as over textual property. Richardson complicates the trajectory I traced in chapter

2 from Moxon to Smith, in chapter 3 from Kirkman to Dodsley, in chapter 4 from mercury to woman writer—from an authority and responsibility vested in the print worker to an authority understood to be held by the godlike Author. My study of Richardson reveals that this authority springs not only, or even mostly, from notions of originality but also from a history of paternal authority. It helps us understand why Smith drew on ideologies of gender to articulate his version of the properly hierarchical text, with the strong, rational roman font presiding over the weaker, sensitive italic; the abstract idea over the material text; the mind over the body; the Author over the printer. In each case, the first term is coded masculine, the second, feminine, the male pen marking the passive female body, giving birth to the literary work.

By Smith's time, gender was a fundamental aspect of the literary market. The gendering of print in itself was not a new phenomenon: Wendy Wall describes a similar dynamic in early modern England, in which the mere naming of a book as a woman's identifies it "as a *feme covert* necessarily in need of supervision by the more authoritative and masculine force of the writer and/or publisher."[58] In fact, she explains, "by using the female body as a metaphor for the newly commodified book, both became defined as unruly objects in need of supervision and governance."[59] However, the rapid growth of the literary market in the eighteenth century meant that suddenly there was now a threatening *excess* of femininity. Novels, meant for private reading and claiming a wide female audience, were especially problematic, as critical commentary on the novel and novel readers' social coding as "feminine" has shown.[60] The public struggle over the *Pamela* continuations is, indeed, representative of this: Terri Nickel comments that "the need to displace *Pamela* often betrays anxiety about the novel's popularity that conceives of that popularity as distinctly feminine."[61] Ironically, she explains, novelistic attempts to rein in the threat of *Pamela* through the constructions of new versions and sequels only exacerbate the problem by constructing a "multiplicitous *Pamela* that escapes homogenous interpretation."[62] This all-encompassing femininity, a femininity without boundaries, is also what underwrote the libertine literature of the time—it is another version of out-of-control feminine sexuality. It is this form of sexuality, as I have commented, that Stallybrass and White describe as being erased in the "new alignment of the male public body and status," that is, the ephemeral body (or bodylessness) of masculine authorship.[63] Thus in Richardson we have an example of a printer-writer, whose thematic concerns involved controlling the sexual behavior of women and promoting the (textualized) virtue of men, trying to maintain his power and authority over a potentially dangerous or endangered feminine textuality.

Of course, this textuality is also a unique form of commodity, that which became known as intellectual property. Richardson's reactions in the *Pamela* case thus also illuminate an aspect of the eighteenth-century development of this concept. To Richardson the printer, feminine textuality was always a form of *material* property made to be sold on the market—though this was the place where propriety, and thus proprietorship, was most needed. Thus the *intellectual* of "intellectual property" is for Richardson that property's status as vulnerable femininity over which the (male) author must assert his authority. This emphasizes the fact that Richardson was not the "nobody" Catherine Gallagher describes as the quintessential eighteenth-century author—he was not the writer always already feminized, disinherited from his birthright through the sale of copyright to a bookseller. Rather, he was a central Somebody, a father *and* a publisher, a capitalist who, in attempting to control *Pamela*, was simultaneously preserving his estate and his family name.

Richardson's positioning thus provides a missing link between the bookseller as owner and the author as owner. His umbrage at having the text work of Pamela "depreciated and debased"—terms that register simultaneously in both financial and morally gendered economies—shows that the eighteenth-century project of making the literary work more abstract and immaterial, and thus more the property of the author who creates its intangible aspects, must be seen in relation to the similar process of "textualizing" the feminine. This connection can be articulated only if we begin to see literary property as *both* a solid, opaque object—a book made of paper and ink, bearing a woman's name in the title and a printer's name below that—*and* a bearer of ideology, representing itself in a shop that is also a patriarchal domain. The contents of the book will always affect its material representation—and vice versa—whether in a printer's diatribe against piracy or in a copyright case brought to court. Of course, not all or even most of the cases brought to court involved novels, and certainly not all print products of this period are examples of "feminization." The popularity of the novel as a feminine form, however, could not help but affect the practice structuring the larger market. The increasingly commercialized culture of print, therefore, can be comprehended only in the context of the gendered politics of eighteenth-century sexual mores and their expression through family politics. Likewise, the eighteenth-century's project of making a bifurcated, hierarchical, and metaphysical gender can be thoroughly understood only when one examines the material economy of books circulating these values. To return to the quotation that serves as the epigraph to this chapter, we can now read in it Richardson's attempt to posit the father's book, clearly imprinted as such through the authority he wields as paternal producer of print, as the best defense against a threatening, polymorphous feminine textuality and the "bastards" that might result. But is such an imprint enough? Richardson's attempts *as a printer* to authorize the circulation of an official *Pamela* were ultimately futile—alternate representations flourished despite his attempts to rein them in. This failure, however, points us forward: eventually, the Law itself—in the form of stricter and more intangible interpretations of the statutes governing copyright and protecting authors—would be called in to regulate the realm of the sexual, textual commodity.

# 6

# THE GHOST IN THE MACHINE: INVISIBLE PRINT IN A DIGITAL AGE

*Give me a good handsome large volume, with a full promising title-page at the head of it, printed on good paper and letter, the whole well bound and gilt, and I'll warrant its selling—You have the common error of authors, who think people buy books to read—No, no, books are only bought to furnish libraries, as pictures, and glasses, and beds and chairs, are for other rooms.*

—HENRY FIELDING, *THE AUTHOR'S FARCE*, 1730

*How we read, and teach reading, are all the more crucial, even instrumentally crucial, in a society where information exchange is becoming the key global industry.*

—PETER BROOKS, *THE 2000 MLA ELECTIONS: CANDIDATE INFORMATION BOOKLET*

Viewing the eighteenth-century print culture of England as many of its denizens viewed it—as bodies laboring to make goods for the market *as well as* rich text circulating mores and meanings—can make us uncomfortable. Difficult issues are engendered by textual materiality. When we acknowledge our texts' status as commodities, as always already an economic construct, we are confronted with our own distaste for the commercial, inherited from Pope and Wordsworth, inflected by Marx, supported by the ivory-tower mythology of humanism as "pure" study. Indeed, when we admit to the ontological existence of books as physical objects built and moved by biological organisms, we face the limits and temporality of the human body itself. We must concede that the timelessness of Art is illusory: as Dunton said, "Books have their time of life as well as we." Such admissions are vexing when we would rather discuss ideas, politics, passions, and stories. Nonetheless, revealing the work of print is imperative if we are to understand both the eighteenth-century *and* the new configurations of text, labor, and economy that confront us in our own time. For in our own increasingly digitized environment of textual production, in which writing technologies, the materiality of language, and the commerce in words are undergoing radical change, we may be well served in returning our attention to past struggles and to other ways of understanding originality, textual circulation, and intellectual work.

Today, as print is reinvented as new media, our text-making modes again bespeak anxiety. The humanities themselves, long affiliated with print as *the* technology of learning, seem to be in crisis. New forms and new definitions of text are restructuring the way humanists do work, get to work, understand the very idea of work—for themselves and for their students. At the same time, of course, the world around the university is rapidly transforming, as digital communication's alliance with transnational corporations has led to radical shifts in everything from geopolitics to identity politics. Bodies, cultures, texts, epistemologies, and disciplines fragment, only to be reconstructed into hybrids and aggregates that form new coalitions and create new hierarchies.[1] The change is simultaneously fascinating, overwhelming, and mundane, frighteningly obvious yet difficult to detect. Old familiar terms like *postmodern condition* seem antiquated and ineffective—debris from an age of innocence.

In the face of such anxiety, humanists do what they have always done: read, write, teach—never mind that terms such as *read, write,* and *teach* are themselves up for grabs. Libraries and bookstores—themselves perhaps relics—fill up with shelf after shelf of new books, all of which struggle to interpret, clarify, organize, and categorize the transfiguration of what were once such natural(ized) daily processes. They vainly seek that always impossible outside perspective that will allow the larger frame of reference necessary to make wise choices in unfamiliar terrain. Failing that, they fall back into comfortable dichotomies that see the unknown only in terms of not known. In most studies—and in many classrooms, committee meetings, and hallway conversations—the new media culture and digitized education are contrasted, for better or worse, depending on the speaker, with print literacy and traditional "brick-and-mortar" classrooms. This is an understandable, and certainly not surprising, pairing. In all but the most sophisticated analyses, however, the *technological* perils or pleasures are always described as being an essential element of the *new*. The familiar—print—becomes the neutral ground against which our new text machines are constructed and compared: print/digital becomes a fixed binary reinscribing nature/technology.

Such comparisons have the effect of "disappearing" print and text work yet again. This transparency can have pernicious consequences. We have seen what happened in the past, what was lost when print was constructed as a transparent medium. Competing models of creativity, the labor of writing, and the role of economics once struggled for dominance—yet the understanding of print as *only* an invisible bearer of transcendent genius has a surprising duration. Indeed, the ideological longevity of print values is produced precisely *because* of print's now naturalized guise of neutrality. By bringing the production values of print to the foreground, however, and revealing their cultural construction in the eighteenth-century literary market, we can begin to confound the nature/technology boundary. Making print visible then allows us to see how the values constructed by the work of eighteenth-century print still circulate in a variety of new media.

Jay David Bolter and Richard Grusin's recent study of technological "remediation" supplies a theoretical model that can help us understand how a specific version of print values continues to affect media culture. They explain how this "complex kind of borrowing in which one medium is itself incorporated or represented in another medium" is the defining characteristic of all new media.[2] Despite their claim that such remediation dates at least back to the Renaissance, however, their discussion focuses mostly on late twentieth-century technologies and their cannibalization of one another, although they do reference painting and photography. In fact, the inclusion of painting and photography are emblematic of this study's privileging of the visual over the textual. While they do focus on the Web's remediation of print information, books are considered simply as one of the "more venerable media" and are not examined as a technology in and of themselves. Bolter and Grusin believe Web developers see print as "played out" and unthreatening and so reproduce it more respectfully.[3] By buying into this view of print as docile, neutralized, perhaps even dead, though, Bolter and Grusin inadvertently continue the project of "disappearing" it. In this, they are merely re-presenting what is a widespread belief, a common cultural blind spot. This construction of print as negligible actually allows it to reemerge as a natural force: print is being unmediated.

To call attention to this dynamic, we need to expand Bolter and Grusin's useful idea of remediation. What might be called "cultural remediation" is the process through which any new medium takes on and uses in its own interests a *specific discursive construction* of a communication technology. No act of this media "borrowing" or incorporation is innocent; rather, it is a means of calling on certain ideas affiliated with older media, ideas that are deployed in specific circumstances for specific aims and effects. For the purposes of this study, understanding cultural remediation allows us insight into the ways in which print's value of naturalized invisibility continues to regenerate. We can see the ways in which, because of its divorce from a specific techno-economic regime and the denial of its complex linguistic historicity, the culture of print discursively solidified in late eighteenth-century England is able to remediate itself in many diverse places, practices, and technologies today.

## THE WORK OF FILM

The first chapter of this study called on the work of film—specifically its practice of providing extensive "credits" to all involved, from directors, screenwriters, and actors to carpenters, caterers, and best boys—to stress the way technological dependence and economic necessity can be acknowledged as a fruitful basis for collaboration among a variety of talented individuals and organizations. Even in this realm, however, the concept of immaterial genius, borrowed from the late eighteenth-century print market and consolidated by the Romantics, can be discursively remediated in order to boost the medium's cultural credibility. For example, in his introduction to a collection of works from the "literary journal" (as it terms itself), *Zoetrope: All Story*, founding editor Francis Ford Coppola, in a rhetorical move much in sympathy with Robert Dodsley's, decries the mechanic aspects of the world in which he made his (quite good) living, in order to deploy the notion of a disembodied creativity encapsulated in the written, literary "story." This, he claims, is what *really* underlies film:

> [I]t is not possible for a good movie to exist without a good story. This is one reason I've always been puzzled that none of the powerful, well-funded major studios make the cultivation of writing their main focus. Even though many of them own publishing companies . . . , none of them that I know of devote serious resources to the cultivation of *literary* work—stories from contemporary writers who help us understand our lives and our times. . . . Hollywood studios want to jump over the literary part and get right to the screenplay, to commence budgeting and casting and everything necessary to justify some cash flow [emphasis in the original].[4]

In casting major studios as the bad guys, Coppola draws on a long history of obscuring the economic basis of the literary by assuming that writers, in the white hats of course, transcend the courser realm of "cash flow." He further positions himself as one affiliated with their goals: "So I decided a few years back that the wisest investment I could make with my own film company, American Zoetrope (which, though old and venerable, remains very small and has few financial resources), would be to take what cash we had and dedicate it to literary cultivation" (ix). In placing his own film company in sympathy with the economics of the literary realm—it too suffers from lack of funding—he promotes his own artistic merit by "investing in" the privileged cultural capital of the literary. If the mention of "cash" and "investment" threatens to sully his project by implying that he had much to gain through this experiment, he clarifies later that he is not just interested in "material" for production: "If we looked only for stories that would make good films, we would be excluding a giant group of writers whose work and ideas and emotions *must* be included to publish the best writing talent of the nation, the culture, the era, but whose particular stories might not be adaptable into movies" (x). Given the collaborative nature of film, and the layers of artistic, financial, and physical work that goes into its production, his emphasis on the intangibles of "idea," "emotion," and "best writing talent" is notable. Coppola is setting himself up as the "muse's midwife."

Interestingly, two pieces in Coppola's collection are not actually short stories at all, but nonfiction, "behind-the-scenes" accounts of the relationship between writing and movies. The first, by David Mamet, works to solidify the ideology promulgated by Coppola in striking ways, actually tapping directly into the familiar vein of anti–Grub Street rhetoric to promote his updated version of aesthetic disinterest. Mamet starts by comparing an increase in the number of screenplays being written to the stock market boom—with disastrous results predicted for both.[5] He goes so far as to suggest that "the end is at hand" for "film as a dramatic medium."[6] In listing the culprits responsible for this demise, Mamet supplies a list of trades and professions, in fact an entire class—"the butcher, the baker, and their progeny"—who have all, to his disgust, written a screenplay. He goes on to assert, in an impassioned diatribe, that these and others with links to more worldly realms of production are corrupting real art: "Certainly, these duffers, our friends the lawyers, doctors and bus drivers, are not writing drama. They write, as do our betters in Hollywood, for gain, transforming this broad land into one large new Grub Street. The urge of these acolytes is not dramatic, but mercantile—to traduce all personal history, to subvert all perception or insight into gain, or the hope of gain" (317). Mamet's frustration may be understandable—his specific object of criticism is the summer action-adventure blockbuster. What is interesting, however, is the way in which his artistic complaint locates its target in both trade and gain—conflating the two in an attempt to suggest an alternative that would, apparently, transcend both. In this scenario, with Hollywood as the "New Grub Street," Mamet assumes these writers *must* be—perhaps because of their lack of author-izing credentials (their amateur status or employment outside the artistic)—improperly motivated. By definition, he seems to imply, lawyers and butchers—here reduced to "duffers," or peddlers of cheap junk—cannot be dramatic artists. The "mercantile urge" underlying these professions taints their writing and categorizes it and them as outside "true" drama.

We might usefully compare Mamet's depiction of mercantile production—the very prolificacy of which threatens to falsely inflate the system and bring the entire edifice crashing down—to James Watson's description, cited in my introduction, of Mrs. Anderson's "illegible and uncorrect" work, produced because "nothing was study'd but gaining of

Money by printing Bibles at any Rate." And just as Watson reminds readers that her corrupt printing literally violates the "Sacred Word of GOD," Mamet uses similar language to clarify his production values. Referring to the false artists, he claims: "This work of writing the screenplay, then, is not an act of creation, but an obeisance—it is a ceremony, a prostration, in which the individual's feelings and thoughts are offered to the golden calf: 'There is no lie I will not tell, no secret I will not reveal, no treasure I will not debase, if you will just buy my screenplay'" (317).

His references to the golden calf and later to the "obeisance to the god of commerce" suggest the Western religio-moral discourse underpinning this construction of unholy conception.[7] The movie screen is the new press, producing illicit and unwholesome offspring; Hollywood is the new Grub Street, a place and set of practices antithetical to the holy intercourse between author and dramatic muse. Not surprisingly, Mamet's essay calls no attention to how its own publication in the *Zoetrope: All Story* journal helps mutually reinforce both Mamet's and Coppola's reputations as "artistic" producers, a move that garners them significant cultural capital.

A second description of the trials and travails of screenwriting included in the *Zoetrope* volume, Salman Rushdie's account of his foiled attempt to adapt *Midnight's Children* into a BBC television series, takes a markedly different approach. Rushdie, certainly among the most renowned of the "talent" Coppola includes in his volume, never denigrates, but is actually quite explicit about, the economic exigencies of moviemaking, the need to collaborate across spheres, the strain of physical and mental energy, the effects of cultural conditions, and the role played by corporate, national, and international politics in the would-be production of his work. He does not reduce (as Mamet might assume) all creativity to commercialism, but acknowledges the multitiered work of many hands, including those willing to supply financial backing. Musing on his ultimate failure to get his screenplay produced, he even alludes to what may be a tangible outcome of the printing of this essay: "But publication is always an act of optimism. . . . And a film brought into half-being may yet manage, somehow, to get itself born."[8] His title itself—"*Midnight's Children*: A Screenplay in Search of a Movie"— alludes to this goal. Rushdie, then, is much like Kirkman, who baldly expressed his desire that the money he garnered from the publication of *The Unlucky Citizen* would transform him into a lucky—that is, financially solvent—citizen. That Rushdie's expansive acknowledgment of the material appears in spite of Coppola's denial of that realm indicates that, despite the approximately 250-year reign of ideas dictated by John Smith's *Printer's Grammar*, the ideology of transparency does not maintain monolithic discursive control. The linguistic struggle continues.

## *Author-izing Hypertext*

This struggle can be glimpsed in the rhetoric surrounding the digital work of textual production as well. Notions of genius emerging from, though not intrinsic to, the print culture of the mid- to late eighteenth century are being recycled into popular views about electronic writing technologies—although the first wave of technophiles resolutely denied this remediation. A brief case study of the rhetoric surrounding early versions of hypertext supplies us with a useful example of this process. Transmitted, before the Web was widely used, through purchased disks run on special software, hypertext, despite its complex web of linkages, was a stand-alone product similar to books. Nonetheless, proponents claimed it virtually embodied the tenets of post-structuralism, positioning it as being all that print was not. Hypertext fiction, for example, was constructed recursively, with no one linear plot prioritized. In general, this new textual format was lauded as potentially collaborative, intertextual, multivocal, and decentered: the ultimate writerly text, freed from the constraints of print. Indeed, its advocates believed that its inception signaled a revolution in reading and writing as significant as the one triggered by Gutenberg's press; Ted Nelson, who coined the term *hypertext* in the 1960s, claimed it would bring about a "rebirth of literacy."[9] The flexible and interactive nature of the hypertext environment was thought to be incompatible with the stability necessary to support the regime of proprietary authorship and the copyright laws depending on that construction. As Jay David Bolter detailed: "As long as the printed book remains the primary medium of literature, traditional views of the author as authority . . . will remain convincing for most readers. The electronic medium, however, threatens to bring down the whole edifice at once. . . . [I]t denies the fixity of the text, and it questions the authority of the author."[10] Because it was interactive and nonlinear, allowing readers to decide which of the many links they would pursue, hypertext was thought to be able to strip the Author of his vestments of solitary genius and originality, concepts that worked to exclude many, like the print workers I discuss, from inclusion in the category of creativity.

We have seen, however, that singular "authorship" was one particular way of understanding the production of print, put forth by parties with vested interests in the deployment of that idea—it was *not* a necessary or inevitable feature of books. Since it is a cultural, rather than technological, attribute, then, there is nothing certain about its demise in the new media. Because print has so long been invisible, though, no one questions what is at stake when print—and print values—are remediated into electronic writing. Indeed, if it is true that the age of print is coming to a close, then we might expect a resurgence of its values, a backlash against what is perceived as the anarchical nature of the electronic medium. Thus we might expect the most popular forms of electronic text to closely resemble print, and those who produce hypertext may look suspiciously like late eighteenth-century authors of books.

Indeed, despite disclaimers to the contrary, there is evidence that hypertext fiction was often viewed, both inside and outside the academy, as "new and improved" works of original genius—by an author who has now enlarged his skills to include programming. *Discover* magazine, for example, dubbed hypertext writers "half hackers, half Hemingways."[11] A pamphlet publicizing Eastgate System's Storyspace, an early program designed for writing and reading hypertext fiction, contained endorsements by users also deploying the language of the solitary genius. One claimed that this system "fulfills the dreams of hypertext visionaries," while another asserted that "I was so impressed that I immediately severed all social ties, opting instead to spend the ensuing months working feverishly on my Great American Hypertext." The same pamphlet also advertised hypertext fiction "signed by the author," the ultimate gesture guaranteeing the unmediated and authentic personality adhering in the work. The formations of canons of greatness were in evidence as well: another Eastgate pamphlet marketed Michael Joyce's *Afternoon, a Story*, with a *New York Times* blurb that situated it at the head of a patrilinear line of descent of other author-ized texts, calling *Afternoon* "the granddaddy of hypertext fiction . . . essential to understanding this new art form." Further, as the first generation of hypertext fiction began to receive notice in scholarly journals, it did so only in terms of the old standards of authorship. One essay, for example, provided a recipe for "determining literariness in interactive fiction," while another bemoaned the fact that "interactive fiction still awaits a major high-culture advocate whose software product wins coverage in the *New York Times Book Review* . . . , [a] literary harbinger, with impeccable credentials and startling creative ability. . . , [a] Whitman figure."[12] Rhetoric such as this relies on conventional notions of authorship and the literary work of art as transcending the bounds of its medium. While calling attention to the new technology as part of the novelty of this work, the discourse of hypertext downplayed its own economic positioning as a product available only to an elite group of computer users. In fact, by privileging its *literary* features—coded, as references to Hemingway, Whitman, and "granddaddies" reveal, as *masculine*—it ignored its reliance on the ultimate ground of digital production, the motherboard. Paradoxically, invisible technology becomes the raw material of nature. Such discourse thus reinscribes the old binaries of (male) culture versus (female) nature.

As the recent dot-com bubble graphically illustrated, however, despite—or maybe because of—this erasure, it is indeed the material realm of economics that fuels our new textual machines. And interestingly, as the popularity of the Internet increased the consumption of digital texts in a seemingly new literary economy, publishers and programmers alike borrowed the intellectual property regime linked to the late eighteenth-century print market to restrict access to and increase their dividends from electronic texts and other electronic forms of information. Those arguing legally for corporate programming interests, for example, explicitly use the tenets of Romantic authorship to argue for tighter copyright restrictions, actually positing programs as "silicon epics" and programmers as "binary bards."[13] Ironically, in calling up this singular notion of authorship, they effectively erase the actual collaborative activity that results in most new computer technology. Nonetheless, their recourse to this "natural" view of authorship supplies a moral aspect to their efforts. For example, the Clinton administration's policy document on the future of the "electronic superhighway," *The National Information*

*Infrastructure: Agenda for Action* insured that the administration would "investigate how to strengthen domestic copyright laws and international intellectual property treaties to *prevent piracy* and to *protect the integrity* of intellectual property [my emphasis]."[14] This piracy is not, of course, like Richardson's, the literal theft of sheets (or bytes). Rather, this promotion of the regulated circulation of electronic texts reveals how certain cultural constructions of authorship, print fixity, and the moral trade in texts are used to protect financial interests. "Integrity," unity, and stability become signifiers that obscure while strengthening such motivations.

Our revised understanding of the work of print in seventeenth- and early eighteenth-century England also helps us see how a lingering "print effect" distilled from a later period still governs versions of both the ethical and efficacious circulation of textual knowledge. Certainly, there are forces working within our own academic institutions to make the Web seem more like a book, complete with copyright and authentic authors. Students are taught "neutral" research techniques that ask them to validate the information they access in reference to its authorial provenance, institutional affiliations, use of print conventions, and so forth. "Knowledge" is understood to be produced "naturally" through these limitations and regulations; the print-based nature of these is seldom acknowledged—except perhaps implicitly in nostalgic lamentations on the superiority of books and dire warnings about their extinction. Print values also structure the very file system that underlies most of our computers. This method of information storage and retrieval is taxonomy with a vengeance, another holdover from print culture's privileging of linear models of categorization, perhaps even its fetishism of the alphabetic. Even the most popular search engines are adopting this way of sorting what seems otherwise to be an overwhelming chaos. Because of the invisible nature of the (print) technology it is grounded in, however, the human and political contexts for such structures are erased, leading us away from the challenging questions: Who designs the topics that organize our information universe? What hierarchies do they support? In this context, the insistence that print—and therefore print values—is obsolete is at best naive, at worst an ideological service that masks the remediation of print, allowing us to deny its effects both at home and at its neocolonial outposts.

## *Disappearing the Digital*

The case studies outlined in each of the previous chapters have illustrated how the construction of print as an invisible, intangible medium worthy of encapsulating the intellectual production of the great required that the physical work and financial investment involved in its making be categorized as unworthy of polite consideration. Certainly, there is much in our current regime of textual production to render *its* material basis visible. For many users, computers are still obviously and obtusely *there*. The technology makes itself visible with each Windows error message and crashed hard drive, with accidentally deleted files and jammed printers. Stock market reports gleefully herald (or mourn) the economic health of the latest dot-com, and some workers—the Bill Gateses and Steve Jobses—are visible celebrities. The technology's link to sexualized bodies receives anxious attention in local news reports on the latest Internet pornography or child-molester-in-chat-room scandal. Schools rush to acquire the latest equipment—or sometimes even the most basic—believing that only the digital path leads to enlightenment. Digital technology is most visible, of course, to those who are excluded from its magical realm and see it as a symbol of yet one more cultural promise denied them. Clearly, the computer is already a mythological creature— but it is still one that walks among us.

The very ubiquity of computers, however, is leading to their disappearance. This is not an inevitable process, but a common one: Bolter and Grusin report that "the logic of transparent immediacy," the illusion that the user "stands in an immediate relationship to the contents of that medium," is one strategically deployed as a promotional tool by each new form of media.[15] Invisibility might be seen, then, as a form of ideological authorization that downplays the mechanic in order to signify authenticity. The extent to which this is already happening within mainstream representations of the digital is highlighted by a recent *New Yorker* letter to the editor, responding to an article about the writing process, which claims, "We now think on screen. . . . [T]he mind and the page are no longer such separate identities."[16] Such statements erase significant distinctions and work to "disappear" the tools that construct the boundary between embodied mind and created media, between nebulous thought and its concrete form on the page.

Similarly, the icons that visually structure our screen space are losing their opacity. Indeed, this function was part of their very conception: Grusin and Bolter note that "[b]y introducing graphical objects into the representation scheme, designers believed they were making the interfaces 'transparent' and therefore more 'natural.'... In fact, the graphical interface referred not only to culturally familiar objects, but specifically to prior media, such as painting, typewriting, and handwriting."[17] We may also note that it is the cultural remediation of the earlier media's *representation* of themselves as "non-media"—mere vehicles for pure expression—that allows this interface to do its current cultural work of immediacy so successfully. Certainly, Graphical User Interfaces, or GUIs, are credited with the computer's widespread appeal as they make new applications fairly simple and convenient to use. Such claims, however, are part of the ideology of the new regime, a statement of empirical cause-and-effect that disguises the ways in which technologies must rhetorically seduce users. This "spell of immediacy" also masks mechanic structures—and their effects. The Windows desktop, for example, mimicking a literal desktop replete with files and a trash can, valorizes the corporate world.[18] Further, immediacy conceals the operations behind our point-and-click world that are considered unnecessary for the average user. For example, most students and many of their professors can surf the Web quite well without ever comprehending that what they are actually viewing are encoded pieces of binary information. With "WYSI-WYG" (what-you-see-is-what-you-get) editors, we can even make our own Web sites without the slightest knowledge of HTML, much less Java, the languages laying the foundations of these pages. Many frequent Web readers have no idea where the information they access is stored or how it is retrieved. This limits, in the long run, what users can do with computers, but, more importantly, it also increases what can be done *to* them. The fact that many people have been and may still be unaware of the ways in which computer "cookies" have been used to gather information about them perhaps best exemplifies this point. Such erasure of the mechanical also works to conceal economic issues such as information ownership, the source of information, and its circulation as part of the transnational movement of capital.

The current dominance of Microsoft's infamous Windows interface only speeds up this process of naturalization. Because users are able to manipulate text so easily, move it between applications, send it to friends or colleagues, or publish it on the Web without (it seems) the interference of a third party, their false sense of control increases. This is especially true as the forms of writing become seemingly less and less tangible, as our texts spill almost effortlessly out of machines about which we understand little and shoot magically across the seemingly ethereal realm of cyberspace. Communication seems—and is made to seem—more divorced than ever from the physical hand writing or working. Machine becomes Web becomes text becomes brain becomes Truth. The nuts and bolts and plastic of the machine on your desk have disappeared, along with its connection with real human bodies. Who made it? Where? Erased from this picture are the modern-day equivalents to John Dunton or Joseph Moxon's Master Printer, those who create software, whom we might more fruitfully consider our collaborators. These workers and their products, after all, allow us to write—we do not make text ourselves. We are always already constrained by the technology *as it is*—by invisible restrictions such as screen shape, keyboard setup, Web editors, or even HTML code, server size, capabilities, and so on. This constraint is *not* inevitable or predetermined: we do possess agency (albeit limited) to work *with* rather than *through* it—but only if it is visible. To reenvision the work of writing is to see it as a collaboration between language and technology—between the words in our heads and the codes, keyboards, and screens that allow us to make pages. This is, of course, cyborg writing: the fruitful coupling of human and machine. If we persist instead in envisioning ourselves working *through* rather than *with* technology, then we merely perpetuate a new version of an old image: dead print on a screen, eagerly awaiting a transcendent author's touch to begin to glow.

More at risk of being forgotten, however, are those, like mercuries and hawkers, at the very bottom of the industrial ladder: those Haraway terms the "women in the integrated circuit." These labels refer not only to those women—usually from so-called developing countries—who labor for computer companies, piecing together circuitry under backbreaking conditions for minimum wages, but to all workers who are "integrat[ed]/exploit[ed] into a world system of production/reproduction and communication called the informatics of domination."[19] Smith's manual presented a book that was a commodity alienated from the worker's body.

Within our global economy, the privileged commodity is now disembodied information itself. Within this economy, Haraway suggests, physical labor "is being redefined as both literally female and feminized, whether performed by men or women. To be feminized means to be extremely vulnerable; able to be disassembled, reassembled, exploited as a reserve labor force; seen less as workers than as servers; . . . leading an existence that always borders on being obscene, out of place, and reducible to sex" (208). In the gendered dystopia Haraway describes, a few white men run companies while women run households and support families, trying to stave off the "feminization of poverty" (209). In other words, the potent mix of gender, work, technology, and text (here read as information), almost three hundred years after Anne Dodd made her pleas from prison, still forms a complex discursive terrain. The erased sign supporting the interests in new forms of text making and text moving is that representing the laboring bodies of women.

## THE MATRIX: RE-EMBODIED TEXT WORK

Analyzing the text work of print shows that alternatives to this pernicious transparency of the media have existed and can still exist. This study has shown that many of the characteristics thought to be inherent to print emerged through discursive struggle, a series of rhetorical moves made by printers, booksellers, and writers, always bound up with a cultural semiotics that was both outside and an intrinsic part of their arguments. Choices were made that did have ideological effects—but none of the choices, and therefore none of the effects, were inevitable. The ideologies became naturalized, however, and therefore very difficult to change, when their link to *material practices* of technology disappeared. By denaturalizing the book, we can reverse this process. By understanding the book's cultural remediation in today's communication technologies, we can gain insight into many of the issues that now challenge us, which I have only briefly suggested here: intellectual property, privacy, alphabetic versus iconic literacies, the disciplinary and hierarchical categorization of knowledge, and the geographic sources and distribution networks of information and power. These all have long, fraught historical relationships to the technologies, economies, and cultural practices that supported and were supported by them.

A restructuring of knowledge itself is required to fully address these issues, for the disciplines themselves are "disappeared" by-products of print. To re-embody and make visible our own institutions requires a radical interdisciplinarity. Not only must connections between disciplines be forged (and be fully supported), but the ramifications of the disciplinary nature of information production must continue to be explored and acknowledged. Lines must be blurred not only within the humanities (as in the "easy" interdisciplinarity of cultural studies) but between the more rigidly distinct categories of knowledge, such as the humanities and science.[20] This realignment also requires a *trans*disciplinarity—that is, partnerships between education and institutions beyond the ivory tower: government, nongovernmental organizations, even, or perhaps especially, the corporate sector.[21] Finally, making knowledge and the technologies it is based in visible again requires that we risk transhistoricism. To be sure, learning about the Internet from a seventeenth-century printer's manual clearly erases all sorts of important distinctions, but it does, at the same time, recover many important and vitally useful similarities. We must rethink what it means to read, write, and teach in our digital age, but only if we first acknowledge the technological regimes and cultural conditions that have allowed those activities to become such a natural and unquestioned part of our cultural landscape. This critical self-consciousness is imperative: the new technologies will soon disappear.

The new affiliations we need to forge may best be represented by a new form of academic cyborg, the Matrix. The Matrix links bodies and economies, histories and geographies, technologies and labor, drawing from them all, but, by keeping each distinct and visible, highlights their differences. The Matrix is a multimedia machine, an operating system designed to produce text work: texts that reveal, indeed revel in, their own construction and the grounds of their production. Forms of Matrix knowledge are by necessity collective and therefore multiple and heterogeneous. The very complexity of this web disrupts the "integrated circuit" of smooth teleologies that resist alternatives and cast out the unsavory. Like Haraway's cyborg, the Matrix "insist[s] on noise and advocate[s] pollution, rejoicing in the illegitimate fusions of animal and machine."[22] Noise interferes with the flow of information, redirects power, forces the dominant discourse to recognize the glitches in its self-perpetuating circuitry.

This study of early information technologies, while recognizing the cultural specificity of the seventeenth- and eighteenth-century London print trade, can thus be seen as noise in our own system. Revealing the discursive work behind the "natural" separation of mind and body, text and machine, shows that the merger of body with technology is not a vision limited to new millennial thinking, but a construct with a significant past. By presenting this fusion as a valid alternative, I have shown that there is nothing inevitable about an ideology that posits a few men as superior (because disinterested and disembodied) owners and controllers of information and relegates women/workers to invisibility. If we realize that the rise of the author and the transparency of print was almost accidental, at best contingent, and never, even in its own time, the only way to understand the production of discourse, we can more usefully and productively create alternatives in our own time.

# $\mathcal{N}$OTES

<br>

## *I. INTRODUCTION: PRINTING PRODUCTION VALUES*

1. James Watson, *The History of the Art of Printing*, ed. D. F. Foxon (1713; reprint, London: Gregg Press, 1965), 3–4, hereafter *History*. Further citations are noted parenthetically.

2. Quoted in David McKitterick, *Print, Manuscript and the Search for Order, 1450–1830* (Cambridge: Cambridge University Press, 2003), 1. McKitterick claims these words, with which Carter opened his 1968 Lyell lectures, "have come to haunt a generation born since" (1).

3. N. Katherine Hayles, *Writing Machines* (Cambridge, MA: MIT Press, 2002), 107.

4. See Michel Foucault, "What Is an Author?" in *Textual Strategies*, ed. Josué Harari (Ithaca, NY: Cornell University Press, 1979), 118.

5. Richard A. Lanham, *The Electronic Word* (Chicago: University of Chicago Press, 1993), 4.

6. Credit must go to the manuscript editor at the University of Washington Press, Jane Lichty, for pointing out to me that there are exceptions to this rule. In mainstream trade publishing, for example, art credit is usually given to cover designers, perhaps because their work does not impinge on, but only complements, an author's prowess. The copyright owner, of course—usually a large multinational corporation—is always mentioned. Increasingly, books include information on the type used and its history, but individual workers are rarely referenced.

Magazines and newspapers, an amalgam of word and image, and more blatantly commercial than books, provide a more obvious example of credit sharing within the print media. Mastheads (which include advertising directors in addition to editors), like film credits, mark the more explicitly collaborative nature of their production. This is true of many academic journals as well, which, though not so explicitly graphic in form, are likewise not singularly authored.

7. Lanham, *Electronic Word*, 4.

8. I investigate licensing, sedition, and the production of power in the print trade in chapter 4.

9. Alvin Kernan, *Samuel Johnson and the Impact of Print* (Princeton, NJ: Princeton University Press, 1987), 48.

10. I am indebted to John Feather, *A History of British Publishing* (London: Croom Helm, 1988), which charts in detail this period of tremendous growth and change.

11. Michel Foucault, "Nietzsche, Genealogy, History," in *Language, Counter-Memory, Practice: Selected Essays and Interviews*, ed. Donald Bouchard (Ithaca, NY: Cornell University Press, 1977), 145.

12. My understanding of the processes through which social constructions become dominant, accruing enough "linguistic capital" to erase the signs of their previously embattled status, is indebted in part to Paula Treichler, who traces this process in the very different twentieth-century American context of shifting definitions of childbirth. See "Feminism, Medicine, and the Meaning of Childbirth," in *Body/Politics: Women and the Discourses of Science*, ed. Mary Jacobus, Evelyn Fox Keller, and Sally Shuttleworth (New York: Routledge, 1990), esp. 116–18.

13. Pierre Bourdieu, *The Field of Cultural Production*, ed. Randal Johnson (New York: Columbia University Press, 1993), 34.

14. Clifford Siskin, *The Work of Writing: Literature and Social Change in Britain, 1700–1830* (Baltimore: Johns Hopkins University Press, 1998), 130.

15. Hayles, *Writing Machines*, 25.

16. N. Katherine Hayles, *How We Became Posthuman: Virtual Bodies in Cybernetics, Literature, and Informatics* (Chicago: University of Chicago Press, 1999), 8.

17. Ibid., 8–9.

18. Instability is a characteristic of texts even in a strict bibliographical sense, as McKitterick relates in his discussion of the introduction of error in print. See *Print, Manuscript*, 97–138.

19. That the reality of Anderson's position may have been different can be read between the lines of Watson's text. Despite the pariah status he assigns her, she evidently possessed enough power to have a warrant taken out against Watson himself to shut down his printing. And rather than Anderson's dying destitute and alone, as one might expect this narrative to conclude, Watson has to admit that she enjoyed her grant for over forty years and "[lately] was become rich and old" (19).

20. In his introduction to *Printing and Parenting in Early Modern England* (Burlington, VT: Ashgate Press, 2004), editor Douglas A. Brooks provides an overview of the scholarship on this history. Mark Rose focuses on the problematic fit between paternity and the market in "Copyright and Its Metaphors," *UCLA Law Review* 50 (2002): 1–16.

21. Paula McDowell, *The Women of Grub Street: Press, Politics, and Gender in the London Literary Marketplace, 1678–1730* (Oxford: Oxford University Press, 1998), 16.

22. Throughout much of my study, I refer to "writers *and* print workers" as if they were two groups. Such a linguistic construction reflects the values of author-centric literary studies and, when applied to this time in history before the modern author was consolidated as such, is anachronistic. In the view of those I write about, the writer was merely one of many workers who made up the print trade, a worker whose contribution to a text was not seen as necessarily categorically different from their own. However, both for the sake of clarity (to remind readers that writers were part of the group "workers") and to stress the embattled nature of the print trade's self-representations (often depicted as worker *versus* writer), I am strategically employing this usage.

23. Also erased in this regime is the role of readers. Discussing medieval marginalia, Evelyn B. Tribble explains that "modern editions which omit such accompanying matter in effect rewrite the text by effacing evidence of its collaborative nature." See *Margins and Marginalia: The Printed Page in Early Modern England* (Charlottesville: University Press of Virginia, 1993), 1.

24. See Kernan, *Samuel Johnson and the Impact of Print*, esp. 49–50. See also Elizabeth Eisenstein, *The Printing Press as an Agent of Change* (Cambridge: Cambridge University Press, 1979), esp. 70–159; and Walter Ong, *Orality and Literacy: The Technologizing of the Word* (New York: Routledge, 1982), esp. 117–38.

25. Kernan, *Samuel Johnson and the Impact of Print*, 51.

26. Jonathan Rose, "SHARP Notes: Getting Started in Book History," *Counter* 2 (Spring 1995): 2. See also John Feather, "The Book in History and the History of the Book," *Journal of Library History* 21 (1986): 12–26. Feather's essay is a defining text for this field, as is Robert Darnton's "What Is the History of the Book?" in *Books and Society in History*, ed. Kenneth Carpenter (New York: R. R. Bowker, 1983).

27. James Raven, "New Reading Histories, Print Culture and the Identification of Change: The Case of Eighteenth-Century England," *Social History* 23 (October 1998): 273.

28. We might point to Pat Rogers as the starting point of this trend. His *Grub Street: Studies in a Subculture* (London: Methuen, 1972), despite its usefulness and specificity in laying out the geographic reality behind the metaphoric "Grub Street," is explicit in its purpose: to help readers better understand Augustan satire in general and Pope's verse in particular.

29. See Adrian Johns, *The Nature of the Book: Print and Knowledge in the Making* (Chicago: University of Chicago Press, 1998). Interestingly, his work

emerges from the history of science rather than literary studies, which allows him to bypass some prejudices while installing others. It thus points to the necessity of interdisciplinary and multidisciplinary work in this area, as difficult as that may be to accomplish.

30. McDowell, *Women of Grub Street*, 12.

31. Other exemplary studies include Jeffrey Masten, "Pressing Subjects; or, The Secret Lives of Shakespeare's Compositors," in *Language Machines: Technologies of Literary and Cultural Production*, ed. Jeffrey Masten, Peter Stallybrass, and Nancy J. Vickers (New York: Routledge, 1997); Jonathan Goldberg, *Writing Matter: From the Hands of the English Renaissance* (Stanford, CA: Stanford University Press, 1990); and Michael Warner, *The Letters of the Republic: Publication and the Public Sphere in Eighteenth-Century America* (Cambridge, MA: Harvard University Press, 1990).

32. In groundbreaking work, Martha Woodmansee elegantly teases out the implications of authors being understood as the sole creators of unique literary and artistic "works," the originality of which warrants their protection under laws of intellectual property known as "copyright" and "authors' rights." See *The Author, Art and the Market: Rereading the History of Aesthetics* (New York: Columbia University Press, 1994), esp. 35–55; and "On the Author Effect: Recovering Collectivity," in *The Construction of Authorship: Textual Appropriation in Law and Literature*, ed. Martha Woodmansee and Peter Jaszi (Durham, NC: Duke University Press, 1993). Mark Rose is responsible for narrowing the scope of Woodmansee's work, narrating the rise of the author as an eighteenth-century English legal construction in his useful and influential *Authors and Owners: The Invention of Copyright* (Cambridge, MA: Harvard University Press, 1993). He analyzes specific court cases that resulted in an abstract understanding of an author's "work," detailing a progression from the limited 1710 Statute of Anne, England's first copyright law, which was based on a material understanding of rights to copy, to the 1774 *Donaldson v. Becket*, which gave credence to the more abstract notion of an author's natural right to his property.

33. Lanham, *Electronic Word*, 5.

34. Ibid.

35. Shoshana Zuboff, *In the Age of the Smart Machine: The Future of Work and Power* (New York: Basic Books, 1988).

36. Hayles, *Writing Machines*, 19.

37. The dating of Moxon's work reminds us that the mechanics of the print process are not always as unified as the final product suggests. The title page of *Mechanick Exercises on the Whole Art of Printing* bears the date of 1683. However, in their edition, Herbert Davis and Harry Carter provide evidence that only

half the work was published at this time, with the second half issued a year later, bound with the earlier sections and original title page. Thus, perhaps in the interest of having his project appear coherent and complete, Moxon himself elides the time-dependent work of print. To highlight this aspect, however, I have preserved the two-year dating.

## 2. *Printers' Manuals and the Bodies of Type*

1. At the time of publication, Moxon was attempting to become the letter founder for the press at Oxford University, which was engaged in a dispute with the Stationers' Company over printing privileges. This, most likely, is why he argues in his preface that printing came to England through Frederick Corseles in Oxford, not through Caxton in London, as was commonly believed. See Joseph Moxon, *Mechanick Exercises on the Whole Art of Printing*, ed. Herbert Davis and Harry Carter (1683–84; reprint, New York: Dover Publications, 1958), xlix-li, hereafter *ME*. Further citations are parenthetical.

2. Feather, "Book in History," 13.

3. Eisenstein, *Printing Press*, xv. See also Adrian Johns's critique, *Nature of the Book*, 18–20.

4. Warner, *Letters*, 5.

5. Ibid., 6.

6. See, e.g., Alvin Kernan's description of Samuel Johnson as a product of print logic in *Samuel Johnson and the Impact of Print*.

7. See Jay David Bolter, *Writing Space: The Computer, Hypertext, and the History of Writing* (Hillsdale, NJ: Lawrence Erlbaum Associates, 1991); George Landow, *Hypertext: The Convergence of Contemporary Critical Theory and Technology* (Baltimore: Johns Hopkins University Press, 1992); and Lanham, *Electronic Word*.

8. Neil Postman, *Technopoly: The Surrender of Culture to Technology* (New York: Random House, 1992), 7.

9. For the importance of rhetoric in assessing Renaissance print culture, see Wendy Wall, *The Imprint of Gender: Authorship and Publication in the English Rennaissance* (Ithaca, NY: Cornell University Press, 1993), 20–21. For the various strategies used in late seventeenth-century England to legitimate print and to authorize the knowledge it disseminated, see Johns, *Nature of the Book*, 138–50.

10. Philip Gaskell, Giles Barber, and Georgina Warrilow, "An Annotated List of Printers' Manuals to 1850," *Journal of the Printing Historical Society* 4 (1968): 13. Herbert Davis and Harry Carter explain that Moxon's volume "was appropriated by compilers of technical encyclopedias and printers' grammars;

so that parts of Moxon, disguised under other names, remained a standard textbook until the great bulk of printing ceased to be a 'handy-work'" (*ME*, vii). For more on the influence of Moxon and Smith, see also Herbert Davis, "Catalogue of an Exhibition of British and American Printers' Manuals at Dartmouth College," *Printing and Graphic Arts* 5 (1957): 1–33; and E. C. Bigmore and C. W. H. Wyman, *A Bibliography of Printing* (London: Bernard Quaritch, 1884).

Moxon's and Smith's manuals can be usefully compared to similar texts written in this period, which also reveal a self-consciousness about printing. These include James Watson's *The History of the Art of Printing* (Edinburgh, 1713); Samuel Palmer's *A General History of Printing* (London, 1732); Conyer Middleton's *A Dissertation Concerning the Origin of Printing in England* (Cambridge, 1735); Joseph Ames's *Typographical Antiquities* (London, 1749); and Philip Luckombe's *History and Art of Printing* (1771), as well as shorter pieces in encyclopedias and dictionaries of the trades or sciences. See also McKitterick, *Print, Manuscript*, 166–86. Moxon's and Smith's manuals, however, are still the most frequently quoted today and exist in recent reprints.

11. Eisenstein, *Printing Press*, 383. See also *ME*, li.

12. See Eisenstein, *Printing Press*, 553–63.

13. For a more detailed description of these and other factors leading to a loss of guild power in this period, see Peter Earle, *The Making of the English Middle Class: Business, Society and Family Life in London, 1660–1730* (Berkeley: University of California Press, 1989), 250–68.

14. For a detailed history of the print trades in this period, see Feather, *A History of British Publishing*, esp. 43–63.

15. Johns discusses the political and symbolic role of Stationers' Hall and the Stationers' Register in preserving their power in *Nature of the Book*, 187–248.

16. See *ME*, xxvii-xxviii, 370.

17. See Earle, *English Middle Class*, 250–68. At the time *Mechanick Exercises* was published, the Licensing Act was in abeyance (it lapsed in 1679 and was not renewed until 1685), but Moxon, as well as many other unofficial printers, published books before this time.

18. We might compare his explicitness with a later London printer's reserve. Describing the fate of Samuel Palmer's *General History of Printing*—announced in 1729 as a monthly series but not completed as planned—George Psalmanazar relates, "He designed to have added a second part, relating to the practical art, which was more suited to his genius . . . but this . . . met with such early and strenuous opposition from the respective bodies of letterfounders, printers, and bookbinders, under an ill-grounded apprehension that the discovery of the mystery of these arts, especially the two first, would render them cheap and

contemptible . . . that he was forced to set it aside." See Psalmanazar, *Memoirs* (1764), 284–85.

19. Moxon's expertise in this scientific realm was cemented when he became hydrographer to the king in 1662. Moxon's two occupations were interdependent, however. Most of the books he sold, whether he served as writer or printer, were popularizations of science—his authored textbook *A Tutor to Astronomie and Geography* (London, 1659) went through five editions in forty years. See *ME*, xxii-xxv, xxxi; and Bigmore and Wyman, *Bibliography*, 56–63. Books like these created a market for the sale of his scientific tools by educating amateurs. Eisenstein explains this linkage: "[T]he output of mathematical-instruments, atlases, globes and 'theatres of machines' should also be related to the new possibility of profiting from disclosing instead of withholding the tricks of the various trades" (*Printing Press*, 557).

20. Eisenstein, *Printing Press*, 558.

21. For more on Moxon's connections to society members, see Johns, *Nature of the Book*, 80–81.

22. *The Advice of W. P. to Mr. Samuel Hartlib for the Advancement of Some Particular Parts of Learning* (1648). See Walter E. Houghton, Jr., "The History of Trades: Its Relation to Seventeenth Century Thought: As Seen in Bacon, Petty, Evelyn, and Boyle," *Journal of the History of Ideas* 2 (1941): 43–44.

23. See Houghton, "History of Trades," 56.

24. See ibid., 44–45.

25. For example, Gaskell, Barber, and Warrilow describe texts such as Moxon's as "practical manuals intended for professional letterpress printers" ("Annotated List," 11). H. Davis believes that Moxon "continued to exert his influence for a couple of centuries through the admirable instruction he had provided for master printers and their workmen" ("Catalogue," 22). Calhoun Winton also significantly notes that "a literate person . . . with a copy of Moxon's *Mechanick Exercises* (1683) in hand could teach himself or herself the trade, from beginning to end" (quoted in Eisenstein, "Printing Press," 154). My point is not that one could not do such, but that it is likely that the average reader of Moxon's text would not.

26. In fact, research on the spread of early modern technical knowledge suggests that practical changes were rarely instigated by printed texts. See Peter Mathias, "Who Unbound Prometheus? Science and Technical Change, 1600–1800," in *Science and Society*, ed. Peter Mathias (Cambridge: Cambridge University Press, 1972), 54–80; and Carlo Cipolla, *Before the Industrial Revolution: European Society and Economy, 1000–1700* (New York: W.W. Norton, 1976). Eisenstein discusses the difficulty of determining audiences of how-to manuals. See *Printing Press*, 64–65, 554–55.

27. Joseph Moxon, *Mechanick Exercises, or The Doctrine of Handy-Works* (1703; reprint, New York: Early American Industries Association, 1979), n.p.

28. McKitterick, *Print, Manuscript*, 171.

29. Moxon, *Handy-Works*, n.p.

30. Quoted in Houghton, "History of Trades," 54.

31. Quoted in ibid., 50.

32. Of course, such distinctions were not new to this period. See, e.g., Patricia Parker, "Rude Mechanicals," in *Subject and Object in Renaissance Culture*, ed. Margreta de Grazia, Maureen Quilligan, and Peter Stallybrass (Cambridge: Cambridge University Press, 1996), 43–82.

33. Philip Ayres, *Vox Clamantis, or An Essay for the Honour, Happiness and Prosperity of the English Society . . . By P. A., Gent* [1684], 109.

34. Moxon, *Handy-Works*, n.p.

35. Nancy Armstrong and Leonard Tennenhouse, linking the writing of Restoration intellectuals with the rise of the middle class, similarly note that Thomas Sprat's *History of the Royal Society* "subordinates those who work with their hands to those who think and write" (*The Imaginary Puritan: Literature, Intellectual Labor, and the Origins of Personal Life* [Berkeley: University of California Press, 1992], 97). However, while their study references "print culture" and the role of the press in creating a public sphere, it mostly deals with "writing" in its general, textual sense, not specifically print as a unique form of information transmission.

36. Moxon, *Handy-Works*, n.p.

37. Johns, for example, notes the way in which Moxon links recent innovations in the press to Tycho Brahe, "the most powerful modern icon of the mathematical sciences" (*Nature of the Book*, 85).

38. That this is still a primary regime is indicated by the popularity of magazines such as *Popular Mechanics*, how-to books of almost infinite variety (enough to warrant their own *New York Times* best-seller list), industry training manuals, and the takeover of vocational education by community colleges. An ideology of a new sort, however, exists simultaneously as many of these forms are replaced by video equivalents (witness complete cable stations devoted to cooking, homemaking, construction projects, or gardening), which replace typography with image, the reading eye with the watching one. How this may morph again as software or Web-based manuals become prominent is yet to be seen.

39. See Thomas Laqueur, *Making Sex: Body and Gender from the Greeks to Freud* (Cambridge, MA: Harvard University Press, 1990), esp. 134–48.

40. This hierarchy is a microcosm of the larger political structure, described by Hobbes in his 1751 *Leviathan* as a giant artificial man made up of individuals who

are the "atoms" of the body politic. The Sovereign, like the Master Printer, rules the social body. A full political reading of Moxon is outside my purview here, but I want to point out that he does, by implication, stress the print shop's position in a larger cultural context. This comment also may reflect Moxon's insecurities about his own position as both Royal Society "intellect" and embodied printer-worker. He reminds his readers that a master printer, such as himself, is different: as soul, he transcends "ignoble" mechanics. At the same time, however, it is clear from Moxon's text that the two aspects, soul and body, cannot exist without each other.

41. Warren Chappel, *A Short History of the Printed Word* (Boston: Nonpareil Books, 1980), 46.

42. D. F. McKenzie discusses the problem with the term *accidental* and the importance of recovering accidentals as textually significant. He is interested, however, in the way these make up a book's "organic form" and so reveal an author's more nuanced intentions. See D. F. McKenzie, *Bibliography and the Sociology of Texts: The Panizzi Lectures, 1985* (London: British Library, 1986), esp. 83–84. I am not trying to pinpoint Moxon's intentions but instead insist that accidentals be taken as part of the typographic sign system that forms the interface between text and reader and therefore cannot help but affect reception. A text is understood to a great extent through its typography, and screening out certain elements of it imposes an anachronistic reading style.

43. I discuss below the role of the compositor in the construction of print meaning.

44. Donna Haraway, "A Manifesto for Cyborgs: Science, Technology and Social Feminism in the 1980s," reprinted in *Feminism/Postmodernism*, ed. Linda J. Nicholson (New York: Routledge, 1990), 191.

45. Robert Darnton discusses a literal example of this: an inky fingerprint left behind by "Bonnemain," one of the printers of the *Encyclopdie*. See *The Business of Enlightenment: A Publishing History of the Encyclopdie, 1775–1800* (Cambridge, MA: Harvard University Press, 1979), 228–30. He also asserts that "in the era of the handmade book there existed a typographical consciousness that disappeared sometime after the advent of automatic typesetting and printing. . . . Every page, every line has its individuality. Each character bears the imprint of a gesture made by someone like Bonnemain" (236). This "typographical consciousness" is one, I have shown, shared by Moxon; that it disappeared in England well before the advent of automated printing I show below.

46. I discuss the changing role of booksellers and the history of copyright in more detail in chapter 3.

47. John Smith, *The Printer's Grammar*, ed. D. F. Foxon (1755; reprint, London: Gregg Press, 1965), 1, hereafter *PG*. Further citations are parenthetical.

48. See Laqueur, *Making Sex*, 149–92.

49. Michael McKeon, "Historicizing Patriarchy: The Emergence of Gender Difference in England, 1660–1760," *Eighteenth-Century Studies* 28 (1995): 302.

50. Ibid.

51. See also Hannah Barker and Elaine Chalus, eds., *Gender in Eighteenth-Century England: Roles, Representations and Responsibilities* (New York: Longman, 1997), esp. 1–28.

52. *The Art of Governing a Wife, with Rules for Batchelors* (London, 1747), 3. For a more detailed and nuanced description of the divided sphere of masculine and feminine behaviors as represented in conduct manuals and other texts, see Robert B. Shoemaker, *Gender in English Society, 1650–1850: The Emergence of Separate Spheres?* (London: Addison Wesley Longman, 1998), 15–44.

53. Philip Dormer Stanhope, *Lord Chesterfield's Letters to his Son and Others*, ed. R. K. Root (1749; reprint, New York: E. P. Dutton and Co., 1929), 39.

54. For example, John Gregory, in *A Father's Legacy to his Daughters* (London, 1774), notes that "Dress is an important article in female life" and advised that "good taste will direct you to dress in such a way as to conceal any blemishes, and set off your beauties, if you have any, to the greatest advantage" (55–56).

55. Ibid., 73.

56. Indeed, women writers could use this construction to argue for their inclusion in the public realm of print. Anne Dutton, in *A Letter to Such of the Servants of Christ, Who May Have Any Scruple about the Lawfulness of Printing Any Thing Written by a Woman* (1743), argues that

> what is printed is published to the *World*, and the Instruction thereby given, is in this regard *Publick*, in that it is presented to every ones View: Yet . . . *Books* are not Read, and the Instruction by them given in the *public Assemblies* . . . : But visit every one, and converse with them in their own *private Houses*. And therefore the Teaching, or Instruction thereby given is *private*: and of no other Consideration than that of Writing a private Letter to a Friend. (Quoted in Lawrence E. Klein, "Gender and the Public/Private Distinction in the Eighteenth Century: Some Questions about Evidence and Analytical Procedure," *Eighteenth-Century Studies* 29 [1995]: 106)

For more on the role of the eighteenth-century domestic woman, charged with overseeing the private-sphere realms of emotion and interiority, see also Nancy Armstrong, *Desire and Domestic Fiction: A Political History of the Novel* (Oxford: Oxford University Press, 1987), esp. 59–95.

57. See Goldberg, *Writing Matter*, esp. 138–39 and 233–34. See also Joseph Loewenstein, "Idem: Italics and the Genetics of Authorship," *Journal of Medieval and Renaissance Studies* 20 (1990): 205–24.

58. For the ways in which eighteenth-century conduct manuals taught women to create themselves as objects of males' desire within the matrimonial system, see Vivien Jones, ed., *Women in the Eighteenth Century: Constructions of Femininity* (London: Routledge, 1990), esp. 14–56. On the economics of middle-class marriage, see Earle, *English Middle Class*, 177–204.

59. For the problem of "excess" implied by sensibility, see John Mullan, *Sentiment and Sociability: The Language of Feeling in the Eighteenth Century* (Oxford: Clarendon Press, 1988), 98. Mullan also claims that, while sensitive men were believed to have suffered physically and mentally by such nervous disorders, women were the primary patients, thought to be prone to more frequent and violent attacks (see 201–40). Mullan also describes how medical literature insisted that laborers and servants did not suffer from these disorders, not being as delicate, refined, or sensitive as women in the upper echelons of society (see 238–39).

60. Elizabeth Singer Rowe's *Letters Moral and Entertaining, in Prose and Verse* (1728) has a brother confessing to his sister that "while I stay'd at Rome, . . . the only loose amour I had, was with a beautiful *Italian*" (quoted in Jones, *Women in the Eighteenth Century*, 26). In fiction, one example of an impassioned Italian is *Sir Charles Grandison*'s Laurana; although this novel also contains the more central character Clemintina, a virtuous Italian, she is also overly passionate in her love for Grandison and eventually goes mad as a result of her unchecked and thwarted desire. Both are in contrast to the sensitive yet sensible Harriet, a healthy English girl who keeps her feelings properly bounded and waits patiently to become the object of Grandison's desire.

61. Chesterfield also contrasts the virtues of Ancient Rome with the debaucheries of modern Italy: in his *Letters to his Son*, he, like many of his contemporaries, looks often to Roman history, which "furnishes more examples of virtue, magnanimity, or greatness of mind, than any other" (Stanhope, *Lord Chesterfield's Letters to his Son and Others*, 4).

62. That the herald can continue to be mutated—if only by its technological context—to suit the needs of the present is indicated not only by the Stationers' Web site itself (http://www.stationers.org/) but also by its use in a recent online advertisement for their 2006 Livery Lecture, delivered by Rupert Murdoch (http://www.paa.org.uk/statdiary.htm).

63. Another angelic scene of printing (albeit in a neoclassical vein) is to be found on the cover of *Universal Magazine*, 1752, as part of a larger picture representing science, art, and knowledge in action (see McKitterick, *Print, Manuscript*, 174). Similarly, Darnton describes the plates on printing in the *Encyclopdie* as showing pristine workrooms with automaton-like workers, as opposed to the reality of a dirty, smelly, and loud work environment. He also notes that the

accompanying article "fails to say much about the craftsmen as human beings and does not mention anything about their ceremonies, humor, and lore," and he explains that "in stripping artisan work down to its technological base—or recasting it as it ought to exist according to a more rational technology—the *Encyclopdie* eliminated a fundamental aspect of it: its culture" (Darnton, *The Business of Enlightenment*, 242).

64. See Woodmansee, *Author, Art and the Market*; and Rose, *Authors and Owners*, esp. 49–66.

65. Margaret Ezell, *Social Authorship and the Advent of Print* (Baltimore: Johns Hopkins University Press, 1999), 11.

66. Eisenstein, *Printing Press*, 18.

67. Ibid., 23.

68. Johns, *Nature of the Book*, 104–5. See also McKitterick, who discusses "the process of printing not as one of straightforward copying but a series of different readings and interpretations each one of which was accounted satisfactory by the agent responsible" (*Print, Manuscript*, 117). Stephen B. Dobranski also discusses John Milton's collaboration with printers and publishers in *Milton, Authorship and the Book Trade* (Cambridge: Cambridge University Press, 1999). See esp. 18–30.

69. Andrew Marvell, *The Rehearsal Transpros'd* (1672), 9.

70. Caleb Stower, *The Printer's Grammar*, ed. D. F. Foxon (1808; reprint, London: Gregg Press, 1965), vi. This emphasis is also apparent in Philip Luckombe's *History and Art of Printing* (1771), also modeled explicitly on Smith.

71. Stower, *Grammar*, 152–59, 371, 382–86.

72. Francis Barker, *The Tremulous Private Body: Essays on Subjection* (Ann Arbor: University of Michigan Press, 1995), 15.

73. Haraway, "A Manifesto for Cyborgs," 191.

74. Zuboff presents a detailed account of the restructuring of the forms of knowledge in the American workplace, a study notable for its prescient analysis so early in the digital era. See *In the Age of the Smart Machine*, esp. 58–96.

75. See C. J. Mitchell, "Women in the Eighteenth-Century Book Trades," in *Writers, Books, and Trade: An Eighteenth-Century Miscellany for William B. Todd*, edited by O. M. Brack, Jr. (New York: AMS Press, 1995), 31.

## 3. CITIZEN, HERO, OR MIDWIFE?
### RE-PRESENTING THE BOOKSELLER

1. Philip Pinkus perhaps encapsulated this view best in the subtitle of his *Grub Street Stripped Bare* (New York: Archon Books, 1968): "The scandalous lives

& pornographic works of the original Grub St. writers, together with the bottle songs which led to their drunkenness, the shameless pamphleteering which led them to Newgate Prison, & the continual pandering to public taste which put them among the first almost to earn a fitful living from their writing alone."

2. For example, the entry for Dodsley in the *Oxford Companion to English Literature*, while mentioning his own publications, notes that "he is chiefly remembered as the publisher of works by Pope, Dr. Johnson, E. Young, Goldsmith, T. Gray, Akenside, and Shenstone" (*The Oxford Companion to English Literature*, 5th ed., ed. Margaret Drabble [Oxford: Oxford University Press, 1985], 280). Tonson's entry is similar. A notable exception to this sort of treatment, however, is Harry M. Solomon's *The Rise of Robert Dodsley: Creating the New Age of Print* (Carbondale: Southern Illinois University Press, 1996). While occasionally succumbing to the rhetoric I describe, Solomon does offer a more complex understanding of this important figure.

3. Solomon, *Rise of Robert Dodsley*, 262.

4. Dustin Griffin has produced similar findings in his study of the patronage system, which often overlapped with that of the booksellers' marketplace, as a "site of contestation." See *Literary Patronage in England, 1650–1800* (Cambridge: Cambridge University Press, 1996), 10–11.

5. James Raven lists a spate of works that are part of this trend, calling Dunton the "founding figure of the genre" ("Selling One's Life: James Lackington, Eighteenth-Century Booksellers and the Design of Autobiography," in Brack, *Writers, Books, and Trade*, 1). Unlike Kirkman's or Dunton's texts, the works Raven discusses were not actually published until the late eighteenth or early nineteenth century, although many of them were written (and prepared for publication) in the first half of the eighteenth century. These early works include Thomas Guy, *A True Copy of the Last Will and Testament of Thomas Guy Esq., late of Lombard Street, Bookseller* (London, 1725); [John Almon], *Memoir of a Late Eminent Bookseller* (London, 1790); *Memoirs of the Life of the Rev. Dr. Trusler, with his Opinions on a Variety of Interesting Subjects . . . Written by Himself* (Bath, 1806); John Henry Prince, *The Life, Pedestrian Excursions and Singular Opinions of J. H. Prince, Bookseller* (London, 1806); and Joseph Hunter, ed., *The Life of Thomas Gent, Printer of York; Written by Himself* (London, 1832). Another similar work that Raven does not mention is William Wagstaffe, *Some Memoirs of the Life of Abel, Toby's Uncle. Composed, Collated, Comprized, Compiled, Digested, Methodized, Written and Illustrated by Dr. Andrew Tripe* (London, 1726), excerpted in Pinkus, *Grub Street Stripped Bare*, 31–51. For a bookseller as writer of popular histories, see Robert Mayer, "Nathaniel Crouch, Bookseller and Historian: Popular Historiography and Cultural Power in Late Seventeenth-Century

England," *Eighteenth-Century Studies* 27 (1994): 391–419. For the ways in which literary biographies of the same period represent similar issues—albeit from the viewpoint of writers—see George Justice, *The Manufacturers of Literature: Writing and the Literary Marketplace in Eighteenth-Century England* (Newark: University of Delaware Press, 2002), esp. 71–111.

6. The following account is indebted to the work of Martha Woodmansee, *Author, Art and the Market* esp. 35–55; John Feather, "The Publishers and the Pirates: British Copyright Law in Theory and Practice, 1710–1775," *Publishing History* 22 (1987): 5–32; Feather, *A History of British Publishing*; and Mark Rose, *Authors and Owners*, 12–65.

7. For depictions of early modern authorship, see Woodmansee, *Author, Art and the Market*; Arthur Marotti, *John Donne, Coterie Poet* (Madison: University of Wisconsin Press, 1986); Ezell, *Social Authorship*; Harold Love, *Scribal Publication in Seventeenth-Century England* (Oxford: Clarendon Press, 1993); Masten, "Pressing Subjects"; David Scott Kastan, *Shakespeare and the Book* (Cambridge: Cambridge University Press, 2001); and Max W. Thomas, "Reading and Writing the Renaissance Commonplace Book: A Question of Authorship," in Woodmansee and Jaszi, *The Construction of Authorship*, 401–15. For an analysis of the commercial and trade-oriented genesis of intellectual property in this period, see Joseph Loewenstein, *The Author's Due: Printing and the Prehistory of Copyright* (Chicago: University of Chicago Press, 2002).

8. Rose, *Authors and Owners*, 14. See Loewenstein, *Author's Due*, esp. 82–88, for the ways in which sixteenth- and seventeenth-century literary practices "served as an engine" for the "history of possessiveness" (82).

9. Rose, *Authors and Owners*, 37, 35. Defoe also seems to base his property claim on the fact that writers could be prosecuted for the seditious texts that they wrote. I discuss the roles of print workers and writers within the discourse of textual regulation in chapter 4.

10. For a brief overview of the problems with determining literacy rates, see Feather, *A History of British Publishing*, 94–96.

11. Johns, *Nature of the Book*, 353.

12. 8 Anne, c. 21.

13. Rose, *Authors and Owners*, 35; my emphasis.

14. See Griffin, *Literary Patronage*, esp. 24–27.

15. Michael Harris asserts that "by 1730 a large proportion of the principal London newspapers was in the hands of the booksellers" and that "by mid-century a virtual monopoly in the market seems to have been established" (*London Newspapers in the Age of Walpole* [London: Associated University Presses, 1987], 66–67). He also claims that booksellers supervised "every stage in the

process of production and distribution" of their newspapers (72) and their influence over editorial policy was "rather greater than is usually assumed" (77). Harris discusses their review of content, their choices of the literary material to excerpt, their management of writers, as well as their own writing. See also James Raven, *Judging New Wealth: Popular Publishing and Responses to Commerce in England, 1750–1800* (Oxford: Clarendon Press, 1992), 47.

16. Johns, *Nature of the Book*, 137. Likewise, Raven comments that "the influence of the booksellers upon both the technical and literary composition should certainly not be underestimated" (*Judging New Wealth*, 46).

17. Margaret Ezell, for example, comments on how such practices on the part of printers and booksellers, which she terms "acts of textual violence" forced some writers to bypass print for scribal publication, but she also accedes that the writers she discusses "sought publication for reasons other than financial ones" (*Social Authorship*, 96, 103).

18. William Roberts, *The Earlier History of English Bookselling* (London: Sampson Low, Marston, Searle, and Rivington, 1889), 107; Feather, *A History of British Publishing*, 57. See also Daniel W. Hollis III, "Francis Kirkman," in *Dictionary of Literary Biography*, vol. 170, *The British Literary Book Trade, 1475–1700*, ed. James K. Bracken and Joel Silver (Detroit: Gale Research, 1996), 146.

19. See Francis Kirkman, *The Unlucky Citizen: Experimentally Described in the Various Misfortunes of an Unlucky Londoner* (London, 1673), hereafter abbreviated *UC*. Subsequent citations are parenthetical. The term *autobiography* is too generically specific (and therefore anachronistic) for this work, which transforms, in its last third, to a collection of amusing tales and anecdotes of other "unluckies."

20. Francis Kirkman, "To His Much Honored Friend Wil. Beeston, Esq.," *The Loves of Clerio and Lozia* (1652), in Strickland Gibson, *A Bibliography of Francis Kirkman with His Prefaces, Dedications and Commendations (1652–80)* (Oxford: Oxford University Press for Oxford Bibliographical Society, 1949), 71.

21. Hollis, "Francis Kirkman," 148. Michael McKeon sees *The Unlucky Citizen* as an important text marking generic and epistemological tensions of the period. See *The Origins of the English Novel, 1600–1740* (Baltimore: Johns Hopkins University Press, 1987), 244–48.

22. Francis Kirkman, "The Epistle dedicatory to the Book-sellers of London," *The English Rogue. Pt. 2* (1668), in Gibson, *Bibliography*, 78; Richard Head and Francis Kirkman, *The English Rogue, Described in the Life of Meriton Latroon* [pts. 1–3] (New York: Dodd, Mead and Co., 1928), 269.

23. Kirkman, "The Epistle dedicatory to the Book-sellers of London," 78.

24. Francis Kirkman, "The Preface," *The Wits* (1673), in Gibson, *Bibliography*, 101; Head and Kirkman, *English Rogue*, 269.

25. Cf. Peter Brooks's description of sexual desire as the underlying energy of narrative in *Reading for the Plot* (New York: Alfred A. Knopf, 1984).

26. Kirkman's self-positioning predates and complicates similar claims implied by a plethora of eighteenth-century novels, the middle-class origins and allegiances of which have been traced by critics as theoretically diverse as Ian Watt, Terry Eagleton, and Nancy Armstrong. See Ian Watt, *The Rise of the Novel: Studies in Defoe, Richardson and Fielding* (Berkeley: University of California Press, 1957); Terry Eagleton, *The Rape of Clarissa: Writing, Sexuality and Class Struggle in Samuel Richardson* (Minneapolis: University of Minnesota Press, 1982); and Armstrong, *Desire and Domestic Fiction*. That such statements as Kirkman's have been regularly overlooked is indicative of the blind spots generated by English studies' genre biases, that is, its emphasis on novels and poetry at the expense of other forms of prose and paratextual materials. These oversights can only be resolved by a form of print/literary culture studies that rigorously examines technology, trade, and tradespeople and not just a few canonical authors' views on publishing.

27. Given the decreasing social and economic role of livery companies in the latter part of the seventeenth century, discussed in the previous chapter, appeals such as Kirkman's may have also worked rhetorically to foster a sense of unity among fellow citizens.

28. Interestingly, as a writer in the Romance tradition he had found it more useful to assert a different sort of social identity. He describes in *The Unlucky Citizen* how he transfigures himself through and on the title page of his second book:

> The Name of the Translator being plac'd on the Title-page in large Characters, there was also added the honoured Word *Gent.* to import that the Translator was a Gentleman, that he was every Inch of him in his own imagination, and did believe that the so printing that word on the Title of the Book, did so much entitle him to Gentility, as if he had Letters Patents for it from the *Heralds-Office*: Nay, did suppose this to be more authentick because more publick. (*UC*, 181–82)

Again, Kirkman claims for print itself a transformative power. See also McKeon's assertion that this work evinces a "profound interest in the self-creative powers of writing and printing" (*Origins of the English Novel*, 246). However, this technological ability also parallels the other forms of self-representation that those without access to print were forced to rely on. Paul Langford, for example, discusses the fluidity of the lower titles during this period, noting that by the mid-eighteenth century "the novelist Richard Graves could claim that 'sir' and 'your Honour' were accorded anyone 'that appears in a clean shirt and powdered wig'" (*A Polite and Commercial People: England, 1727–1783* [Oxford: Oxford University Press, 1992], 66).

29. Brean S. Hammond, *Professional Imaginative Writing in England, 1640–1740* (Oxford: Clarendon Press, 1997), 5.

30. Gibson, *Bibliography*, 53.

31. Pinkus, *Grub Street Stripped Bare*, 82. Few literary critics or book historians have thoroughly investigated Dunton's life and works. J. Paul Hunter does cede some critical space to him in *Before Novels: The Cultural Contexts of Eighteenth-Century English Fiction* (London: W. W. Norton, 1990); his importance to the periodical press of the period has been more centrally argued in Urmi Bhomik, "Facts and Norms in the Marketplace of Print: John Dunton's *Athenium Mercury*," *Eighteenth-Century Studies* 36 (2003): 345–65. Other works include Robert Adams Day, "Richard Bentley and John Dunton: Brothers under the Skin," *Studies in Eighteenth-Century Culture* 16 (1986): 125–38; William C. Wright, "Sir Thomas Browne's *Pseudoxia Epidemica* and English Coffee House Journalism," *Journal of Popular Culture* 12 (1978): 36–41; Albert B. Cook III, "John Bunyan and John Dunton: A Case of Plagiarism," *Papers of the Bibliographical Society of America* 71 (1977): 11–28; and Stephen Parks, *John Dunton and the English Book Trade: A Study of His Career with a Checklist of His Publication* (New York: Garland, 1976). Historians of publishing mine his autobiography for factual details about the workings of the print trade and gossipy anecdotes used to flesh out biographies of turn-of-the-century printers, booksellers, and publishers, but rarely do they consider the scope of the entire text or examine its claims as culturally situated arguments.

32. Hunter, *Before Novels*, 332–34.

33. John Dunton, *The Life and Errors of John Dunton Citizen of London . . . to Which Are Added . . . Selections from his Other Genuine Works* (1705; reprint, New York: Burt Franklin, 1969), 1:iii–iv, hereafter *LE*. Subsequent citations are noted parenthetically.

34. Dunton's views were not merely idiosyncratic, however, but reflective of the broader social practices of his period. Lennard Davis links Dunton's textual appropriations to a larger cultural change developing out of the burgeoning ideology of the print era, a "growing interest in the preservation of an individual life by typography." He explains, "To have a life recorded in print was in a sense to have it validated and enshrined," and "to truly 'be' one had to be set in print—to have a preserved existence one had to be where one was not, that is, in the embalmment and embodiment of print" (*Factual Fictions: The Origins of the English Novel* [New York: Columbia University Press, 1983], 143–44).

35. The following "new life" chapter for this stage is quite vague and never

touches on business dealings. Instead, he provides a guide, almost a conduct manual, for choosing a spouse, though this cannot be seen as correcting his life because he asserts again and again what a perfect union he obtained with his first wife. He also supplies a long rambling testament to moral character in general, offering little concrete examples from his own life.

36. In fact, he states at one point that, "as to Bookselling and Traffick, I dare stand the test, with the same allowances that every man under the same circumstance with me would wish to have, for the whole Trading part of my Life" (*LE*, 159). He protests his professional honesty often throughout the text.

37. Here he might be seen as a precursor to another member of the print trade, who also freely mixed morality and family economics in his own writing: Samuel Richardson.

38. Dunton does not mark all writers as the "enemy." They did provide an essential service as part of the print trade, and projects ran more smoothly when a bookseller could count on reliable writers. Interestingly, most of the writers Dunton praises are not professional writers at all, but religious men, scholars, or aristocratic dabblers.

39. This relationship between writer and bookseller may have provided the foundation for current corporate "work for hire" laws, in which employers retain the copyright for all work done or texts created by their employees.

40. Siskin, *The Work of Writing*, 161. See also 158–63.

41. Hammond describes how this manner of thinking informed nineteenth-century notions of literary tradition. See *Professional Imaginative Writing*, esp. 201.

42. See Johns, *Nature of the Book*, 138–47.

43. For the details on Dodsley's life, I am, unless otherwise indicated, indebted to Solomon's *Rise of Robert Dodsley*.

44. See David Fordyce, letter to Robert Dodsley, February 11, 1747–48, in *The Correspondence of Robert Dodsley, 1733–1764*, ed. James E. Tierney (Cambridge: Cambridge University Press, 1988), 121, and, also in Tierney, 121n3. Thomas Gray was also especially condescending in his letters to Dodsley; Tierney notes that he "had little regard for either [Dodsley's] learning or literary ability" (149n1). This prejudice survives even today: Michael Suarez, for example, notes that "it is not difficult to imagine that Dodsley's gentlemen editors . . . assisted the fledgling bookseller . . . by adjudicating in matters of literary taste" (Michael Suarez, S.J., ed., in Robert Dodsley, *A Collection of Poems by Several Hands* [1748–58; reprint, London: Routledge, 1997], 19).

45. Matthew Pilkington, letter to Robert Dodsley, October 1, 1748 (Tierney, *Correspondence*, 124).

46. See, e.g., John Brown, letter to Robert Dodsley, October 17, 1745 (Tier-

ney, *Correspondence*, 88); and Robert Dodsley, letter to John Gilbert Cooper, December 19, 1749 (Tierney, *Correspondence*, 132).

47. For example, see Suarez's description of the delays in publishing later volumes of *A Collection of Poems by Several Hands* while Shenstone amended and corrected his poems (Suarez, 49–67).

48. Thus John Brown feels free to insist, "I know not whether the Title I have fixed on may promote the Sale of the Essays or not, but it is the most expressive of the Design, and therefore I am determined to retain it." Brown, letter to Dodsley, October 17, 1745 (Tierney, *Correspondence*, 88). Cf. Dunton's use of the word "design," discussed above.

49. Solomon, *Rise of Robert Dodsley*, 88

50. Suarez, 8.

51. Ironically, it was Lord Chesterfield—famously linked with Dodsley in Samuel Johnson's rejection of patrons in favor of print—who used his patronage to influence John Rich to produce Dodsley's play. See Solomon, *Rise of Robert Dodsley*, 187.

52. See Marotti, *John Donne, Coterie Poet*; and Love, *Scribal Publication*. Ezell comments on the persistence of these practices in *Social Authorship*. What I find interesting is that Dodsley is doing so even from the center of the print trade itself. In this his activities also resemble the printer-novelist Samuel Richardson's sharing of early manuscript drafts of his works among his friends.

53. At the time Dodsley was writing, the society's chief awards were in the categories of agriculture, chemistry, colonies and trade, manufactures, and mechanics and polite arts (painting and the plastic arts); specific awards went for spinning and carpet manufacture, and it encouraged tree planting for timber to supply the shipbuilding industry. Tierney notes that the only prizes for "arts" in Dodsley's day were for children's drawings (*Correspondence*, 221); later in the society's history it developed an emphasis on industrial design. For a timeline of the organization, now (still misleadingly) known as the Royal Society of Arts, see the Royal Society of the Arts, "RSA History—Key Dates and Events," http://www.rsa.org.uk/rsa/history.asp/.

54. Dodsley, letter to Jacob, Lord Viscount Folkestone, President of the Society for the Encouragement of Arts, Manufactures and Commerce, March 17, 1756 (Tierney, *Correspondence*, 220–21).

55. Dodsley, letter to George Box, Secretary of the Society for the Encouragement of Arts, Manufactures and Commerce, June 21, 1757 (Tierney, *Correspondence*, 281–82).

56. See, e.g., Dodsley, letter to William Shenstone, February 9, 1756 (Tierney, *Correspondence*, 218).

57. In fact, his perceived alliance with this camp raised the ire of the Pope following, especially William Warburton, who saw Dodsley as turning his back on his onetime benefactor. See Solomon, *Rise of Robert Dodsley*, 134–39.

58. Edward Young, *Conjectures on Original Composition in a Letter to the Author of Sir Charles Grandison*, in Edmund D. Jones, ed., *English Critical Essays: Sixteenth, Seventeenth and Eighteenth Centuries* (1759; reprint, London: Oxford University Press, 1975), 274, 189.

59. Solomon, *Rise of Robert Dodsley*, 217.

60. Ibid., 255.

61. Future historians narrowed Dodsley's role even more: Solomon comments on his representation in the nineteenth and twentieth centuries as an "amiable bookseller . . . an honest simpleton, deferential both to rank and genius" (ibid., 262). See also 256–61. As we have seen, Dodsley's own self-presentation, though mutable and more complex, did contain elements of this role.

62. Raven contrasts this to earlier periods, in which more balanced views of trade were represented, and to earlier notions of the noble merchant. See *Judging New Wealth*, 7–9, 90–93. His work details the scapegoating of business as a response to a number of economic and social changes in the later part of the eighteenth century.

63. Ibid., 5.

64. Quoted in ibid., 46.

65. Another late-century commentator makes reference to such a threat in verse, following the appropriation of discourse by the lower classes to its "logical" conclusion: "And if the rustics grew refined, / Who would the humble duties mind? / They might, from scribbling odes and letters, / Proceed to dictate to their betters." James West, "To the Hon. Mrs. C[ockayn]e" (1791), quoted in Siskin, *The Work of Writing*, 130.

66. McDowell, *Women of Grub Street*, 289.

67. See Siskin, *The Work of Writing*, especially his discussion of eighteenth-century changes in notions of labor and writing (130–52). He comments on the naturalization of "the division of labor into physical and mental" produced through claims "for the poet's work of writing, the higher (and thus deeper) motivation of love instead of money" (114).

## 4. From Authorized Print to Authoritative Author: The Regulated Trade

1. Foucault, "What Is an Author," 124.

2. On the French trade, see Carla Hesse, who claims that "the first revolu-

tionary effort to give legal recognition to the author's claim on the text, then, was *not* a grant of freedom to the author, but the imposition of accountability and responsibility. Politically, it formed part of a conservative pro-order move, a police measure" ("Enlightenment Epistemology and the Laws of Authorship in Revolutionary France, 1777–1793," *Representations* 30 [Spring 1990]: 120).

3. Susan Stewart, *Crimes of Writing: Problems in the Containment of Representation* (New York: Oxford University Press, 1991), 12.

4. Some sections of this chapter originally found form in Lisa Maruca, "Political Propriety and Feminine Property: Women in the Eighteenth-Century Text Trades," *Studies in the Literary Imagination* 34 (2001): 79–99.

5. Foucault, "What Is an Author," 138.

6. For the following account of censorship in England I rely on John Feather, "From Censorship to Copyright: Aspects of the Government's Role in the English Book Trade, 1695–1775," in *Books and Society in History*, ed. Kenneth Carpenter (New York: Bowker, 1983), and Feather, *A History of British Publishing*; Alan Downie "The Growth of Government Tolerance of the Press to 1790," in *Development of the English Book Trade, 1700–1899*, ed. Robin Myers and Michael Harris (Oxford: Oxford Polytechnic Press, 1981); Laurence Hanson, *Government and the Press, 1695–1763* (Oxford: Clarendon Press, 1936); and Frederick Seaton Siebert, *Freedom of the Press in England, 1476–1776: The Rise and Decline of Government Control* (Urbana: University of Illinois Press, 1965), esp. 237–324.

7. Quoted in Siebert, *Freedom of the Press*, 242.

8. Quoted in ibid., 254.

9. See Downie, "Growth of Government Tolerance," 49; see also Simon Varey, "Revisiting a Masterpiece: *Government and the Press, 1695–1763*," *Studies in the Literary Imagination* 34 (2001): 49–61.

10. Downie, "Growth of Government Tolerance," 51.

11. Michel Foucault, *The History of Sexuality, Volume One: An Introduction*, trans. Robert Hurley (New York: Vintage Books, 1980), 92.

12. Harold Weber claims that print became the omnipresent medium of discourse only with the Restoration. He believes that Charles's return marks the first time in England that history could no longer be understood apart from the printed word. "The transformation of the English monarchy during the seventeenth century," he asserts, "was not simply played out against a backdrop of changes in the production, marketing and consumption of printed matter, but was itself part of these very changes" (*Paper Bullets: Print and Kingship under Charles II* [Lexington: University Press of Kentucky, 1996], 5).

13. Roger L'Estrange, *Truth and Loyalty Vindicated* (1662), in *Freedom of*

*the Press: Sir Roger L'Estrange's Tracts and Others 1660–1681*, ed. Stephen Parks (New York: Garland, 1974), 54–55; all further citations are noted parenthetically as *Truth*.

14. For a description of the development of page layout in the eighteenth century, see Nicolas Barker, "Typography and the Meaning of Words: The Revolution in the Layout of Books in the Eighteenth Century," in *Buch und Buchhandel im Europa im achzehten Jahrhundert* [The Book and Book Trade in Eighteenth-Century Europe], ed. Giles Barber and Bernhard Fabian (Hamburg: Hauswedell, 1981). For a discussion of the linkage of "mise-en-page," the conceptual space of texts, and linguistic theory in the seventeenth century, see Richard W. F. Kroll, "Mise-en-Page, Biblical Criticism, and Inference during the Restoration," *Studies in Eighteenth-Century Culture* 16 (1986): 3–40.

15. I am not making the point that gothic type is always essentially representative of the monarch's voice. While that is true in this pamphlet, it is frequently used in other works of the 1660s, including L'Estrange's, to emphasize words and phrases more noticeably than the italic. It did evolve as a way to signal authority more generally, however, as we see in its continuation in legal texts throughout the eighteenth century. Typography also seems to be used during this period to retain oral inflection and emphasis, which lends more credence to the suggestion that oral and print cultures were not separate but overlapping domains.

Unfortunately, political questions rarely enter standard histories of typography, which rely largely on a narrative of increased legibility, empirically considered. See, e.g., Harry Carter, *A View of Early Typography up to about 1600* (Oxford: Clarendon Press, 1969), and any of the works of Stanley Morison (*First Principles of Typography* [New York: Macmillan, 1936]; *On Type Designs Past and Present: A Brief Introduction* [1926; reprint, London: Ernest Benn, 1962]; *Letter Forms, Typographic and Scriptorial: Two Essays on Classification, History, and Bibliography* [London: Nattali and Maurice, 1968]; or *Selected Essays on the History of the Letter-Forms in Manuscript and Print*, ed. David McKitterick [New York: Cambridge University Press, 1981]). An exception is David McKitterick, "Old Faces and New Acquaintances: Typography and the Association of Ideas," *Papers of the Bibliographic Society of America* 87 (1993): 163–86. Though he provides more questions than answers, he does call for a study of typography that goes beyond using it as a "tool for location and dating" (179), and he is especially interested in readers and "typographic literacy" (166). For one example of a cultural rather than empirical approach to typography, see John L. Flood, "Nationalistic Currents in Early German Typography," *Library* 15 (June 1993): 125–41, an overview of the political uses of the gothic in Germany.

16. For a different use of the pointing hand, see Tribble, *Margins and Marginalia*, 25.

17. Roger L'Estrange, *Considerations and Proposals in Order to the Regulation of the Press* (1663), in Parks, *Freedom of the Press*, 57. All further citations are noted parenthetically as *Considerations*.

18. In a similar vein, Adrian Johns notes, "In the making of a book, authorship . . . was distributed over a number of individuals and groups. . . . [A]uthorities more helpfully formalized this . . . by recognizing Stationers themselves as authors" (*Nature of the Book*, 138).

19. Weber, *Paper Bullets*, 155.

20. *Oxford English Dictionary*, definition 1c; see also 1d.

21. Loewenstein, *Author's Due*, 211.

22. Quoted in Weber, *Paper Bullets*, 174.

23. Downie, "Growth of Government Tolerance," 48.

24. Quoted in Weber, *Paper Bullets*, 174–75.

25. Feather, "Censorship," 186.

26. Margaret Hunt, "Hawkers, Bawlers, and Mercuries: Women and the London Press in the Early Enlightenment," *Women and the Enlightenment* (New York: Institute for Research in History, 1984), 54.

27. Quoted in Michael Treadwell, "London Trade Publishers, 1675–1750," *Library*, 6th ser., 4 (June 1982): 125.

28. Quoted in Hanson, *Government and the Press*, 51–52.

29. Quoted in ibid., 58.

30. Henry Fielding, *The Author's Farce*, in *The Complete Works of Henry Fielding, Esq.: Plays and Poems*, vol. 1, ed. William Ernest Henley (New York: Barnes and Noble, 1967), 221.

31. Ibid., 222.

32. Some sources do refer to them as just "publishers," though the role should not be confused with the function we call publishing today. Their job can be more aptly described as distributing or retailing.

33. Quoted in Treadwell, "London Trade Publishers," 100.

34. For more on the careers of the Baldwins, see Leona Rostenberg, *Literary, Political, Scientific, Religious and Legal Publishing, Printing and Bookselling in England, 1551–1700: Twelve Studies*, 2 vols. (New York: Burt Franklin, 1965); for the Nutt family's involvement in the trade, see John Horden, "'In the Savoy': John Nutt and His Family," *Publishing History* 24 (1988): 5–26.

35. Treadwell defines "regularly" as appearing in at least twenty imprints during a year; the regularity of appearance in imprints is one way he determines a roster of publishers in this period. See "London Trade Publishers," esp. 105.

36. Paula McDowell's groundbreaking work details the political role of women in the print trades (see *Women of Grub Street*, esp. 33–62), as do case studies by Maureen Bell on women in the opposition press. See "Elizabeth Calvert and the 'Confederates,'" *Publishing History* 32 (1992): 5–49; "Women and the Opposition Press after the Restoration," *Writing and Radicalism*, ed. John Lucas (London: Longman, 1996); and "Women in the English Book Trade 1557–1700," *Leipziger Jahrbuch zur Buchgeschichte* 6 (1996): 13–45. C. J. Mitchell also provides a useful summary of women's contributions in "Women in the Eighteenth-Century Book Trades." For overviews of women workers in general during the seventeenth and eighteenth centuries, see Alice Clark, *Working Life of Women in the Seventeenth Century* (London: Routledge, 1919); Ivy Pinchbeck, *Women Workers and the Industrial Revolution, 1750–1850* (London: Frank Cass, 1930); and Maxine Berg, *The Age of Manufactures, 1700–1820: Industry, Innovation and Work in Britain*, 2nd ed. (London: Routledge, 1994), 136–69.

37. Quoted in Earle, *English Working Class*, 161.

38. Ibid., 160. For more details on the position of the *feme sole* in the book trade, see McDowell, *Women of Grub Street*, 42–43.

39. Hunt, "Hawkers, Bawlers, and Mercuries," 48.

40. Mitchell admits to several problems with his numbers: women existing in the lowest rungs of the trade hierarchy are rarely recorded; some women used their husbands' or fathers' names; others go by their nongendered initials. Furthermore, his percentage refers only to owners of businesses, not all workers. In family-run businesses (as most were), male ownership would obscure female participation, which might be close to 50 percent.

41. Notably, Treadwell believes that publishers developed out of binders, many of who were traditionally women. See "London Trade Publishers," 130–31.

42. Quoted in David Foxon, *Pope and the Early Eighteenth-Century Book Trade*, rev. and ed. James McLaverty (Oxford: Clarendon Press, 1991).

43. For more details on mercuries and hawkers, see also Johns, *Nature of the Book*, 154–56.

44. Treadwell, "London Trade Publishers," 102.

45. Mitchell puzzles over the reasons women made up such a small proportion of booksellers, since "the hurdles seem less demanding than the specialized skills required of printers, engravers, and binders." He notes that wholesale work in particular was so unspecialized, that Joseph Collyer, in his *The Parent's and Guardian's Directory, and the Youth's Guide in the Choice of a Profession or Trade* (1761), warns away apprentices, who he says "will learn nothing but the manner of picking up parcels, and the titles of those books for which there is the greatest demand" ("Women in the Eighteenth-Century Book Trades," 36).

This is corroborated by *The London Tradesman* (1747), which claims of shop-keepers that "but a moderate share of wit serves their turn in general" (quoted in Earle, *English Working Class*, 98). Since the job was not too physically demanding for women, we must assume that other social conventions kept them from entering.

46. Treadwell, "London Trade Publishers," 130.

47. Frederick Siebert notes that "no single method of restricting the press was as effective as the law of seditious libel as it was developed by the common-law courts of the late seventeenth century" (*Freedom of the Press*, 296). Even though Feather grants that censorship "was neither universal nor oppressive" ("Censorship" 180), affecting only about one percent of published texts, he also acknowledges that the threat of prosecution did stifle the production of potentially libelous material.

48. Historians are divided as to whether the Stamp Act indeed constituted a form of indirect censorship or merely the government's capitulation to and economic exploitation of the press's popularity. See Downie, "Growth of Government Tolerance"; and cf. Siebert, *Freedom of the Press*, 305–18. For my purposes, the government's intentions do not matter: the fact that each newspaper had to be imprinted made it easy for the law to trace it at least as far as its publisher or mercury.

49. Feather claims, for example, that the ballad was one of the most important forms of Jacobite propaganda. Sold by hawkers and mercuries, it represented "the cheapest, quickest, and most effective way of reaching a mass urban audience" ("Censorship," 177).

50. Johns, *Nature of the Book*, 155.

51. Hanson, *Government and the Press*, 50.

52. Joan W. Scott, "Gender: A Useful Category of Historical Analysis," in *Coming to Terms: Feminism, Theory, Politics* (New York: Routledge, 1989), 95–96.

53. In contrast, McDowell, Hunt, and Bell, all celebrate the many dedicated women working in the trade as political activists. See McDowell, *Women of Grub Street*; Hunt, "Hawkers, Bawlers, and Mercuries"; and Bell, "Women and the Opposition," "Calvert," and "Women in the English Book Trade."

54. Discussing eighteenth-century class divisions at all is problematic, and no one, as far as I know, has taken up the issue in publishing history (in general, this field has shown little interest in the broader theoretical concerns of social history). Most of the terms used to describe class structure refer to agrarian life, the miserable poor, or "mechanick" workers. See, e.g., Donna Landry, *The Muses of Resistance: Laboring-Class Women's Poetry in Britain, 1739–1796* (Cambridge: Cambridge University Press, 1990), 9. Little work has been done, however, on

what might be called the "service class," on the border between the middle and lower classes. Incomes varied widely within the print trade (and even within individual occupations) at a time when, E. P. Thompson reports, money often meant more than other class markers (see "Eighteenth-Century English Society: Class Struggle without Class?" *Social History* 3 [May 1978]: 138–40). Even among publishers and mercuries, some may have had the ability to hire one or more servants, employees, or workers who served as both—another badge of middle-class affiliation, according to Earle (*English Working Class*, 4)—while others merely relied on family members. Similarly, some publishers like Mary Cooper were able to use their money for the middle-class strategy of, as Earle terms it, "accumulation and improvement" (4–5), while others lived hand to mouth. Education levels also meant little, as did the type of work. Earle notes that among the lower middle class, within which he includes small shopkeepers, "incomes were often lower than those of many 'mechanicks' and this fact seems to emphasize the problem of treating the 'mechanick part of mankind' as a unitary group. . . . The independent artisan who owned a workshop had most of the attributes of the middle class even if he did work with his hands" (329). Despite these discrepancies, Thompson notes that "many urban artisans evinced the 'vertical' consciousness of the 'the trade' (rather than the 'horizontal' consciousness of a 'mature' industrial working class)" ("Class Struggle without Class," 148). Thus social and cultural affiliation may have meant more than per annum income, though it is difficult to tell whether booksellers would have related to mercuries as business equals or inferiors. More work on the rhetorical construction of class needs to be done before the class dynamics of this trade can be properly assessed.

55. See McDowell, *Women of Grub Street*, 33–42. Earle claims this was true of most small businesses of the period (*English Working Class*,112). Johns notes, however, that in the seventeenth century, despite the link between family life and trade, the public work / private dwelling distinction was kept rigid, since "privacy" connoted "illicit, secret or seditious" (*Nature of the Book*,128). This early modern concept of privacy, I believe, was transformed by the new ideology of respectable domestic (private) femininity.

56. Johns, *Nature of the Book*, 79.

57. Quoted in Hunt, "Hawkers, Bawlers, Mercuries," 57–58.

58. McDowell, *Women of Grub Street*, 18.

59. McDowell does in fact describe Elinor James, a seventeenth-century printer, as seeing "sexual ideology [as] . . . a weapon that she could not simply disregard" (ibid., 212).

60. Feather, "Censorship," 186.

61. Quoted in Bell, "Women and the Opposition," 40.

62. Quoted in Bell, "Calvert," 18.

63. Ibid., 3.

64. Mitchell, "Women in the Eighteenth-Century Book Trades," 31.

65. As Adrian Johns notes, discussing mercuries, hawkers, and chapmen (who sold print matter in the country), "All these agents were problematic, for three connected reasons: they were mobile, many of them were women, and they thrived outside the householder elite entrusted with governing urban life. Both economically and culturally, then, they made that elite uneasy" (*Nature of the Book*, 156).

66. Thompson, "Class Struggle without Class," 149.

67. See Jane Spencer, *The Rise of the Woman Novelist: From Aphra Behn to Jane Austen* (Oxford: Basil Blackwell, 1987); Janet Todd, *The Sign of Angelica: Women, Writing and Fiction, 1660–1800* (New York: Columbia University Press, 1989); and Cheryl Turner, *Living by the Pen: Women Writers in the Eighteenth Century* (London: Routledge, 1992).

68. See Turner, *Living by the Pen*, 95.

69. Todd, *Sign of Angelica*, 126.

70. Quoted in Spencer, *Rise of the Woman Novelist*, 80.

71. Ibid., 77.

72. Quoted in Turner, *Living by the Pen*, 52. Novels became so associated with feminine values that what was expected in those by women writers was extended to apply to men as well. Thus the preface of Penelope Aubin's *A Collection of Entertaining Histories and Novels* (1739) explains the ways in which Aubin's work is illustrative of a general set of "Rules . . . for constituting a good Novel," in which all aspects of the text are virtuously arranged:

> First, A Purity of Style and Manners, that nothing may be contained in them that has the least Tendency to pollute or corrupt the inexperienced Minds, for those whose Diversion they are intended. Secondly, That the Subjects should be such as naturally recommend all the Duties of social Life, and inforce an universal Benevolence to Mankind. Thirdly, That when a guilty Character is introduced, it should in the Conclusion appear to be signally punished or distressed, that others may be deterred from the Pursuits of those Follies, or Mistakes, which have been the Occasion of its Misfortunes. Fourthly, that Virtue or Innocence, on the contrary, be not finally permitted to suffer; but that a Prospect at least should be opened, either here or hereafter, for its Reward, in order to encourage everyone who reads it to Imitation. And, lastly, that the whole have, at least, an Air of Probability, that the Example may have the greater Force

upon the minds it is intended to inform. (Quoted in Turner, *Living by the Pen*, 49)

Terry Eagleton, among others, has discussed the "feminization of discourse" as it pertains more broadly to this period. See Eagleton, *The Rape of Clarissa*.

73. McDowell is notable for looking at other forces exerting pressure on women to write. Discussing women who were Quakers or members of other radical sects, for example, she argues that "[a]t a time when women's virtues were increasingly understood to "open fairest in the shade," a profound sense of religious calling made public expression, both oral and printed, appear a 'duty' to women of diverse ideological allegiances and socioeconomic backgrounds" (*Women of Grub Street*, 122).

74. See Armstrong, *Desire and Domestic Fiction*.

75. Catherine Gallagher, *Nobody's Story: The Vanishing Acts of Women Writers in the Marketplace 1670–1820* (Berkeley: University of California Press, 1994), 156–59.

76. Ibid., xxiii.

77. Feather, "Publishers and Pirates," 5.

78. Todd, *Sign of Angelica*, 126.

79. Catherine Ingrassia, *Authorship, Commerce, and Gender in Early Eighteenth-Century England: A Culture of Paper Credit* (Cambridge: Cambridge University Press, 1998), 105. It is likely that Haywood, herself at times a bookseller and erstwhile distributor, borrowed this rhetorical coin from her fellow tradeswomen.

80. Quoted in Turner, *Living by the Pen*, 31.

81. See Christine Battersby, *Gender and Genius: Towards a Feminist Aesthetic* (Bloomington: Indiana University Press, 1989); Anne K. Mellor, *Romanticism and Gender* (New York: Routledge, 1993); Marlon Ross, *The Contours of Masculine Desire: Romanticism and the Rise of Women's Poetry* (New York: Oxford University Press, 1989); and Martha Woodmansee, *Author, Art and the Market*, 103–9.

## 5. *The Printer as Author: Samuel Richardson, Intellectual Property, and the Feminine Text*

1. Wall, *Imprint of Gender*, 5.

2. See William Merrit Sale, Jr., *Samuel Richardson: A Bibliographical Record of His Literary Career with Historical Notes* (New Haven, CT: Yale University Press, 1936), vii-xiii; Sale, *Samuel Richardson: Master Printer* (Ithaca, NY: Cornell University Press, 1950), 86–105; and T. C. Duncan Eaves and Ben D. Kimpel, *Samuel Richardson: A Biography* (Oxford: Clarendon Press, 1971),

37–86. My description of Richardson's career below is also indebted to these sources.

3. This is not the view of standard biographies, which radically differentiate his two careers as printer and novelist, with the latter taking precedence and the former supplying an interesting life story or at best merely the information that allows us to slot him as "middle class" (Watt, *Rise of the Novel*, 59). Even Sale, whose interest in Richardson as a printer resulted in two large-scale and important works, makes the disclaimer that if Richardson "had not begun the writing of *Pamela* in November, 1739, [the] details of his career as printer would never have become a matter of general concern" (Sale, *Bibliographical Record*, vii).

4. A significant exception is Lennard Davis, who notes that "Richardson's life was so implicated in the technology of typography—in the taint of ink, press, and production—that it is not surprising that his work should carry the imprint of his trade." Even his account, however, focuses more on vague notions such as the authority and impersonality of print than on what I try to examine, Richardson's self-representation as a printer and the business practices and ideology that resulted from that role. Davis, *Factual Fictions*, 174.

Another departure is William B. Warner, *Licensing Entertainment: The Elevation of Novel Reading in Britain, 1684–1750* (Berkeley: University of California Press, 1998). Warner sees Richardson's novels as part of eighteenth-century media culture, usefully highlighting the conjunction between the physicality of reading, the discursive construction of novels, and Richardson's role as one positioned to manipulate new media practices. Nonetheless, in his analysis of Richardson's novel writing, he explains how Richardson "must teach readers how to read"(187)—and what they seem to be reading is text, not books. His descriptions of the print market as uncontrolled, open to multiple meanings, and "influenced by any who can get their writings printed" (181) privilege it as a semiotic system seemingly divorced from economic conditions, oblivious to material concerns, and untouched by print workers other than writers.

5. See, e.g., William B. Warner, *Reading Clarissa: The Struggles of Interpretation* (New Haven, CT: Yale University Press, 1979); Terry Castle, *Clarissa's Ciphers: Meaning and Disruption in Richardson's "Clarissa."* (Ithaca, NY: Cornell University Press, 1982); Eagleton, *The Rape of Clarissa*; Armstrong, *Desire and Domestic Fiction*; Madeleine Kahn, *Narrative Transvestism: Rhetoric and Gender in the Eighteenth-Century English Novel* (Ithaca, NY: Cornell University Press, 1991); and Tassie Gwilliam, *Samuel Richardson's Fictions of Gender* (Stanford, CA: Stanford University Press, 1993).

6. See William B. Warner, "The Institutionalization of Authorship: Rich-

ardson's Battle with the Irish Booksellers" (paper presented at the "Intellectual Property and the Construction of Authorship" conference, Cleveland, 1991), 1–2.

7. Ibid., 5.

8. Samuel Richardson, *The Case of Samuel Richardson, of London, Printer* (1753), in *English Publishing, the Struggle for Copyright, and the Freedom of the Press: Thirteen Tracts*, ed. Stephen Parks (New York: Garland, 1975), 2–3. The very title of this set of collected works positions Richardson's tract as a direct descendent of copyright law.

9. Thus Warner neatly ends his reading of Richardson's pamphlet in "Institutionalization" with a reminder that, a few years later, Richardson encouraged his friend Edward Young to write "Conjectures on Original Composition," that landmark text that defines the genius as a solitary, unique individual and his work as organic inner expression.

10. Richardson, *The Case of Samuel Richardson*, 1–2.

11. Ibid., 2n.

12. Ibid., 2.

13. Quoted in John Nichols, *Literary Anecdotes of the Eighteenth Century* (London, 1812), 4:593.

14. James Grantham Turner, "Richardson and His Circle," in *Columbia History of the Novel*, ed. John Richetti (New York: Columbia University Press, 1994), 79.

15. Cf. Woodmansee's description of Samuel Johnson's collaborations, including ghostwriting ("Author Effect," 281–88).

16. Eaves and Kimpel, *Samuel Richardson*, 46. For the printer's and the bookseller's roles in newspapers, see Harris, *London Newspapers in the Age of Walpole*, esp. 66–106.

17. Samuel Richardson, *The Richardson-Stinstra Correspondence*, ed. William C. Slatterly (Carbondale: Southern Illinois University Press, 1967), 99.

18. Davis, *Factual Fictions*, 186.

19. Richardson was not the first to do this, of course. The popularity of conduct literature had been exploited for quite sometime. My purpose in emphasizing Richardson's involvement in this process is to redirect critical focus, which for decades has tended to privilege Richardson the moralist over Richardson the savvy marketer. Warner also shifts our attention to the "Pamela ad campaign" directed by a "print media worker," but he focuses mostly on his strategies for redirecting novelistic discourse (*Licensing Entertainment*, 200–201).

20. Warner similarly terms this a "media event." See ibid., 176–80.

21. For example, Armstrong, *Desire and Domestic Fiction*, and Eagleton, *The*

*Rape of Clarissa*, both discuss the way his novels participated in middle-class interests; Castle, *Clarissa's Ciphers*, and Gwilliam, *Fictions of Gender*, analyze the way they responded to anxieties of gender.

22. Compared to the massive amount of literature devoted to Richardson studies in general, especially that devoted to *Pamela* and *Clarissa*, little work beyond the biographical and bibliographical has focused on any of the *Pamela* spin-offs, the continuations, or the other popular forms that jumped on the *Pamela* bandwagon. Exceptions include article- and chapter-length studies by Janet E. Aikins, "Re-presenting the Body in *Pamela II*," in *New Historical Literary Study: Essays on Reproducing Texts, Representing History*, ed. Jeffrey N. Cox and Larry J. Reynolds (Princeton, NJ: Princeton University Press, 1993); Terry Castle, *Masquerade and Civilization: The Carnivalesque in Eighteenth-Century English Culture and Fiction* (Stanford, CA: Stanford University Press, 1986); Miriam Dick, "Joseph Highmore's Vision of *Pamela*," *English Language Notes* 24 (June 1987): 33–42; Richard Gooding, "*Pamela*, *Shamela*, and the Politics of the *Pamela* Vogue," *Eighteenth-Century Fiction* 7, no. 2 (1995): 109–30; Viktor Link, "The First Operatic Versions of *Pamela*," *Studies on Voltaire and the Eighteenth Century* 267 (1989): 273–81; Terri Nickel, "*Pamela* as Fetish: Masculine Anxiety in Henry Fielding's *Shamela* and James Parry's *The True Anti-Pamela*," *Studies in Eighteenth-Century Culture* 22 (1992): 37–49; Betty A. Schellenberg, "Enclosing the Immovable: Structuring Social Authority in *Pamela* Part II," *Eighteenth-Century Fiction* 4, no. 1 (1991): 27–42; and James Grantham Turner, "Novel Panic: Picture and Performance in the Reception of Richardson's *Pamela*," *Representations* 48 (Fall 1994): 70–96.

23. Furthermore, in 1740 *Gyles v. Wilcox* established abridgements as new works and therefore not copyright violations. The underpinnings of this law, based on a literal interpretation of the term *copy* in the Statute of Anne, might also seem to apply to any new form of a previous work. To be classified as a legal infringement, a work had to be a word-for-word copy, not just the use of previously expressed ideas.

24. Eaves and Kimpel, *Samuel Richardson*, 135.

25. See David A. Brewer, *The Afterlife of Character, 1726–1825* (Philadelphia: University of Pennsylvania Press, 2005).

26. Warner, *Licensing Entertainment*, 228.

27. Eaves and Kimpel, *Samuel Richardson*, 136.

28. Samuel Richardson, *Pamela* (1741; reprint, London: J. M. Dent and Sons, 1969), 2:v, hereafter *P*. All further citations are parenthetical.

To call this *Pamela II*, as many do, is convenient, but historically inaccurate. The "sequel" was first published as *Pamela, or, Virtue Rewarded*, vols. 3 and 4—

the same fundamental title as the first *Pamela*, though there were slight changes in the longer subtitles, which varied from edition to edition. It was first released separately (December 7, 1741), but was published with the first two volumes as a complete set a few months later (May 10, 1742). Although volumes 3 and 4 were occasionally sold in editions by themselves, presumably to complete the sets of the many original buyers of *Pamela*, no subsequent edition of the first *Pamela* (vols. 1 and 2) was ever sold again without the accompanying volumes 3 and 4. (See Sale, *Bibliographical Record*, 13–34, for complete bibliographical and publishing information for the four volumes.) This, I believe, shows that Richardson did not consider it a separate work, as the spurious title *Pamela II* implies, but a completion that merely made *Pamela* two volumes longer. This challenges our common notions concerning a work's organic "wholeness" and integrity, supposedly frozen in the stability of print.

29. Janet Aikins uses this passage to note that the "depiction of Sir Simon hurling a book at his daughter's face . . . posits a complex equation between the consumption of books and human procreation" ("Representing the Body in *Pamela II*," 152). While she is interested, as I am, in the links between the material text and the politics of a gendered body, her essay explores the relationship between the illustrations in the octavo edition and the rhetoric of Pamela's pregnancy.

30. See Rose, "Copyright and Its Metaphors," and *Authors and Owners*, 38–40.

31. Rose, *Authors and Owners*, 39.

32. Richard G. Swartz, "Patrimony and the Figuration of Authorship in the Eighteenth-Century Literary Property Debates," *Works and Days* 7, no. 2 (1989): 40–41.

33. Ibid., 30. A corrective to this is Judith Roof's study linking notions of paternity in current copyright law to those underlying abortion statutes. She finds that the interests being served in both are those of the *male* (pro)creator. Her discussion of the anxieties underlying these laws is suggestive:

> While the flashy Frankenstein desire to endow what one creates with a life of its own provides an obvious impetus for birthing metaphors, it also spawns the fear that what one creates will escape control, lose itself, or attach itself to another creator. To allay such apprehensions, paternal gestation seals any doubt about paternity or authority by forging an inalienable "natural" link between the "paternal" owner/artist and his or her property/creation. ("The Ideology of Fair Use: Xeroxing and Reproductive Rights," *Hypatia* 7 [Spring 1992]: 63)

34. Eaves and Kimpel, *Samuel Richardson*, 135.

35. Sale, *Bibliographical Record*, 27.

36. Ibid., 28.

37. Although Lawrence Stone charts the rise of the companionate marriage throughout the eighteenth century, he does acknowledge that practice often differed widely from theory and that many arranged or parentally approved marriages still existed. In most cases, a daughter or son had veto power or was able to select from a limited circle of her or his parents' choices. Richardson's *Familiar Letters* (1741) contains a missive from father to daughter advising against a marriage to a man financially beneath her. James Fordyce, in *Sermons to Young Women* (1766), decries the practice of marrying merely for money, but seems to find it a common one: "The times in which we live are in no danger of adopting a system of romantic virtue. The parents of the present generation, what with selling their sons and daughters in marriage, and what with teaching them by every possible means the glorious principles of Avarice, have contrived pretty effectually to bring down from its former flights that idle, youthful, unprofitable passion . . . in preference to all the wealth of the world" (quoted in Jones, *Women in the Eighteenth Century*, 178).

38. Sale, *Bibliographical Record*, 28.

39. John Kelly, *Pamela's Conduct in High Life* (London: Printed for Ward and Chandler, 1741), x-xi.

40. *Pamela in High Life, or Virtue Rewarded* (London: Printed for Mary Kingman, 1741), 9–10.

41. Eaves and Kimpel, *Samuel Richardson*, 144.

42. Turner, "Novel Panic," 76; Castle, *Masquerade*, 138.

43. See Armstrong, *Desire and Domestic Fiction*, esp. 108–34. She claims this specifically in reference to Pamela: "[I]t is not a creature of flesh and blood that Mr. B—— encounters in the body naked and supine on the bed, but a proliferation of female words and feelings. . . . Mr. B——'s repeated failures suggest that Pamela cannot be raped because she is nothing but words" (116).

44. For a larger view of the exchange of women between patriarchal families, see Gayle Rubin, "The Traffic in Women: Notes on the 'Political Economy' of Sex," in *Toward an Anthropology of Women*, ed. Reiter Raynor (New York: Monthly Review Press, 1978).

45. Ezell documents the persistence of this form of manuscript production and dissemination into the eighteenth century in *Social Authorship*.

46. Eagleton describes Richardson's collaborative coterie as an ideological "family," of which Richardson is patriarch. See *The Rape of Clarissa*, 11–13.

47. I depart from Castle's assertion that the obviously pregnant Pamela is a

focal point at the masquerade. While she does attract suitors, she stands in one place and wards them off dully. The costumed flirts who approach her are never taken seriously as a sexual threat, perhaps because her pregnant body is too clearly marked as the property of another man.

48. *Pamela in High Life*, 246.

49. Warner, *Licensing Entertainment*, 229.

50. Peter Stallybrass and Allon White, *The Politics and Poetics of Transgression* (Ithaca, NY: Cornell University Press, 1986), 83–84.

51. Ibid., 87.

52. See Jones, *Women in the Eighteenth Century*, 57–97.

53. Stallybrass and White, *Politics and Poetics*, 92–93.

54. Gallagher, *Nobody's Story*, 133. Gallagher also discusses this construction and the ways in which writers such as Aphra Behn and Delarivier Manley exploited this image to increase their popularity; see 1–144.

55. Janelle Greenberg describes the legal status of women in the first half of the eighteenth century. Of course, as she points out, "in no period of English history, at least since the Norman Conquest, have women been given the legal status of chattel." A married woman, however, that is, a *feme covert*, did not exist as an independent person in the law, but was considered as part of the "same legal category as wards, lunatics, idiots, and outlaws"; her rights were subsumed into and superseded by those of her husband ("The Legal Status of the English Woman in Early Eighteenth-Century Common Law and Equity," *Studies in Eighteenth-Century Culture* 4 [1975]: 172). Therefore all personal property she brought into the marriage or acquired after the marriage (with certain exceptions specified in marital settlements) became his absolutely. Greenberg further notes that the ideology supporting this legal status was one of paternalism: "the *feme covert* related to her husband as a child to her parents" (175). Thus husband and father structurally held the same position in relation to the wife/daughter.

56. Ann Louise Kibbie, "Sentimental Properties: *Pamela* and *Memoirs of a Woman of Pleasure*," *English Literary History* 58 (1991): 562.

57. Sale, *Bibliographical Record*, 27.

58. Wall, *Imprint of Gender*, 62.

59. Ibid., 282.

60. See, e.g., Armstrong, *Desire and Domestic Fiction*; and Eagleton, *The Rape of Clarissa*, 13–17.

61. Nickel, "*Pamela* as Fetish," 39.

62. Ibid., 47.

63. Stallybrass and White, *Politics and Poetics*, 95.

## 6. The Ghost in the Machine: Invisible Print in a Digital Age

1. A useful summary of this process is Ronald J. Deibert, *Parchment, Printing and Hypermedia: Communication in World Order Transformation* (New York: Columbia University Press, 1997), esp. 113–202.

2. Jay David Bolter and Richard Grusin, *Remediation: Understanding New Media* (Cambridge, MA: MIT Press, 1999), 45.

3. See ibid., 199–203.

4. Francis Ford Coppola, "Introduction," in *Francis Ford Coppola's Zoetrope: All Story*, ed. Adrienne Brodeur and Samantha Schnee (New York: Harcourt, Inc., 2000), viii.

5. Cf. Catherine Ingrassia's study of how representations of bad credit, bad writing, and women were linked, especially in the time of the South Sea Bubble in *Authorship, Commerce, and Gender in Early Eighteenth-Century England: A Culture of Paper Credit* (Cambridge: Cambridge University Press, 1998).

6. David Mamet, "The Screenplay and the State Fair," in Brodeur and Schnee, *Zoetrope*, 317.

7. Ibid., 318. Mamet further describes the summer film as a pagan "solstice festival" in which Nemesis, standing in for Drama, is "ritualistically murdered" (319).

8. Salman Rushdie, "*Midnight's Children*: A Screenplay in Search of a Movie," in Brodeur and Schnee, *Zoetrope*, 75. The discourse this "birth" takes part in is not the paternalistic author's intangible one but one based in material processes.

9. Quoted in Landow, *Hypertext*, 170.

10. Bolter, *Writing Space*, 153.

11. Carl Zimmer, "Floppy Fiction," *Discover*, November 1989, 34.

12. Neil Randall, "Determining Literariness in Interactive Fiction," *Computers and the Humanities* 22 (1988): 183; Richard Ziegfeld, "Interactive Fiction: A New Literary Genre?" *New Literary History* 20 (Winter 1989): 341.

13. See Pamela Samuelson, "Writing as Technology" (paper presented at the conference "Cultural Agency/Cultural Authority: Politics and Poetics of Intellectual Property in the Post-Colonial Era," Bellagio, Italy, March 8–12, 1993).

14. Ronald H. Brown, *The National Information Infrastructure: Agenda for Action*, version 1.0 (Washington, DC: Government Printing Office, 1993), 3.

15. See Bolter and Grusin, *Remediation*, 24–31.

16. October 2, 2000.

17. Bolter and Grusin, *Remediation*, 32.

18. See Cynthia L. Selfe and Richard J. Selfe, Jr., "The Politics of the Interface: Power and Its Exercise in Electronic Contact Zones," *College Composition and Communication* 45 (1994): 480–504.

19. Haraway, "A Manifesto for Cyborgs," 205.

20. The problems and possibilities of such restructuring are explored in Julie Thompson Klein, *Crossing Boundaries: Knowledge, Disciplinarities and Interdisciplinarities* (Charlottesville: University Press of Virginia, 1996).

21. The term *transdisciplinarity* has been used to suggest a variety of convergences. Here, I refer to "a new mode of knowledge production that fosters a synthetic reconfiguration and recontextualization by drawing on expertise from a wide range of organizations and stakeholders . . . , and collaborative partnerships for sustainability that cross the boundaries of social sectors as well as disciplines." ("Interdisciplinarity," in *The Encyclopedia of Science, Technology, and Ethics,* ed. Carl Mitcham (New York: Macmillan, 2005). See also Julie Thompson Klein et al., eds, *Transdisciplinarity: Joint Problem Solving among Science, Technology and Society* (Basel: Birkhäuser, 2001).

22. Haraway, "A Manifesto for Cyborgs," 218.

# BIBLIOGRAPHY


*The Advice of W. P. to Mr. Samuel Hartlib for the Advancement of Some Particular Parts of Learning.* 1648.

Aikins, Janet E. "Re-presenting the Body in *Pamela II.*" In *New Historical Literary Study: Essays on Reproducing Texts, Representing History*, edited by Jeffrey N. Cox and Larry J. Reynolds. Princeton, NJ: Princeton University Press, 1993.

Ames, Joseph. *Typographical Antiquities.* London, 1749.

Armstrong, Nancy. *Desire and Domestic Fiction: A Political History of the Novel.* Oxford: Oxford University Press, 1987.

Armstrong, Nancy, and Leonard Tennenhouse. *The Imaginary Puritan: Literature, Intellectual Labor, and the Origins of Personal Life.* Berkeley: University of California Press, 1992.

*The Art of Governing a Wife, with Rules for Batchelors.* London, 1747.

Aubin, Penelope. *A Collection of Entertaining Histories and Novels.* 1739.

Ayres, Philip. *Vox Clamantis, or An Essay for the Honour, Happiness and Prosperity of the English Society . . . By P. A., Gent.* [1684].

Barker, Francis. *The Tremulous Private Body: Essays on Subjection.* Ann Arbor: University of Michigan Press, 1995.

Barker, Hannah, and Elaine Chalus, eds. *Gender in Eighteenth-Century England: Roles, Representations and Responsibilities.* New York: Longman, 1997.

Barker, Nicolas. "Typography and the Meaning of Words: The Revolution in the Layout of Books in the Eighteenth Century." In *Buch und Buchhandel in Europa im achzehnten Jahrhundert* [The Book and Book Trade in Eighteenth-Century Europe], edited by Giles Barber and Bernhard Fabian. Hamburg: Hauswedell, 1981.

Battersby, Christine. *Gender and Genius: Towards a Feminist Aesthetic.* Bloomington: Indiana University Press, 1989.

Bell, Maureen. "Elizabeth Calvert and the 'Confederates.'" *Publishing History* 32 (1992): 5–49.

———. "Women and the Opposition Press after the Restoration." In *Writing and Radicalism*, edited by John Lucas. London: Longman, 1996.

———. "Women in the English Book Trade, 1557–1700." *Leipziger Jahrbuch zur Buchgeschichte* 6 (1996): 13–45.

Berg, Maxine. *The Age of Manufactures, 1700–1820: Industry, Innovation and Work in Britain.* 2nd ed. London: Routledge, 1994.

Bhomik, Urmi. "Facts and Norms in the Marketplace of Print: John Dunton's *Athenium Mercury*." *Eighteenth-Century Studies* 36 (2003): 345–65.

Bigmore, E. C., and C. W. H. Wyman. *A Bibliography of Printing*. London: Bernard Quaritch, 1884.

Bolter, Jay David. *Writing Space: The Computer, Hypertext, and the History of Writing*. Hillsdale, NJ: Lawrence Erlbaum Associates, 1991.

Bolter, Jay David, and Richard Grusin. *Remediation: Understanding New Media*. Cambridge, MA: MIT Press, 1999.

Bourdieu, Pierre. *The Field of Cultural Production*. Edited by Randal Johnson. New York: Columbia University Press, 1993.

Brack, O. M., Jr., ed. *Writers, Books, and Trade: An Eighteenth-Century Miscellany for William B. Todd*. New York: AMS Press, 1995.

Brewer, David A. *The Afterlife of Character, 1726–1825*. Philadelphia: University of Pennsylvania Press, 2005.

Brodeur, Adrienne, and Samantha Schnee, eds. *Francis Ford Coppola's Zoetrope: All Story*. New York: Harcourt, Inc., 2000.

Brooks, Douglas A., ed. *Printing and Parenting in Early Modern England*. Burlington, VT: Ashgate Press, 2004.

Brooks, Peter. *Reading for the Plot*. New York: Alfred A. Knopf, 1984.

Brown, Ronald H. *The National Information Infrastructure: Agenda for Action*. Version 1.0. Government Printing Office: Washington, DC, 1993.

Butler, Judith. *Gender Trouble: Feminism and the Subversion of Identity*. New York: Routledge, 1990.

Carpenter, Kenneth, ed. *Books and Society in History*. New York: R. R. Bowker, 1983.

Carter, Harry. *A View of Early Typography up to about 1600*. Oxford: Clarendon Press, 1969.

Castle, Terry. *Clarissa's Ciphers: Meaning and Disruption in Richardson's "Clarissa."* Ithaca, NY: Cornell University Press, 1982.

———. *Masquerade and Civilization: The Carnivalesque in Eighteenth-Century English Culture and Fiction*. Stanford, CA: Stanford University Press, 1986.

Chappel, Warren. *A Short History of the Printed Word*. Boston: Nonpareil Books, 1980.

Cipolla, Carlo. *Before the Industrial Revolution: European Society and Economy, 1000–1700*. New York: W. W. Norton, 1976.

Clark, Alice. *Working Life of Women in the Seventeenth Century*. London: Routledge, 1919.

Cook, Albert B., III. "John Bunyan and John Dunton: A Case of Plagiarism." *Papers of the Bibliographical Society of America* 71 (1977): 11–28.

Coppola, Francis Ford. "Introduction." In Brodeur and Schnee, *Francis Ford Coppola's Zoetrope*.

Darnton, Robert. *The Business of Enlightenment: A Publishing History of the Encyclopdie, 1775–1800*. Cambridge, MA: Harvard University Press, 1979.

————. "What Is the History of the Book?" In Carpenter, *Books and Society in History*.

Davis, Herbert. "Catalogue of an Exhibition of British and American Printers' Manuals at Dartmouth College." *Printing and Graphic Arts* 5 (1957): 1–33.

Davis, Lennard. *Factual Fictions: The Origins of the English Novel.* New York: Columbia University Press, 1983.

Day, Robert Adams. "Richard Bentley and John Dunton: Brothers under the Skin." *Studies in Eighteenth-Century Culture* 16 (1986): 125–38.

Deibert, Ronald J. *Parchment, Printing and Hypermedia: Communication in World Order Transformation.* New York: Columbia University Press, 1997.

Dick, Miriam. "Joseph Highmore's Vision of *Pamela*." *English Language Notes* 24 (June 1987): 33–42.

Dobranski, Stephen B. *Milton, Authorship and the Book Trade.* Cambridge: Cambridge University Press, 1999.

Dodsley, Robert. *A Collection of Poems by Several Hands.* 1748–58. Reprint, edited by Michael F. Suarez, S.J. London: Routledge, 1997.

Downie, Alan. "The Growth of Government Tolerance of the Press to 1790." In *Development of the English Book Trade, 1700–1899*, edited by Robin Myers and Michael Harris. Oxford: Oxford Polytechnic Press, 1981.

Drabble, Margaret, ed. *The Oxford Companion to English Literature.* 5th ed. Oxford: Oxford University Press, 1985.

Dunton, John. *The Life and Errors of John Dunton Citizen of London . . . to Which Are Added . . . Selections from His Other Genuine Works.* 1705. Vol. 1. Reprint, New York: Burt Franklin, 1969.

Dutton, Anne. *A Letter to Such of the Servants of Christ, Who May Have Any Scruple about the Lawfulness of Printing Any Thing Written by a Woman.* 1743. Quoted in Lawrence E. Klein, "Gender and the Public/Private Distinction in the Eighteenth Century: Some Questions about Evidence and Analytical Procedure," *Eighteenth-Century Studies* 29 (1995): 106.

Eagleton, Terry. *The Rape of Clarissa: Writing, Sexuality and Class Struggle in Samuel Richardson.* Minneapolis: University of Minnesota Press, 1982.

Earle, Peter. *The Making of the English Working Class: Business, Society and Family Life in London, 1660–1730.* Berkeley: University of California Press, 1989.

Eaves, T. C. Duncan, and Ben D. Kimpel. *Samuel Richardson: A Biography.* Oxford: Clarendon Press, 1971.

Eisenstein, Elizabeth. *The Printing Press as an Agent of Change.* Cambridge: Cambridge University Press, 1979.

Ezell, Margaret. *Social Authorship and the Advent of Print.* Baltimore: Johns Hopkins University Press, 1999.

Feather, John. "The Book in History and the History of the Book." *Journal of Library History* 21 (1986): 12–26.

————. "From Censorship to Copyright: Aspects of the Government's Role in the English Book Trade 1695–1775." In Carpenter, *Books and Society in History*.

———. *A History of British Publishing*. London: Croom Helm, 1988.

———. "The Publishers and the Pirates: British Copyright Law in Theory and Practice, 1710–1775." *Publishing History* 22 (1987): 5–32.

Fielding, Henry. *The Author's Farce*. In *The Complete Works of Henry Fielding, Esq.: Plays and Poems*. Vol. 1, edited by William Ernest Henley, 191–263. New York: Barnes and Noble, 1967.

Flood, John L. "Nationalistic Currents in Early German Typography." *Library* 15 (June 1993): 125–41.

Fordyce, James. *Sermons to Young Women*. 1766. Quoted in Jones, *Women in the Eighteenth Century*, 178.

Foucault, Michel. *The History of Sexuality; Volume One: An Introduction*. Translated by Robert Hurley. New York: Vintage Books, 1980.

———. "Nietzsche, Genealogy, History." In *Language, Counter-Memory, Practice: Selected Essays and Interviews*, edited by Donald Bouchard. Ithaca, NY: Cornell University Press, 1977.

———. "What Is an Author?" In *Textual Strategies*, edited by Josué Harari. Ithaca, NY: Cornell University Press, 1979.

Foxon, David. *Pope and the Early Eighteenth-Century Book Trade*. Revised and edited by James McLaverty. Oxford: Clarendon Press, 1991.

Fuderer, Laura Sue. *Eighteenth-Century British Women in Print: Catalog of an Exhibit*. Notre Dame, IN: Department of Special Collections, University Libraries of Notre Dame, 1995.

Gallagher, Catherine. *Nobody's Story: The Vanishing Acts of Women Writers in the Marketplace 1670–1820*. Berkeley: University of California Press, 1994.

Gaskell, Philip, Giles Barber, and Georgina Warrilow. "An Annotated List of Printers' Manuals to 1850." *Journal of the Printing Historical Society* 4 (1968): 11–32.

Gibson, Strickland. *A Bibliography of Francis Kirkman with His Prefaces, Dedications and Commendations (1652–80)*. Oxford: Oxford University Press for Oxford Bibliographical Society, 1949.

Goldberg, Jonathan. *Writing Matter: From the Hands of the English Renaissance*. Stanford, CA: Stanford University Press, 1990.

Gooding, Richard. *Pamela, Shamela*, and the Politics of the *Pamela* Vogue." *Eighteenth-Century Fiction* 7, no. 2 (1995): 109–30.

Greenberg, Janelle. "The Legal Status of the English Woman in Early Eighteenth-Century Common Law and Equity." *Studies in Eighteenth-Century Culture* 4 (1975): 171–82.

Gregory, John. *A Father's Legacy to his Daughters*. London, 1774.

Griffin, Dustin. *Literary Patronage in England, 1650–1800*. Cambridge: Cambridge University Press, 1996.

Gwilliam, Tassie. *Samuel Richardson's Fictions of Gender*. Stanford, CA: Stanford University Press, 1993.

Hammond, Brean S. *Professional Imaginative Writing in England, 1640–1740*. Oxford: Clarendon Press, 1997.

Hanson, Laurence. *Government and the Press, 1695–1763.* Oxford: Clarendon Press, 1936.

Haraway, Donna. "A Manifesto for Cyborgs: Science, Technology and Social Feminism in the 1980s." Reprinted in *Feminism/Postmodernism,* edited by Linda J. Nicholson. New York: Routledge, 1990.

Harris, Michael. *London Newspapers in the Age of Walpole.* London: Associated University Presses, 1987.

Hayles, N. Katherine. *How We Became Posthuman: Virtual Bodies in Cybernetics, Literature, and Informatics.* Chicago: University of Chicago Press, 1999.

———. *Writing Machines.* Cambridge, MA: MIT Press, 2002.

Head, Richard, and Francis Kirkman. *The English Rogue, Described in the Life of Meriton Latroon.* [Pts. 1–3]. 1672. Reprint, New York: Dodd, Mead and Co., 1928.

Hesse, Carla. "Enlightenment Epistemology and the Laws of Authorship in Revolutionary France, 1777–1793." *Representations* 30 (Spring 1990): 109–37.

Hollis, Daniel W., III. "Francis Kirkman." In *Dictionary of Literary Biography.* Vol. 170, *The British Literary Book Trade, 1475–1700,* edited by James K. Bracken and Joel Silver. Detroit: Gale Research, 1996.

Horden, John. "'In the Savoy': John Nutt and His Family." *Publishing History* 24 (1988): 5–26.

Houghton, Walter E., Jr. "The History of Trades: Its Relation to Seventeenth Century Thought: As Seen in Bacon, Petty, Evelyn, and Boyle." *Journal of the History of Ideas* 2 (1941): 33–60.

Hunt, Margaret. "Hawkers, Bawlers, and Mercuries: Women and the London Press in the Early Enlightenment." *Women and the Enlightenment.* New York: Institute for Research in History, 1984.

Hunter, J. Paul. *Before Novels: The Cultural Contexts of Eighteenth-Century English Fiction.* London: W. W. Norton, 1990.

Ingrassia, Catherine. *Authorship, Commerce, and Gender in Early Eighteenth-Century England: A Culture of Paper Credit.* Cambridge: Cambridge University Press, 1998.

Jaszi, Peter, and Martha Woodmansee. "The Ethical Reaches of Authorship." *South Atlantic Quarterly* 95 (Fall 1996): 947–77.

Johns, Adrian. *The Nature of the Book: Print and Knowledge in the Making.* Chicago: University of Chicago Press, 1998.

Jones, Vivien, ed. *Women in the Eighteenth Century: Constructions of Femininity.* London: Routledge, 1990.

Justice, George. *The Manufacturers of Literature: Writing and the Literary Marketplace in Eighteenth-Century England.* Newark: University of Delaware Press, 2002.

Kahn, Madeleine. *Narrative Transvestism: Rhetoric and Gender in the Eighteenth-Century English Novel.* Ithaca, NY: Cornell University Press, 1991.

Kastan, David Scott. *Shakespeare and the Book.* Cambridge: Cambridge University Press, 2001.

Kelly, John. *Pamela's Conduct in High Life.* London: Printed for Ward and Chandler, 1741.

Kernan, Alvin. *Samuel Johnson and the Impact of Print*. Princeton, NJ: Princeton University Press, 1987.

Kibbie, Ann Louise. "Sentimental Properties: *Pamela* and *Memoirs of a Woman of Pleasure*." *English Literary History* 58 (1991): 561–77.

Kirkman, Francis. "The Epistle dedicatory to the Book-sellers of London." In *The English Rogue. Pt. 2*. 1668. Reprinted in Gibson, *A Bibliography of Francis Kirkman*.

———. "The Preface." In *The Wits*. 1673. Reprinted in Gibson, *A Bibliography of Francis Kirkman*.

———. "To His Much Honored Friend Wil. Beeston, Esq." In *The Loves of Clerio and Lozia*. 1652. Reprinted in Gibson, *A Bibliography of Francis Kirkman*.

———. *The Unlucky Citizen: Experimentally Described in the Various Misfortunes of an Unlucky Londoner*. London, 1673.

Klein, Julie Thompson. *Crossing Boundaries: Knowledge, Disciplinarities and Interdisciplinarities*. Charlottesville: University Press of Virginia, 1996.

Klein, Julie Thompson, et al., eds. *Transdisciplinarity: Joint Problem Solving among Science, Technology and Society*. Basel: Birkhäuser, 2001.

Kreissman, Bernard. *Pamela-Shamela: A Study of the Criticisms, Burlesques, Parodies, and Adaptations of Richardson's "Pamela."* Lincoln: University of Nebraska Press, 1960.

Kroll, Richard W. F. "Mise-en-Page, Biblical Criticism, and Inference during the Restoration." *Studies in Eighteenth-Century Culture* 16 (1986): 3–40.

Landow, George. *Hypertext: The Convergence of Contemporary Critical Theory and Technology*. Baltimore: Johns Hopkins University Press, 1992.

Landry, Donna. *The Muses of Resistance: Laboring-Class Women's Poetry in Britain, 1739–1796*. Cambridge: Cambridge University Press, 1990.

Langford, Paul. *A Polite and Commercial People: England, 1727–1783*. Oxford: Oxford University Press, 1992.

Lanham, Richard A. *The Electronic Word*. Chicago: University of Chicago Press, 1993.

Laqueur, Thomas. *Making Sex: Body and Gender from the Greeks to Freud*. Cambridge, MA: Harvard University Press, 1990.

L'Estrange, Roger. *Considerations and Proposals in Order to the Regulation of the Press*. 1663. Reprinted in Parks, *Freedom of the Press*.

———. *Truth and Loyalty Vindicated*. 1662. Reprinted in Parks, *Freedom of the Press*.

Link, Viktor. "The First Operatic Versions of *Pamela*." *Studies on Voltaire and the Eighteenth Century* 267 (1989): 273–81.

Loewenstein, Joseph. *The Author's Due: Printing and the Prehistory of Copyright*. Chicago: University of Chicago Press, 2002.

———. "Idem: Italics and the Genetics of Authorship," *Journal of Medieval and Renaissance Studies* 20 (1990): 205–24.

Love, Harold. *Scribal Publication in Seventeenth-Century England*. Oxford: Clarendon Press, 1993.

Luckombe, Philip. *History and Art of Printing*. 1771.

Mamet, David. "The Screenplay and the State Fair." In Brodeur and Schnee, *Francis Ford Coppola's Zoetrope*.

Marotti, Arthur. *John Donne, Coterie Poet*. Madison: University of Wisconsin Press, 1986.

Maruca, Lisa. "Political Propriety and Feminine Property: Women in the Eighteenth-Century Text Trades." *Studies in the Literary Imagination* 34 (2001): 79–99.

Marvell, Andrew. *The Rehearsal Transpros'd*. 1672.

Masten, Jeffrey. "Pressing Subjects; or, The Secret Lives of Shakespeare's Compositors." In *Language Machines: Technologies of Literary and Cultural Production*, edited by Jeffrey Masten, Peter Stallybrass, and Nancy J. Vickers (New York: Routledge, 1997).

Mathias, Peter. "Who Unbound Prometheus? Science and Technical Change, 1600–1800." In *Science and Society*, edited by Peter Mathias. Cambridge: Cambridge University Press, 1972.

Mayer, Robert. "Nathaniel Crouch, Bookseller and Historian: Popular Historiography and Cultural Power in Late Seventeenth-Century England." *Eighteenth-Century Studies* 27 (1994): 391–419.

McDowell, Paula. *The Women of Grub Street: Press, Politics, and Gender in the London Literary Marketplace, 1678–1730*. Oxford: Oxford University Press, 1998.

McKenzie, D. F. *Bibliography and the Sociology of Texts: The Panizzi Lectures, 1985*. London: British Library, 1986.

———. "Printers of the Mind: Some Notes on Bibliographical Theories and Printing-House Practices." *Studies in Bibliography* 22 (1969): 1–75.

McKeon, Michael. "Historicizing Patriarchy: The Emergence of Gender Difference in England, 1660–1760." *Eighteenth-Century Studies* 28 (1995): 295–322.

———. *The Origins of the English Novel, 1600–1740*. Baltimore: Johns Hopkins University Press, 1987.

McKitterick, David. "Old Faces and New Acquaintances: Typography and the Association of Ideas." *Papers of the Bibliographic Society of America* 87 (1993): 163–86.

———. *Print, Manuscript and the Search for Order, 1450–1830*. Cambridge: University of Cambridge Press, 2003.

Mellor, Anne K. *Romanticism and Gender*. New York: Routledge, 1993.

Middleton, Conyer. *A Dissertation Concerning the Origin of Printing in England*. Cambridge, 1735.

Mitcham, Carl, ed. *The Encyclopedia of Science, Technology, and Ethics*. New York: Macmillan, 2005.

Mitchell, C. J. "Women in the Eighteenth-Century Book Trades." In Brack, *Writers, Books, and Trade*.

Morison, Stanley. *First Principles of Typography*. New York: Macmillan, 1936.

———. *Letter Forms, Typographic and Scriptorial: Two Essays on Classification, History, and Bibliography*. London: Nattali and Maurice, 1968.

———. *On Type Designs Past and Present: A Brief Introduction*. 1926. Reprint, London: Ernest Benn, 1962.

———. *Selected Essays on the History of the Letter-Forms in Manuscript and Print*. Edited by David McKitterick. New York: Cambridge University Press, 1981.

Moxon, Joseph. *Mechanick Exercises on the Whole Art of Printing.* 1683–84. Reprint, edited by Herbert Davis and Harry Carter. New York: Dover Publications, 1958.

———. *Mechanick Exercises, or The Doctrine of Handy-Works.* 1703. Reprint, New York: Early American Industries Association, 1979.

Mullan, John. *Sentiment and Sociability: The Language of Feeling in the Eighteenth Century.* Oxford: Clarendon Press, 1988.

Nichols, John. *Literary Anecdotes of the Eighteenth Century.* Vol. 4. London, 1812.

Nickel, Terri. "*Pamela* as Fetish: Masculine Anxiety in Henry Fielding's *Shamela* and James Parry's *The True Anti-Pamela.*" *Studies in Eighteenth-Century Culture* 22 (1992): 37–49.

Ong, Walter. *Orality and Literacy: The Technologizing of the Word.* New York: Routledge, 1982.

Palmer, Samuel. *A General History of Printing.* London, 1732.

*Pamela in High Life, or Virtue Rewarded.* London: Printed for Mary Kingman, 1741.

Parker, Patricia. "Rude Mechanicals." In *Subject and Object in Renaissance Culture,* edited by Margreta de Grazia, Maureen Quilligan, and Peter Stallybrass. Cambridge: Cambridge University Press, 1996.

Parks, Stephen. *John Dunton and the English Book Trade: A Study of His Career with a Checklist of His Publications.* New York: Garland, 1976.

———, ed. *Freedom of the Press: Sir Roger L'Estrange's Tracts and Others, 1660–1681.* New York: Garland, 1974.

Pinchbeck, Ivy. *Women Workers and the Industrial Revolution, 1750–1850.* London: Frank Cass, 1930.

Pinkus, Philip. *Grub Street Stripped Bare.* New York: Archon Books, 1968.

Postman, Neil. *Technopoly: The Surrender of Culture to Technology.* New York: Random House, 1992.

Psalmanazar, George. *Memoirs.* 1764.

Randall, Neil. "Determining Literariness in Interactive Fiction." *Computers and the Humanities* 22 (1988): 183–91.

Raven, James. *Judging New Wealth: Popular Publishing and Responses to Commerce in England, 1750–1800.* Oxford: Clarendon Press, 1992.

———. "New Reading Histories, Print Culture and the Identification of Change: The Case of Eighteenth-Century England," *Social History* 23 (October 1998): 268–87.

———. "Selling One's Life: James Lackington, Eighteenth-Century Booksellers and the Design of Autobiography." In Brack, *Writers, Books, and Trade.*

Richardson, Samuel. *The Case of Samuel Richardson, of London, Printer.* 1753. Reprinted in *English Publishing, the Struggle for Copyright, and the Freedom of the Press: Thirteen Tracts,* edited by Stephen Parks. New York: Garland, 1975.

———. *Pamela.* Vol. 2. 1741. Reprint, London: J. M. Dent and Sons, 1969.

———. *The Richardson-Stinstra Correspondence.* Edited by William C. Slatterly. Carbondale: Southern Illinois University Press, 1967.

Roberts, William. *The Earlier History of English Bookselling*. London: Sampson Low, Marston, Searle, and Rivington, 1889.

Rogers, Pat. *Grub Street: Studies in a Subculture*. London: Methuen, 1972.

Roof, Judith. "The Ideology of Fair Use: Xeroxing and Reproductive Rights." *Hypatia* 7 (Spring 1992): 63–73.

Rose, Jonathan. "SHARP Notes: Getting Started in Book History." *Counter* 2 (Spring 1995): 2–3.

Rose, Mark. *Authors and Owners: The Invention of Copyright*. Cambridge, MA: Harvard University Press, 1993.

———. "Copyright and Its Metaphors." *UCLA Law Review* 50 (2002): 1–16.

Ross, Marlon. *The Contours of Masculine Desire: Romanticism and the Rise of Women's Poetry*. New York: Oxford University Press, 1989.

Rostenberg, Leona. *Literary, Political, Scientific, Religious and Legal Publishing, Printing and Bookselling in England, 1551–1700: Twelve Studies*. 2 vols. New York: Burt Franklin, 1965.

Rowe, Elizabeth Singer. *Letters Moral and Entertaining, in Prose and Verse*. 1728. Quoted in Jones, *Women in the Eighteenth Century*, 26.

Rubin, Gayle. "The Traffic in Women: Notes on the 'Political Economy' of Sex." In *Toward an Anthropology of Women*, edited by Reiter Raynor. New York: Monthly Review Press, 1978.

Rushdie, Salman. "*Midnight's Children*: A Screenplay in Search of a Movie." In Brodeur and Schnee, *Francis Ford Coppola's Zoetrope*.

Sale, William Merrit, Jr. *Samuel Richardson: A Bibliographical Record of His Literary Career with Historical Notes*. New Haven, CT: Yale University Press, 1936.

———. *Samuel Richardson: Master Printer*. Ithaca, NY: Cornell University Press, 1950.

Samuelson, Pamela. "Writing as Technology." Paper presented at the conference "Cultural Agency/Cultural Authority: Politics and Poetics of Intellectual Property in the Post-Colonial Era," Bellagio, Italy, March 8–12, 1993.

Schellenberg, Betty A. "Enclosing the Immovable: Structuring Social Authority in *Pamela* Part II." *Eighteenth-Century Fiction* 4, no. 1 (1991): 27–42.

Schneller, Beverly. "Using Newspaper Advertisements to Study the Book Trade: A Year in the Life of Mary Cooper." In Brack, *Writers, Books, and Trade*.

Schwoerer, Lois G. "Women and the Glorious Revolution." *Albion* 18 (Summer 1986): 195–218.

Scott, Joan W. "Gender: A Useful Category of Historical Analysis." In *Coming to Terms: Feminism, Theory, Politics*. New York: Routledge, 1989.

Selfe, Cynthia L., and Richard J. Selfe, Jr. "The Politics of the Interface: Power and Its Exercise in Electronic Contact Zones." *College Composition and Communication* 45 (1994): 480–504.

Shoemaker, Robert B. *Gender in English Society, 1650–1850: The Emergence of Separate Spheres?* London: Addison Wesley Longman, 1998.

Siebert, Frederick Seaton. *Freedom of the Press in England, 1476–1776: The Rise and Decline of Government Control*. Urbana: University of Illinois Press, 1965.

Siskin, Clifford. *The Work of Writing: Literature and Social Change in Britain, 1700–1830.* Baltimore: Johns Hopkins University Press, 1998.

Smith, John. *The Printer's Grammar.* 1755. Edited by D. F. Foxon. Reprint, London: Gregg Press, 1965.

Solomon, Harry M. *The Rise of Robert Dodsley: Creating the New Age of Print.* Carbondale: Southern Illinois University Press, 1996.

Spacks, Patricia Meyer. *Imagining a Self: Autobiography and Novel in Eighteenth-Century England.* Cambridge, MA: Harvard University Press, 1976.

Spencer, Jane. *The Rise of the Woman Novelist: From Aphra Behn to Jane Austen.* Oxford: Basil Blackwell, 1987.

Stallybrass, Peter, and Allon White. *The Politics and Poetics of Transgression.* Ithaca, NY: Cornell University Press, 1986.

Stanhope, Philip Dormer. *Lord Chesterfield's Letters to his Son and Others.* 1749. Reprint edited by R. K. Root. New York: E. P. Dutton and Co., 1929.

Stewart, Susan. *Crimes of Writing: Problems in the Containment of Representation.* New York: Oxford University Press, 1991.

Stone, Lawrence. *The Family, Sex and Marriage in England, 1500—1800.* Abridged. New York: Harper and Row, 1977.

Stower, Caleb. *The Printer's Grammar.* 1808. Edited by D. F. Foxon. Reprint, London: Gregg Press, 1965.

Suarez, Michael, S.J., ed., In Robert Dodsley, *A Collection of Poems by Several Hands.* 1748–58; reprint, London: Routledge, 1997.

Swartz, Richard G. "Patrimony and the Figuration of Authorship in the Eighteenth-Century Literary Property Debates." *Works and Days* 7, no. 2 (1989): 29–54.

Thomas, Max W. "Reading and Writing the Renaissance Commonplace Book: A Question of Authorship." In Woodmansee and Jaszi, *The Construction of Authorship,* 401–15.

Thompson, E. P. "Eighteenth-Century English Society: Class Struggle without Class?" *Social History* 3 (May 1978): 133–65.

Tierney, James E., ed. *Correspondence of Robert Dodsley, 1733–1764.* Cambridge: Cambridge University Press, 1988.

Todd, Janet. *The Sign of Angelica: Women, Writing and Fiction, 1660–1800.* New York: Columbia University Press, 1989.

Treadwell, Michael. "London Trade Publishers, 1675–1750." *Library,* 6th ser., 4 (June 1982): 99–134.

Treichler, Paula. "Feminism, Medicine, and the Meaning of Childbirth." In *Body/ Politics: Women and the Discourses of Science,* edited by Mary Jacobus, Evelyn Fox Keller, and Sally Shuttleworth. New York: Routledge, 1990.

Tribble, Evelyn B. *Margins and Marginalia: The Printed Page in Early Modern England.* Charlottesville: University Press of Virginia, 1993.

Turner, Cheryl. *Living by the Pen: Women Writers in the Eighteenth Century.* London: Routledge, 1992.

Turner, James Grantham. "Novel Panic: Picture and Performance in the Reception of Richardson's *Pamela*." *Representations* 48 (Fall 1994): 70–96.

———. "Richardson and His Circle." In *Columbia History of the Novel*, edited by John Richetti. New York: Columbia University Press, 1994.

Varey, Simon. "Revisiting a Masterpiece: *Government and the Press, 1695–1763*." *Studies in the Literary Imagination* 34 (2001): 49–61.

Wall, Wendy. *The Imprint of Gender: Authorship and Publication in the English Renaissance*. Ithaca, NY: Cornell University Press, 1993.

Warner, Michael. *The Letters of the Republic: Publication and the Public Sphere in Eighteenth-Century America*. Cambridge, MA: Harvard University Press, 1990.

Warner, William B. "The Institutionalization of Authorship: Richardson's Battle with the Irish Booksellers." Paper presented at the "Intellectual Property and the Construction of Authorship" conference, Cleveland, 1991.

———. *Licensing Entertainment: The Elevation of Novel Reading in Britain, 1684–1750*. Berkeley: University of California Press, 1998.

———. *Reading Clarissa: The Struggles of Interpretation*. New Haven, CT: Yale University Press, 1979.

Watson, James. *The History of the Art of Printing*. 1713. Edited by D. F. Foxon. Reprint, London: Gregg Press, 1965.

Watt, Ian. *The Rise of the Novel: Studies in Defoe, Richardson and Fielding*. Berkeley: University of California Press, 1957.

Weber, Harold. *Paper Bullets: Print and Kingship under Charles II*. Lexington: University Press of Kentucky, 1996.

West, James. "To the Hon. Mrs. C[ockayn]e." 1791. Quoted in Siskin, *The Work of Writing*, 130.

Woodmansee, Martha. *The Author, Art and the Market: Rereading the History of Aesthetics*. New York: Columbia University Press, 1994.

———. "On the Author Effect: Recovering Collectivity." In Woodmansee and Jaszi, *The Construction of Authorship*.

Woodmansee, Martha, and Peter Jaszi, eds. *The Construction of Authorship: Textual Appropriation in Law and Literature*. Durham, NC: Duke University Press, 1993.

Wright, William C. "Sir Thomas Browne's *Pseudoxia Epidemica* and English Coffee House Journalism." *Journal of Popular Culture* 12 (1978): 36–41.

Young, Edward. *Conjectures on Original Composition in a Letter to the Author of Sir Charles Grandison*. 1759. Reprinted in *English Critical Essays: Sixteenth, Seventeenth and Eighteenth Centuries*, edited by Edmund D. Jones. London: Oxford University Press, 1975.

Ziegfeld, Richard. "Interactive Fiction: A New Literary Genre?" *New Literary History* 20 (Winter 1989): 341–72.

Zimmer, Carl. "Floppy Fiction." *Discover*, November 1989, 34–36.

Zuboff, Shoshana. *In the Age of the Smart Machine: The Future of Work and Power*. New York: Basic Books, 1988.

# *INDEX*

*Page numbers in bold type refer to illustrations.*